PREFACE

This is the story of my life's journey, beginning in childhood in post-war Liverpool. It was an interesting, although austere, place in which to grow up. Times were tough in our working-class community. Liverpool bore the marks of the Blitz, and there were many challenges. War rationing continued into the post-war period. There was a shortage of suitable housing and many families, like ours, lived in multi-generational homes. We had a rented terraced house: 57 Grey Rock Street, Everton. It was next to Boundary Lane (where Ogden's Tobacco factory was a local employer), and it was not far from Liverpool's football ground. I lived at Grey Rock Street from 1947 to 1967, when we moved just before our street was demolished under the city's "slum clearance" scheme.

It was a considerably different world to the middle-class one in which my three children grew up. My story preserves precious memories of my grandparents, parents, relatives, friends, events and circumstances, for my children, grandchildren, relatives (including those in the US), friends and a wider readership to enjoy. I include photos and a sketch of our streets.

My story is not written in isolation from other autobiographies, biographies, social histories, etc., which I've enjoyed reading. However, this is my unique contribution to social life in post-war, working-class Liverpool, and tells how I achieved social mobility, principally through education. I reflect on class, education, religion, and science.

Even now, despite so many changes in society and the wider world, my story is strikingly relevant to today's important issues.[1]

---

[1] This is illustrated in the Education Committee's *The forgotten: how White working-class pupils have been let down, and how to change it* and the Social Mobility Commission's response (June 2021).

MEMORIES OF POST-WAR LIVERPOOL

Living, Learning, and Leaving

To Eileen

I hope you enjoy my book.

Best wishes.

Rob

Robert S. Dutch

HEDDON PUBLISHING

First published in the United Kingdom 2023 by Heddon Publishing

www.heddonpublishing.com

A catalogue record for this book is available from the British Library

ISBN 978-1-913166-71-7 (paperback)

Cover Design: Catherine Clarke
Cover images courtesy of the author

To my maternal grandparents, Alfred and Elizabeth Thompson, who shared their home at 57 Grey Rock Street, Everton, with Mum and Dad's growing family.

And to Mum and Dad for constant love and support.

FOREWORD

When teaching a university-level course on the New Testament in Bristol, I came across Robert Dutch, who contributed a fascinating illustrated lecture on the social scene in ancient Corinth. Who would have imagined that such an expert historian of the ancient world might have previously been a nuclear scientist who originally came from a working-class academically-unpromising background in inner-city Liverpool after failing his 11-plus exam? There cannot be many people in the world who have written expert and knowledgeable books both on nuclear energy and the historical context of the New Testament! How did it come about? This book is not just an interesting history of one modest man who became a committed Christian en route, but a book that touches on issues of great relevance to today – from education and "levelling up", to nuclear energy and its safety, via faith and science. I am grateful for Robert's help and friendship in my teaching and writing, and glad to recommend this intriguing account of his personal and academic journey.

Rev Dr David Wenham

Formerly Lecturer in New Testament in Wycliiffe Hall Oxford and Trinity College Bristol

CONTENTS

Preface   1

1 - 57 Grey Rock Street, Liverpool 6   3

2 - A Working-Class Community   18

3 - Grandparents, Parents and Other Relatives   39

4 - Primary School Years   61

5 - Weekends in the Wirral   84

6 - Secondary Modern School Years   101

7 - Duke of Edinburgh's Award: Struggles, Survival and Stickability   134

8 - Grammar School Years   181

9 - University of Salford   205

10 - Moving South: Working as a Scientist and Starting to Settle   241

11 - Scientist, Tutor, Engineer, Theologian   274

12 - Reaching Retirement and Reflections   307

Our Streets   330

Lilian Dutch (née Thompson) family tree   331

Summary of Education   332

Acknowledgements   333

CHAPTER 1

57 Grey Rock Street, Liverpool 6

A Liverpool lad, born and bred in post-war Liverpool – a "baby boomer", summer-born baby and Scouser. That's me. I was born in Mill Road Hospital in 1947, where, being before the free National Health Service (NHS) was born on 5th July 1948, my parents paid for my delivery. This came to four pounds and ten shillings. I still have a copy of the bill! Liverpool – its people, communities, churches and schools – laid the foundation for my life. Now in my mid-seventies, it's time to write my story of a post-war working-class community, unimaginably different from the one in which my children grew up. In doing so, I am "preserving family memories" and contributing to social history. But this is not intended as a comprehensive record of life in 1940s-70s Britain (others have written that).[2] Rather, it focuses on my unique story, beginning in Liverpool (then in Lancashire but now in Merseyside), with me in the North, struggling at school and studying, before moving to the South for employment. There were struggles, surprises, and successes ahead.

Our household

I grew up in 57 Grey Rock Street, Liverpool 6 (in Everton) and spent twenty years (1947-67) living there.[3] Initially, our

---

[2] For example, Alan Titchmarsh, *When I was a Nipper: A Personal Journey Through Disappearing Britain* (BBC Books, 2011), Paul Feeney, *A 1950s Childhood: From Tin Baths to Bread and Dripping* (Stroud: The History Press, 2011), and Derek Tait, *1960s Childhood: Moon Landings, The Kinks and the 1966 World Cup* (Stroud: Amberley, 2014).

[3] There were no postcodes with letters and numbers until they were rolled-out across the UK in the 1960s. See 'Postcodes to celebrate 50th

household consisted of my maternal grandparents (Alfred and Elizabeth Mary Thompson), my parents (Stanley and Lilian), and two children (me and my sister Anne, two years younger). My second sister, Christina, was born in 1956. Stan and Lil, and we three children, were all born in Liverpool.

Three-generational households were very common; with post-war Britain's housing shortage, we were not unique. In 1947 alone (the year I was born) Andrew Marr notes that there were 400,000 weddings and 881,000 babies born; in the first five post-war years there were an additional million children born.[4]

Grey Rock was one of three "Rock streets" (Grey Rock, Red Rock and White Rock) sandwiched between Boundary Lane (home of Thomas Ogden's Imperial Tobacco factory) and Norwood Grove. At the north end of our streets ran Whitefield Road, and at the other, West Derby Road.

We had a privately-rented terraced house comprising two floors, with three upstairs bedrooms. The ground floor had two living rooms, a kitchen, and an outside toilet in the backyard. Between this toilet and the kitchen was the small shed (with a door from the kitchen). Initially, the house had no bathroom.

My grandparents, Alfred (born 1887) and Elizabeth (née Thomas, born 1892) had moved to Grey Rock Street from 55 Barry Street around 1934, with their two children, Alfred William (born 1914) and Lilian (born 1921). But the streets were older, as an 1890 map shows.[5] The Mortality Map of Cholera in 1866 shows our streets up to Norwood Grove, while an 1858 map shows only Boundary Lane.[6] An aerial

---

year', BBC News 30 December 2008. Accessed 10 August 2022 at BBC NEWS | UK | Postcodes to celebrate 50th year

[4] Andrew Marr, *A History of Modern Britain* (London: Pan Books, 2008), pp.73-74.

[5] Both Barry Street and Grey Rock are shown in the '1890: Plan of Liverpool – North Sheet'.

[6] Elizabeth J. Stewart, *Courts and Alleys: A history of Liverpool courtyard housing* (Liverpool: Liverpool University Press, 2019). See the 1858

view of 1930 shows them. Kelly's Directory of Liverpool & Birkenhead, 1894, lists Grey Rock Street as from 193 West Derby Road to 163 Whitefield Road. On the west side, houses were numbered 1 to 139 at Whitefield Road, while on the east they were numbered 2 to 128 (the Rock Hotel).[7]

Alfred William married Edith May Connor (from 30 Red Rock Street) at St Margaret's Anglican Church on 5th August 1939. Edie's father John Connor, a labourer, witnessed the wedding, as did Alfred Thompson. At the time of the 1939 Register, they were living at 62 Grey Rock Street. Grandad Alfred's parents (my great-grandparents) James Thompson and his wife Jane (née Millar) had moved to Liverpool from Scotland, where they were born to Scottish parents, while Elizabeth's parents were Charles Thomas (born in 1855 in Cork, Ireland, like his father Charles) and Elizabeth Ellen (née Renkin, born 1862 in Liverpool) – who was the only one born in Liverpool.

We had no front garden, but a little tiled area with a wooden fence – the iron railings had been removed for the war effort. The front door was set back and didn't open immediately onto the street. Our front door was next to our neighbours' (No. 59) where Mr Max Winer (born 1897) and Mrs Charlotte Winer lived. Set in the ground by our doors were manhole entrances to coal cellars. Curtained windows faced the street from the ground-floor front room and main bedroom.

Our sturdy main door led to a small porch with an inner

Hilliars Guide for Strangers and Visitors Through Liverpool in '1858: Hilliars Guide to Liverpool'. Accessed 10 August 2022 at 1858: Hilliars Guide to Liverpool • Historic Liverpool (historic-liverpool.co.uk)

[7] For a brilliant selection of old photos of Grey Rock, Red Rock and White Rock Streets, see the Ged Fagan website: 'Inacityliving'. Accessed 13 April 2023 at https://inacityliving.blogspot.com/2012/11/in-city-living-1.html. However, for 70 photos inside Ogden's on Boundary Lane, see Colin Lane, 'Look inside former Ogden's Tobacco factory', Liverpool Echo 2 February 2016. Accessed 10 August 2022 at Look inside former Ogden's Tobacco factory - Liverpool Echo

door. The main door had a lock, brass doorknob, knocker and letterbox regularly cleaned by Mum, who also cleaned the front steps. The front door was often unlocked so we children could go into the porch and then into the house through the unlocked inner door. We appreciated this, as it gave quick access to our home if we were running away from children trying to hurt us!

After the porch door, a short corridor led to two doors and the stairs for the bedrooms. By the stairs stood a small grandfather clock, which looked good and ticked away with its swinging pendulum. Our front room (also known as the parlour) was the first door on the left in the corridor, and this room faced the street, with a good window. This room was my grandparents'. Later, it was used as the "best room". There was a glass cabinet where delicate ornaments and crockery were displayed. The furniture included chairs (when I was a teenager, we had a settee in the bay window) and a Singer sewing machine, which we children liked to "operate" by seeing how fast we could move the foot pedal that powered it. My sister Anne recalls that Gran took in clothes to sew, and earned a little extra money that way.

Also, there was an upright piano for parties, if anyone could play it. The parlour initially had a coal fire, and eventually an electric fire set inside the grate. Around the fire was the fireplace, and on top stood a brown wooden clock. It had two keyholes inside the glass face, which opened on a hinge. Dad used the large key to wind it up, so it ran non-stop for eight days. It chimed at least every hour. There were no silent, battery-operated clocks then. We were naturally accustomed to hearing ticking clocks in our rooms. When I grew up, the parlour was used to store my bicycle and also for studying, since it had a table and electric fire (much appreciated on cold evenings). On one wall hung a nice framed black-and-white portrait photograph of Mum.

The rooms were wallpapered, but there was a problem if we tried to redecorate by removing the old paper: doing this could pull off plaster. The solution was to repaper over the top, so the layers of paper gradually got thicker over the years. I recall making a nice wooden corner unit at secondary school to hold an ornament, yet this would not fit, because although I made it 90 degrees, the walls were too irregular.

The next door, by the stairs, led to our small living room (often called the kitchen). It had a coal fire with an inbuilt cooking range made from iron and coloured black. We toasted bread in front of this fire, and baby Christina would be bathed before it, to keep her warm. By the fire there was a rug, under which Mum often put clothes, especially jumpers, to dry flat thanks to people walking over them. Above was a hoist system for drying clothes. The rail rack would be lowered from the ceiling, clothes put on it, and then hoisted back up, where the clothes remained to dry (not forgetting to tie the hoist ropes, otherwise the rail came down rather quickly). As you can imagine, the room could be damp.

Most floors were covered with "lino" (linoleum) and rag rugs put on top for warmth. My sister Anne recalls: 'The rag rugs weren't sewn, they were sort of "woven" using thick strands from old coats and other thick clothing. I remember Gran showing me how it was done.' We did not have wall-to-wall carpets or expensive wooden floors.

The family dining table, chairs and sideboard occupied this room. Initially, we had a lovely integrated wireless (radio) and record player unit. When I was about six, we had our first TV (a black-and-white 14" screen which showed a very limited selection of programmes, but we still enjoyed them). Mum wielded her solid metal iron on the ironing board (before the days of electric and steam). A large sash window opened into the small, paved backyard.

The door, with a small window, led into the kitchen (often called the back kitchen), with its gas cooker, storage cupboards and sink with a gas heater above for quick hot water from the tap. There was no central hot water and heating system. We had a largish cylindrical gas boiler used

7

for doing the weekly washing. A dolly peg (which resembled three legs mounted on one end of a handle) was used to stir the washing, and a hand-turned mangle was used to squeeze water from it. Long tongs were used to handle hot, wet clothes. Later, we had a "modern" washing machine, a single tub (no spinner) with a top mangle (two rollers). Washing dried on a line in the backyard. Unfortunately, air pollution sometimes spoilt our clean clothes. When taken down, they had black sooty spots on them from the coal burnt in homes and smoke/smuts going up chimneys! Again, Anne remembers that when we had our first refrigerator (fridge), people came to our house to see it. Apparently, this also happened when we had our first TV. So, she reckons, we can't have been that poor. Fortunately, Dad worked hard as a bricklayer; a skilled job needed for rebuilding Britain. Other men in our area were skilled, semi-skilled, or unskilled.

Further, without a fixed bath and no shower, the kitchen was used for privacy when people had "a good wash" or a bath. Once a week it was family bath night, and the large tin bath was brought in from the backyard (where it hung on the whitewashed wall) and filled with hot water. We took it in turns to have a bath (in the dark) using the same water, topped up with hot. We would take it in turns to have the first bath, so every few weeks I got the clean hot water! Once everyone was bathed, the water was scooped out of the bath (which had no drain), and emptied away. The tin bath was returned to the backyard wall. This is so different from today, with daily showers, baths or washes.

Our kitchen was also used as an occasional workshop. One year, Dad carefully made me a green wooden fort for Christmas. It had four towers, battlements for the soldiers to stand on, and a drawbridge over the moat at the front. I had hours of fun playing with it. Eventually, Mum asked if I would give it to a family across our street as a present for their little boy, which I did. Money was short.

From the kitchen, a door went into the little backyard. We

had a vine climbing up the back wall of the house, a privet tree, and a largish kennel with a glass skylight giving sunlight for Trixie our dog. This was fine for Trixie, but once I had a serious accident there (see chapter 4). There was no garden as such, no grass to mow, and not many flowers. One tiny patch (perhaps five feet long by two feet wide) was available, and was used when we owned small tortoises ("land turtles"). Anne recalls racing them in the backyard. Anyone entering the backyard took care because dog mess often needed cleaning up – a horrible job. We also had a cat.

For American readers, I should say that our "backyard" may be very different from the backyards you may be familiar with! Perhaps a large, paved area with table/dining chairs, a gas barbecue, grass, trees, bushes, and maybe even a swimming pool, as I experienced when visiting relatives in the US. Instead, our backyard was a small area for drying washing and giving access to an outside lavatory or "lav" (toilet) and a narrow back alley.

The outside tiny toilet was a trial, but at least our house had one for just us – no need to share with neighbours. There was no heating in it, no wash basin, and it was perishing in the winter; but fortunately, it did flush into the mains sewers! We went down the backyard whatever the weather – snow, rain or shine. It had a wooden seat (often cold and damp). Newspaper was used to give insulation above the wood if the seat was iced up – I remember when it was. Instead of toilet tissue, newspaper sufficed. I cannot recall if it had a light. Insects and spiders could be lurking in the shadows, waiting for us. One lady we knew, who liked watching horror films at the pictures, was terrified when it came to using the toilet in the dark yard ('Who could be there?'). To be fair, intruders could climb backwalls and get into yards. In fact, we had a break-in once, with the intruder getting into the kitchen. Mum disturbed him when she came in the front door and he fled, thankfully, with only our wireless.

There were ways that people tried to prevent intruders

using rear alleys to climb over walls. Sharp broken glass pieces were set into mortar on the top bricks to deter them. Nevertheless, I recall seeing one boy carefully walking along the glass – a dangerous practice, since a slip could result in injury, risking deep cuts before falling on a hard floor below the wall. We didn't have glass on our wall and cats happily walked along it, but their nightly wailing could be dreadful.

The backyard had a painted wooden door that opened into the narrow alley behind the houses on our side of Grey Rock and Boundary Lane. The dustbin stood in the backyard, and this was collected weekly by dustmen ("bin men") who came along the alley. Dustbins were metal then, since people threw hot ashes in from the coal fires when they cleared them to light new fires. A plastic bin would melt, but they were not around anyway. There was not much recycling then. A neighbour faithfully kept the alley cleaned, otherwise it was smelly and nasty, from litter and dog-fouling.

Sometimes, our parents or grandparents whitewashed the backyard walls, to make them bright and clean. The whitewash was made in a small tin bath using candles and caustic soda (nasty stuff), I think, and painted on the walls to give a rough but clean finish. The yard was the place where, with a small axe, I chopped the wood we used for lighting coal fires. One of my morning jobs was to rake out the coal fire (from the backroom) and shovel hot ashes into the dustbin. Then I laid the fire with newspaper at the base, followed by the wood and then coal. I lit the paper and got a draught up the chimney, and hoped it would light quickly. Finally, the backyard caught some sun, so we could sit or play outside to enjoy its warmth.

We had a small cellar, mainly for storing coal and housing the coin-operated electric and gas meters. Other small items were kept there too (e.g. a gas mask from the Second World War). This cellar was accessed from the kitchen via a wooden door and stairs down to the earthen floor; above were the joists supporting the floorboards. Fortunately, the earth was dry, not damp. Coal was delivered through the manhole next to our front door. The cover was removed, and coalmen emptied sacks into the hole so the coal fell into the cellar with clouds of dust. They took the empty sacks away. When the electricity went off – annoying if we were watching TV – it was often the job of us children to go down into the dark cellar and put a shilling (now a 5p coin) in the meter to get the lights back on. If we were lucky, we had a torch and did not fall down the stairs. Not good if creepy-crawlies terrified you!

On the first floor were three bedrooms (no bathroom, shower or toilet), and a storage chest stood on the landing. At the front was our parents' room, with two freestanding wardrobes which smelled of mothballs, a dressing table with drawers, and a large mirror; when I was older, I used to practise conjuring tricks in front of this mirror. Anne recalls the furniture was mahogany.

Access to the roof space (loft) was via the bedroom ceiling hatch. It wasn't easy, although once firemen had to use it. It was my fault! I was messing about with the fire in the hearth, causing large flames to set alight to the chimney. People stood in the street, watching flames and smoke pouring out. The fire brigade arrived and extinguished the fire, but had to climb into the loft to check nothing was smouldering that may relight, with possible fatalities. A policeman interviewed Mum to investigate if we should be prosecuted but we weren't. It was an accident; we didn't intentionally start the fire to avoid paying a chimney sweep. I learnt my lesson – don't play with fire!

In our parents' room, there was a double bed, and a single bed between it and a built-in cupboard. When Anne and I were little, we lay in bed and kept watch on the wardrobes, worried in case someone was hiding. There never was! Dad often lay with us and sang us to sleep. Also, Dad had a framed painting on the wall of HMS *Grey Fox* – the ship he sailed on during the Normandy D-Day landings (6th June

1944), across to Omaha Beach, escorting the US forces.

The middle bedroom was smaller, with a bed, a freestanding wardrobe, and a small dressing table. Through a window, we looked over the backyards (not inspiring, but at least we could just see the sky, and once I got to wish when I saw a falling star).

The small rear bedroom at the top of the stairs became my room. It was just wide enough to get a bed across the room's width, and pushed to the rear wall of the house (a wall that felt damp sometimes). Alternatively, the bed fitted along the left wall and under the only window, with views across the narrow backyards to our neighbour's brick wall. It was a wooden sash window, painted and single-glazed. My parents fitted a combined electric heater and lamp in the ceiling. This was such a benefit when I was studying at my small table.

As we lacked an inside toilet, the bedrooms had "gazunders" (also called a "po"), which we used and emptied each morning down the toilet. Not a nice experience. Until Dad fitted an inside toilet (and bath) in the shed years later, this was our best option, or we would have to go downstairs to the outside toilet at night. Not good for children.

Living in a terraced property sometimes gave us problems with mice, as they could easily run house-to-house. Dad and Gran dealt with these rodents and kept the house vermin-free and clean. Thanks to their vigilance, we were not overrun. Sometimes rats appeared in the back alleys, and I recall killing one in a neighbour's shed, using a brush (it may have come from houses that were being demolished).

We did, fortunately, have mains water, electricity and gas. But in No. 57 there was no central heating, no double-glazed windows, and no loft insulation. Wasn't it cold? Too true! Two ground-floor coal fires provided some warmth, supplemented with electric fires and hot water bottles, with much heavy bedding. There were no warm duvets then. We used layers of blankets and eiderdowns, but their weight pinned us young children down – it was difficult to breathe. Some houses lit portable paraffin heaters, which were easy to use but a fire risk, and they emitted a funny smell. The problem with coal fires was that they needed to be regularly fed with coal and had to be emptied and relit each morning. When it was windy, smoke from the chimney could be blown back into the room, which was bad for breathing, and left dust all over the furniture. We remained vigilant to ensure hot coals did not fall out and start a fire, or a child, or clothing (not fire-retardant then) didn't fall into the fire. We used fireguards; smoke detectors and carbon monoxide detectors didn't exist. Coal fires were not usually lit in bedrooms, and on some cold mornings ice appeared inside the windows.

The absence of telephones in homes seems unimaginable today. We did not have one, and nor did our neighbours. During our years in Liverpool, if we wanted to make a call – for example to the doctors' – we walked to West Derby Road and used the red GPO (General Post Office) public phone box. This had a button A and B system to pay your money, and we spoke to the operator. If there was a queue, we just patiently waited our turn. Our phone area was Anfield.

If someone entered Grey Rock Street from West Derby Road, our house was located on the left (west) side, in the central block of terraced houses. An old black streetlamp stood outside our home, using a gas mantle with town gas. A man checked it sometimes by leaning a ladder on its outstretched arm. Older kids who could reach the arm swung on it for fun.

Our streets were not wide, but as most people did not own cars that was no problem. Each side of the street had a flagged pavement and next to the kerb was the gutter, which took the rainwater down the drains. Children regularly played in the street, learnt to ride bicycles there, and had fights. There was one cleared bomb site ("debris" or "oller") in our street, and we used it as a space to play. It was bombed in the Second World War by the German Luftwaffe, and remained empty all the years we lived there. Apparently, it had previously been a corner shop. Each Guy Fawkes night (5th November), it was the place to build bonfires and light fireworks. Sometimes, children lit bonfires in the middle of the streets, which did not do the cobble stones/tarmac any good (sometimes the fire brigade came and put them out). Opposite the bomb site was the local corner shop.

Streets were cleaned by council workers. Milkmen delivered morning milk (whole, not semi-skimmed) in one-pint glass bottles. When these were empty, we washed them and put them on the doorstep for collection and refilling (this was early recycling). For US readers, postmen delivered mail through letterboxes to homes. This was pretty straightforward, as the distance from the pavement to the front door of our house was only a few steps. Boys delivered morning and evening newspapers to homes. However, postmen and paperboys had to be wary of dogs outside houses, as they might bite (it happened to me). The rag-and-bone man came to exchange old clothes for cash. There was a lemonade/Corona seller, and an ice-cream seller, too. Some deliveries were by horse and cart.

The rent man came weekly to collect his cash, as did the milkman and the friendly "man from the Pru" (Prudential) for our parents' insurance. Meter readers read and emptied our gas and electric meters (usually we got some cash handed back). Door-to-door salesmen sold their wares – that is how our parents bought their first vacuum cleaner, after they were given a demonstration. Sometimes ambulances or fire engines arrived at homes. Police officers walked the beat.

Overview of our social context

When I was a lad, Liverpool was a major international port, with a long history back to 1207 and King John. Clearly, this detail cannot be covered here, but it is summarised elsewhere.[8] My more modest context is recent events.

Living in post-war Liverpool was a struggle for families. Rationing continued in many ways, and was sometimes worse than during the war. Almost immediately after Victory over Japan (VJ) Day in 1945, America cancelled its Lend-Lease arrangement with Britain, which had provided financial support during the war.[9] It then offered a huge loan, which had to be accepted, given Britain's situation; although twenty-three Labour MPs in parliament voted against accepting America's tough terms.[10]

Energy supplies were problematic. Marr remarks that in the 1940s, most of Britain's energy was supplied by coal. With disruptions in coal supplies, factories closed and people couldn't heat their homes. In 1947, Britain's coal production was far below its pre-war output.[11] Even after the 1940s, air pollution from smoke, smells, soot and smog was bad in our streets.

Housing remained the foremost single issue towards the top of the national agenda from the 1940s into the 1950s. Through the German bombing, 500,000 British homes were destroyed or made unusable. Millions were damaged, so that the government considered that about 750,000 new homes were required.[12]

Moreover, it was not just the quantity of houses. Many cities, Liverpool included, had slums that desperately needed clearing. Families and the baby boom required good quality homes. On the poor quality, Kynaston summarises the 1951 Census of 12.4 million dwellings in England and

---

[8] 'History of Liverpool', VisitLiverpool. Undated. Accessed 8 August 2022 at History of Liverpool - VisitLiverpool

[9] In the UK, the 75th anniversary of VJ Day occurred on 15th August 2020 (Japan's surrender in 1945).

[10] David Kynaston, *A World to Build* (London: Bloomsbury, 2008), pp.103, 133-134. He covers 'Austerity Britain 1945-48'.

[11] Marr, *History*, pp.68-69.

[12] Marr, *History*, p.73.

Wales. He records that even the government's estimate of the number of new houses needed was a considerable underestimate. For "Liverpool and Bootle", his table from the Census shows: (1) occupied dwellings with three rooms or fewer – twelve per cent, (2) households with no fixed bath – thirty-seven per cent, and (3) households without exclusive use of a lavatory – seventeen per cent. Some areas of the country had worse figures.[13]

One solution, which still did not meet the country's need but was welcomed, was the rapid building of "prefabs" (prefabricated bungalows built to meet the housing shortage). These homes were quickly assembled on site, with fewer resources than terraced brick-built houses, and therefore cost much less. Marr notes that from 1945-1949 more than 156,000 were assembled.[14] I had a friend that lived in one and I was surprised how pleasant it was, with an inside bathroom/toilet. It beat the standard of our house.

In 1947, National Service replaced "wartime conscription"' and teenage men were called up for military training. This lasted until 1963, and during this period over two million were trained.[15] Some were bored, and some were buried, having actually lost their lives in overseas hostilities. Mum, like many other parents, was delighted when she heard on the radio that National Service was to be abolished before it affected her own family (it was brought to an end before I was old enough to be called up). I recall her telling me about it – she was so pleased. Mum lived through the Second World War, with its worries, and knew deprivation, danger and deaths.

The book *Yesterday's Britain*, edited by Jonathan

---

[13] David Kynaston, *Smoke in the Valley* (London: Bloomsbury, 2008), p.305.

[14] Marr, *History*, pp.74-75. And Jonathan Bastable (ed.), *Reader's Digest Yesterday's Britain: The Illustrated Story of How We Lived, Worked and Played* (1st edition with amendments; London: Reader's Digest, 1999) pp.194-195.

[15] Marr, *History*, p.116.

Bastable, captures the change to a new decade from the 1940s to the 1950s, which started with ongoing austerity and rationing, but then was regarded as a peaceful change, mainly to better things. People were told, and believed, they had 'never had it so good.'[16]

Struggles, surprises and successes played their part in an age of austerity. But we had hope, love and joy within a small but secure family.

---

[16] Jonathan Bastable (ed.), *Reader's Digest Yesterday's Britain*, p.204 in 'The best is yet to come'. Prime Minister Harold Macmillan said: 'Most of our people have never had it so good' (p.203).

CHAPTER 2

A Working-Class Community

Our community

Our house certainly wasn't in a wealthy area, but neither was it terribly poor. There were no tenements or flats nearby: terraced brick houses with grey-slated roofs faced each other across narrow streets.

Chimneys poured out polluting smoke into the atmosphere, from the coal fires which kept us warm. Streets were originally made with cobble stones, but later some roads were tarmacked. Gas streetlamps provided illumination. There were few cars parked in the streets in the 1950s and early 60s, as they were too expensive for most people. Over the years, as TVs became more popular, aerials appeared on chimneys.

Streets had their corner shops and pubs, but our nearest main shopping area was West Derby Road, with its individual shops before the days of supermarket chains. West Derby Road's shops (and pubs) were on the ground floor of three-storey buildings and often had white awnings that came out above the big windows, providing some protection for shoppers from the sun and rain. There were parks, churches and schools. Local employment opportunities existed in Ogden's Imperial Tobacco factory. The Ogden office block was built in 1899 in Boundary Lane and opened in 1901 – it closed in March 2007 and is now a Grade II listed building.[17] Also, there was the Barker and Dobson chocolate factory (at Franklin Place off Whitefield Road), which closed in 1985. Our Liverpool 6 was in

---

[17] See British Listed Buildings, 'Ogden Imperial Tobacco Ltd Office Block - A Grade II Listed Building in Everton, Liverpool'. Undated. Accessed 8 August 2022 at Ogden Imperial Tobacco Ltd Office Block, Everton, Liverpool (britishlistedbuildings.co.uk)

Everton, away from the city's docks, but on foggy nights we heard ships' foghorns on the Mersey.[18]

Churches and convent

Although our local streets housed a predominantly white working-class community, we were mixed in terms of religion. Four local churches were important: (1) St Michael's Roman Catholic (RC) Church (along West Derby Road next to Horne Street, opposite the Palladium Cinema), (2) Norwood Grove Congregational Church (corner of West Derby Road and Norwood Grove, (3) St Margaret's Anglican Church, Anfield (junction of Belmont Road and Rocky Lane) and (4) Newsham Park Chapel (Sheil Road). St Margaret's was rebuilt after a huge fire, which I witnessed, in 1961. Norwood Grove was eventually demolished.

We had lovely neighbours, Mr and Mrs Winer. Their front door was adjacent to ours, so we saw them often. Mrs Winer was a Roman Catholic and Mr Winer a Jew. I think he fought in the First World War, and he still had shrapnel in his body; he told me that a piece had taken years to work its way out. Liverpool had a large Jewish community, but I don't know which synagogue he attended. When the Winers had a new tape recorder (using tape which they wound on two reels/spools – years before cassettes were invented), they invited us in to record. It was so new and funny hearing our voices! Mrs Winer's daughter, Marie Lawler, lived locally (off Breckfield Road South), with her sons Ken and John. Their church was St Michael's.

There was a RC convent (St Joseph's Home for the Aged Poor) on Belmont Road, Walton on the Hill, run by nuns known as the Little Sisters of the Poor. The 1891 Census

---

[18] On Everton's development, decline and demolition see local journalist Ken Rogers, *The Lost Tribe of Everton & Scottie Road* (TrinityMirror Media, 2012). Also see Home - The Lost Tribe of Everton

records those who worked there and the "inmates" living on charity.[19] As a paperboy, I delivered newspapers there. It was up the road from our church, St Margaret's.

Mrs Winer told me that her grandson John was learning Latin – services in the Roman Catholic Church then were still in Latin. I was impressed, as learning the Queen's English presented enough challenges to Liverpudlians like me.

Mum and Dad were married in St Margaret's Church after the Second World War, on 14th September 1946. Family photos (in black-and-white) show this joyful day, with so many people: relatives, friends and neighbours. My certificate shows I was baptised (christened) at the same church in summer 1947 by the vicar Rev F. Jolley. When Anne and I grew up, we attended Sunday School from 3-4pm for many years. We walked there along West Derby Road. In the large main church building, we learnt Bible stories about Jesus' life, faith, and Christianity. Sunday School teachers (women and men) taught classes. The annual Sunday School outings by coach (called a charabanc) to places such as Southport and Chester Zoo, were much appreciated. Also, our time at Sunday School gave Mum and Dad a rest! Annual prizes were given for good attendance.

As I got older, I attended Sunday morning services with a school friend (Reggie Gabbutt from Red Rock). Also, Norwood Grove Congregational Church played a part in my life. I enjoyed attending its weekly uniformed Life Boys (the "Junior Reserve of the Boys' Brigade", until 1966, when it was renamed "The Junior Section"), and periodically I walked to their Sunday morning services. My cousin Alf also attended Norwood's Life Boys and Boys' Brigade. When Anne grew up, she walked, with a friend, to Newsham Park Chapel.

Church ministers visited members of their parish at home.

---

[19] For comment by Doedoe who worked there see: 'Reply #6 on Tuesday 27 December 11'. Accessed 11 August 2022 at St Josephs Home, Walton on the Hill (Lancashire) 1 RootsChat.Com

Rev Levick, the young minister at St Margaret's, visited us on his bicycle. He was friendly and interesting. I recall talking to him about the American pioneer and legend Davy Crockett, who was all the rage then. I had a Davy Crockett hat (a racoon skin with a tail down my neck), like many boys, and one Sunday when he was speaking, Rev Levick mentioned our chat. Clearly, he did listen to children.

At the end of White Rock Street near Whitefield Road, there was a Methodist Church school and hall. We went and had fun playing games. I suppose it was a children's/youth club. The hall was still standing, though unused, decades later when I photographed it, but when we returned in late 2014, the site had been cleared.

State schools (primary and secondary) had Christian worship in morning school assemblies, with the whole school gathered together. This included Bible readings, prayers and hymns (Jewish children, of course, didn't attend). Often, head teachers talked to children about important issues, not limited to religious topics but addressing things such as personal safety. Besides morning assemblies, we had Scripture or Religious Education (RE) classes, which included discussion of ethical issues.

Churches and schools taught about Jesus, faith and Christianity, but not in a way that I felt forced to believe. Indeed, when I was older and considered confirmation at St Margaret's, I started learning the catechism, with its questions and answers. I could state the answers, but did I believe them? As I was unsure (agnostic, I suppose), I did not go for confirmation and no pressure was put on me by our parents or church ministers to continue. That said, Sunday School, morning worship and RE classes developed knowledge and understanding in many lives.

Opposite us in No. 52 lived Mrs Butler with her children: Billy, Stephen, Dot, Eileen and Joan, and their grandparents. Billy, the eldest, who became a famous Liverpool DJ, tells amusing stories about attending Sunday School.[20] Stephen became a friend.

Schools

Our state primary school was Whitefield Road School, at the end of Boundary Lane. As we lived in the next street, it was an easy walk. The new school intake was in late August, and I was barely four years old when I started in 1951. The school day was long (9am–4pm), five days a week, but I just had to get on with it! My first day was challenging (see chapter 4).

Roman Catholic children could attend St Michael's Catholic School off West Derby Road, across the road from St Michael's Church. This school had nuns on the staff, and church attendance was expected. I had a friend who went there. Our church, St Margaret's, also had its attached school.

At ten or eleven, children took the selective 11-plus exams, to determine what secondary school they should attend when they finished primary schooling. This was either a grammar school (if you passed), or a secondary modern school (if you failed). Occasionally, technical schools were available. Boys attended our local Newsham Secondary Modern School for Boys (on Sheil Road). Girls also attended but had a separate playground and classes. The boys' school was mainly on the first floor and the girls' school on the ground floor. Children often left school for work in the first term that they reached the compulsory leaving age (fifteen).

Our cousins, Edna and Alfred Thompson, who lived in Red Rock Street, passed the 11-plus and travelled by bus to their grammar schools. Edna went to the prestigious girls' school Holly Lodge, and Alf to the Liverpool Collegiate School in Everton. Alf recalls 'walking to the Collegiate to save the (1d or 2d) bus fare'. Billy Butler also attended the Collegiate.

---

[20] Billy Butler, *Billy Butler M.B.E. (Mrs Butler's Eldest)* (Trinity Mirror Sports Media, 2010).

Shops and shopping

Our local streets and West Derby Road had many small shops. Grey Rock Street and the other "Rock Streets" were split into three sections via four passages (wide enough for a horse and cart or motor car to go through, and a tiny pavement for pedestrians). Two passages on opposite sides of the street to our home connected Grey Rock and Red Rock Streets while, on our side, two further passages connected Grey Rock and Boundary Lane. We lived in this middle section. (There is a sketch of the streets after chapter 12.) Cousin Alf recalls that children only played in their part of the street.

We had a nearby corner shop across the passageway into Boundary Lane – just four houses between our house and the passage, then the shop. If we walked through this passage into Boundary Lane there was another corner shop on the right, selling sweets, cigarettes, etc. If we turned right and went up Boundary Lane, we came to the fish and chip shop (the "chippie"). Always a favourite, with its chips, fish, fishcakes, mushy peas, etc., and the lovely smell that came with them. Chips were sprinkled with salt and vinegar, then wrapped in white paper, and then newspaper, to keep them warm. Sometimes newspaper print got on the chips, but we simply scraped it off and enjoyed them!

Instead of turning from Grey Rock into Boundary Lane, we often turned into Red Rock Street. At the right-hand corner in Grey Rock there was the "oller" or "holler" (a cleared bomb site from the Second World War), where the shop was destroyed. In Red Rock, the first corner had another shop. Alf recalls going to the shop for his mum to buy a couple of Woodbine cigs ("Woodies"). Back then, children buying cigarettes for Mum was okay. The smallest packs held five cigarettes but, if asked, shopkeepers would split packs into "a couple of loosies". Alf and I recall the friendly shopkeeper, Roger. We often bought sweets there. Roger was African, with prominent "tribal tattoo" marks on both cheeks. Perhaps for many children, he was the first Black man they met.

If we continued along the passage from Red Rock to White Rock Street, there was another shop on the right-hand corner. We children visited it for its "pink ice cream" (strawberry flavour) as a treat, instead of the usual vanilla. At the top of Red Rock Street on Whitefield Road, I recall when I was an older teenager visiting a launderette with Auntie Edie to wash clothes.

Further up at 80 Grey Rock on the corner passage into Red Rock Street was a dairy (although milk was also delivered daily to doors). On the corners by this dairy were another shop, and a pub. At the top of Grey Rock near Whitefield Road, another shop existed, possibly selling bicycles – memories are too distant to recall with conviction. With so many shops nearby, we children could easily nip out and run errands for our parents.

At the junction of Grey Rock and West Derby Road, there was a narrow alley, wide enough for pedestrians to go through into Red Rock. Here stood our blacksmith's forge. We watched him with his hot forge and tools, making horseshoes and the like. Also, nearby a lady sold fruit and vegetables from her handcart.

On West Derby Road there were newsagents (Rayners was one), selling comics and so on, and employing paperboys to deliver morning and evening newspapers plus Sunday papers. Further along stood a general shop selling flour, fruit and vegetables, with sacks containing produce standing on the shop floor. There was also a gentlemen's clothing shop, and pubs. If we turned left along West Derby Road, there were more shops! In the small section between Grey Rock and Red Rock was the newsagents where I worked as a paperboy. Newsagents sold fireworks for Guy Fawkes Night.

Further along was the butcher's, which employed schoolboys to deliver customers' orders by bicycle. A school friend worked there part-time, delivering meat carried in the metal basket/pannier at the front of the bike. It was a well-paid job. We had another butcher's shop, where we watched them slice meat using a large, sharp cutting wheel. Laws applied to employing school-age children, and we had to keep them.

There was a chemist's shop (now often called a pharmacy). As a teenager interested in chemistry, I purchased small quantities of chemicals there for home experiments. The chemist asked questions before selling anything.

Opposite the chemist, on another corner (Tweed or Berwick Street?), was a bicycle shop with a selection of shiny new bikes. In my teens, I bought my Carlton bicycle there through weekly payments from my paper round. There was also a small garage selling Regent petrol.

Almost opposite Grey Rock was one of our favourite places, the small café and ice-cream shop. We could order and sit inside at tables, or stand on the pavement and buy, through a sliding window, ice creams to take away. Further along was the men's barber's shop (opposite Boundary Lane) where, with no pre-booking, I spent boring hours as a child waiting for a "short back and sides", which was about the only style available. The barber put a piece of wood across the top of the arms on the adult chair and I sat there quietly while he cut my hair. Optional Brylcreem (original) hair cream was applied to keep what little was left of our hair in place. Men had haircuts, with their hair singed, and shaves. Many smoked, so it was smelly!

Near the barber's there was a zebra crossing for pedestrians, but we could cross without using it since the road was straight, not too wide, and illuminated. However, when the fogs/smog came, and on dark evenings, it was dangerous. I once crossed the road virtually blind and then quickly jumped as someone sounded a horn. Fortunately, I was not hit, but the experience scared me.

Up from the barber's was our dentist's surgery, which we attended with trepidation, aware of the awful pain that accompanied fillings or extractions (the feared "school dentist" also treated us). I had fillings and extractions over the years. Fillings were frightening. No painkilling injections were offered. I sat in the chair clenching my fists while the dentist worked. The whirling drill, the smell and the bits floating in the mouth put off vast numbers of children, and adults, from making regular visits. Fluoride toothpaste was not known, and dental hygiene was poor.

Boredom in the barber's and dread in the dentist's; but there were better shops. A record shop which Mum and I went to sold 1960s records (45 rpm vinyl) with singers such as Elvis Presley, Cliff Richard, Helen Shapiro (*Walking Back to Happiness*), the Beatles (consisting of course of local lads John Lennon, Paul McCartney, George Harrison and Ringo Starr) or instrumentalists, e.g. the Shadows. Money was short, so we carefully chose just one single record per visit. The shopkeeper was friendly, willing to help, and amusing. Playing records and persuading ourselves to buy was a pleasant experience.

On another corner stood a lovely toy shop with great selections (but it wasn't cheap). I remember staring in the corner window at toy soldiers placed against a scenic background of the Battle of Waterloo (1815). The foot-soldiers and horsemen were plastic and well-painted (lead soldiers often broke). I bought some when I could. For cheaper soldiers, my friends and I visited Woolworth's on Saturdays in town (at London Rd) for plain plastic soldiers to paint – an option which allowed us to buy more. Painting them and having battles was fun. We also made plastic Airfix aeroplane kits. Lewis's was a great store to visit, with its escalators!

We had a second-hand shop (I bought an airgun there when I was old enough to hold a licence, aged thirteen). Cousin Alf recalls buying second-hand comics, which he swapped with Billy Butler. There was a splendid sweet shop, brightly illuminated and spacious, with luscious sweets made on the premises. The lights, colours, selections and smells still linger with me over sixty years later. Coconut ice was a favourite.

Scattered along West Derby Road were pubs and shops. I guess we had a post office and pawnbroker's, but I cannot recall details; although sometimes Dad had to pawn items. Money was given in exchange for items pawned, and a receipt. Then when owners could afford to, they could buy belongings back for an additional charge.

Further along West Derby Road (towards town), at the junction of Brunswick Road and Everton Road, was our bank, on the corner of Walker Street and next to the Hippodrome Cinema, opposite Grant Gardens. It was a simple single-storey building called the Liverpool Savings Bank. My parents opened an account for me when I was small, and we kept it running into my teenage years. At one stage my account had £10 – that was a lot of money then. The bank and cinema were a short walk or a couple of bus stops from our house. If we walked from Grey Rock to the bank, we passed the Locarno Ballroom (1948-64). It was first built as the Liverpool Olympia (1905-48) for an indoor circus and theatre. In the war it was a Royal Navy depot, before being sold as a ballroom and eventually becoming the Mecca Bingo Hall (1964-90).

The Locarno was next to the Grafton Ballroom "Grafton Rooms" (opened in 1924 as a large dancehall), which was famous for hosting singers and bands such as Gerry & the Pacemakers and the Beatles. The Grafton provided entertainment during the Second World War, even during air raids! It had boom years in the 1950s, and the Fab Four last played there on 12th June 1963. Sadly, I never saw them.

Finally, it's important to mention that for the women in our community (who were generally responsible for shopping), visiting the shops was not always easy. During, and after, the Second World War, there were food shortages, queueing and rationing, with meat rationed until 1954.

Shops offered whale and tinned snoek (a South African fish), but these were often unappreciated. Even so, Marr notes that people were healthier, as the rationing system had considerably improved the working-class diet, and children grew taller.[21]

Doctors

Funnily enough, our family didn't have a local doctors' surgery. We took the bus to Everton Valley, to the practice of Dr Yardumian, his son, and young Dr Melrose.[22] This choice may have come about from my grandparents previously living in 55 Barry Street, Kirkdale. Barry Street ran between Walton Road and Walton Lane at Stanley Park, and it was a short walk to the doctors' surgery from there. My guess is that they found the doctors to be "good" before the National Health Service (NHS) and so stayed with them after they moved. Prior to the introduction of the NHS, patients may have had to pay for their own treatment, although thankfully for the least well-off there was some provision to gain access to medical care.[23] The surgery's big house had a long path with steps up to the front door, and the three surgery rooms and main waiting room were on the ground floor. A smaller waiting area in a dim, dark-brown painted hallway had interesting wall-mounted pictures of

---

[21] Andrew Marr, *A History of Modern Britain* (London: Pan Books, 2008), p.54.

[22] Dr Yardumian senior was probably Dr Garrie Yardumian (born 1879 in Turkey) who had a general practice in Liverpool for over 50 years. See 'Garabed Yeghia Yardumian', University of Glasgow. Accessed 10 August 2022 at University of Glasgow :: Story :: Biography of Garabed Yeghia Yardumian

[23] An excellent short article is available online by Barry Doyle and Rosemary Cresswell, 3 July 2018. Accessed 24 May 2023 at What was healthcare like before the NHS? (theconversation.com)

gleaming early motor cars with drivers and passengers.

After what seemed a long bus-ride, we sat bored in the surgery until finally called – there was no appointment system. Without a receptionist, people had to remember where they were in the queue. Of course, if buses stopped running because of smog, there was no easy way of getting there or back – you could walk or cycle. Liverpool's smogs were terrible. People would have difficulty finding their way home, as seeing even a few feet ahead was challenging. Torches were useful. To try and protect their health, folk would breathe through handkerchiefs held over their mouths and noses, or through scarfs wrapped around their faces. The smog caused coughing and breathlessness, especially among people suffering from respiratory conditions such as bronchitis, which was common. It even got inside people's homes, so there was no escape. Of course, part of the problem was that people kept warm at home by burning coal, which created smoke and pollution from sulphur impurities. People probably died from adverse health impacts just as high excess deaths occurred across all age groups during, and after, the Great Smog of London in 1952. Some government workers in the capital were issued with Martindale masks, which we now know were good at removing smoke particulates but not the toxic gas sulphur dioxide.

During the Great Smog, sometimes bus drivers were guided by a passenger, the conductor, or a police officer, walking ahead and holding a flare. I can't recall seeing this happen in Liverpool, but if (for safety) buses were simply parked at the side of the road and left, the passengers would have to walk. Of course, leaving abandoned vehicles at the side of the road meant that other drivers and cyclists could run into them, because of the poor visibility.

Kynaston notes that car ownership was low – a "middle-class luxury". When I was a toddler, there were only around two million cars on the UK's roads.[24] I remember travelling on Liverpool's trams with Mum to visit Auntie Lizzie – the first, which was horse-drawn, ran in November 1869 and the last electric tram on 14th September 1957.[25]

Parks

Often, we children played in the streets (e.g. football or hide-and-seek), or on the hollers. Sometimes this included parents – Billy Butler recalls playing rounders with his mam in our street, and she smashed a neighbour's window! But we had two parks nearby. Across West Derby Road was Sheil Park, with its entrance opposite the Congregational Church on Norwood Grove. There weren't any gates or fences there. On the left were prefabs. On the right were tennis courts (where cousin Edna played; I didn't know how to), and a bowling green. Here, men such as Grandad and Uncle Alf played bowls, for exercise, 'fresh air', and socialising. In the centre were children's swings, a roundabout and a slide. There was also a small pond/toy boating lake. Cousin Alf recalls 'picking mint for Aunt Ed' (who lived in his shared house) and 'fishing with a net in Sheil Park and bringing jam jars of sticklebacks home to keep in a bathtub out the back'. The park-keeper kept an eye on things to make sure all was okay. You didn't want to get told off by him!

Through Sheil Park we crossed Sheil Road to reach Newsham Park (a 121-acre Victorian park), with its vast green space for playing, jogging, relaxing and rowing on the boating lake, where we fed ducks dry bread. We loved the visiting funfairs with rides and stalls. Pupils at Newsham

---

[24] David Kynaston, *Smoke in the Valley* (London: Bloomsbury, 2008), p.114. Covers 'Austerity Britain 1948-51'.
[25] See 'The Last Tram in Liverpool – 1957', 16 September 2012. Accessed 10 August 2022 at The Last Tram in Liverpool - 1957 (Facebook Search "The Four Squares") - YouTube

Secondary Modern School used Newsham Park to play football and cricket, as the school had no playing fields, and did timed walks around the park's perimeter for the Duke of Edinburgh's Award.

Pictures

The pictures, "flicks" or cinemas were very popular, and provided mass entertainment (TV in its infancy could not easily compete with them). Picture houses were everywhere. Marr reckons the country had 4,600 cinemas in its "post-war peak".

The Palladium Cinema (our nearest) was at West Derby Road on the corner of Butler Street, opposite St Michael's Church. The stalls sat 655 and the circle 250, with just one large screen. It opened on 10th May 1913, but not until April 1929 did it have a "talkie" film. By 1954, it had CinemaScope,[26] a revolutionary technique that helped cinemas compete with TV. It used lenses that allowed wide image filming to compress the images onto standard 35mm film and then, when projected, (anamorphic) lenses would expand the film to produce its full image in a stunning widescreen format for audiences. *The Robe* was the first film to use CinemaScope. The animated film *Lady and the Tramp* used it. The technique was a major hit that took over Hollywood.

We used to stand outside and look at the small black-and-white photographs that showed scenes from the films in a bid to entice us in. I enjoyed seeing many films there. Sadly, the cinema was compulsorily purchased and demolished for road-widening in 1967. The last showing was the spectacular film *The Ten Commandments*, with Charlton

---

[26] For a full description see Rafael Abreu, *What is a CinemaScope?* 31 May 2020. Accessed 14 May 2023 at What is CinemaScope? Definition and Examples for Filmmakers (studiobinder.com).

Heston playing Moses.[27]

The Hippodrome along West Derby Road was another favourite. Others were within a short bus ride, or we walked; going up Grey Rock, crossing Whitefield Road brought us to Breckfield Road South and Breck Road. Just around the corner was the Theatre Royal cinema. There was the Lido on Belmont Road, and many more. The highest film-rating was an X certificate, and we had to be sixteen to attend, but older films were different from today's eighteen ratings, which are more explicit and violent.

I attended Saturday morning or afternoon matinees for 6d (the old sixpence), often at the Lido on Belmont Rd. But boys often behaved badly. Individuals and groups ran around, climbed over seats, shouted, etc. We didn't dare wear caps, as in the dark these were grabbed and thrown upwards, possibly to never be seen again. Managers stopped films and warned children with various threats to behave or else! Films were changed regularly. Typically, shows included newsreels, adverts (including trailers for new films), and two films: the main one and a supporting one (unlike modern cinemas that usually show one film). Sometimes, supporting films could be good quality. For example, we saw *Robin Hood* and *Lady and the Tramp*, both Disney films, together.

Regrettably, there were no restrictions on smoking. Clouds of smoke rose across the screen. Smoke lingered on clothes, but we were used to it; it was a world where non-smokers were expected to breathe others' smoke. Smokers' fingers were stained brown by the nicotine (no filter-tipped cigarettes). Few seemed to worry about annoyance, smelly clothes, and health risks. Doctors smoked in their surgeries – Dr Yardumian (senior) certainly did. It would take excessive early deaths before researchers Richard Doll and

---

[27] Ken Roe, 'Palladium Cinema', Cinema Treasures. Undated. Accessed 9 October 2022 at Palladium Cinema in Liverpool, GB - Cinema Treasures.

A. Bradford Hill established the link between smoking and lung cancer and some action started.[28]

Pubs and clubs

Pubs, like shops, were everywhere in Liverpool; for socialising, drinking, smoking, eating plain crisps, and playing darts. We were required to be eighteen years old to drink. Closing time was usually 10.30pm and "last orders" was shouted as a warning to order and drink up. Men drank their pints (or halves) of bitter (or mild), smoked and talked. Often, they played friendly darts matches or darts competitions in teams. Most men we knew didn't drink to excess, except perhaps on New Year's Eve and special occasions. Up to the early 1970s, New Year's Day wasn't a public holiday, and I still recall the odd experience of working in my first job on 1st January 1971. Often, Liverpool's docks had mass absenteeism on New Year's Day, until the 1974 public holiday started. Excess drinking could bring tragedies to families if men spent their weekly cash pay packets before going home.

Our local pub was The Red Rock, at 42 Red Rock.[29] Here, men met for a pint and smoke, but they could take their wives and girlfriends. Dad had photographs taken with his darts team. After I was of legal drinking age, I sometimes drank there. Local pubs were friendly, but more basic than these days, with fewer food choices.

Different clubs existed, e.g. Irish, bingo, dance, self-defence, church youth clubs and rival football clubs (Liverpool and Everton). When Liverpool played at Anfield, at the end of the

---

[28] Kynaston, *Smoke*, pp.272-273. Also see Naomi Oreskes and Erick M. Conway, *Merchants of Doubt: How a Handful of Scientists Obscured the Truth on Issues from Tobacco Smoke to Global Warming* (London: Bloomsbury, 2010), chapter 1 'Doubt is Our Product'.
[29] Liverpool History, 'The Red Rock, Red Rock St L6', (Pub at No. 42 - 1967). Accessed 10 August 2022 at Pin page (pinterest.co.uk)

match cars would queue along Boundary Lane (next to our street) to get on to West Derby Road; despite this being an era when car ownership was limited. Alf recalls regular Saturday afternoon visits to see Liverpool play. The ground was within walking distance. Once, as a teenager, I saw Liverpool. We stood on the steps behind the goal (in the Kop) and were jostled constantly. As I was small, it was difficult to see over supporters' heads. In the 1960s, I attended the original famous Cavern club. On Friday evenings, with school friends, I watched professional wrestling at Liverpool's Stadium in Bixteth Street.

At the junction of Boaler Street and West Derby Road, the large Emmanuel Anglican Church (established 1867, demolished 1974) stood on an island. I once attended its Cubs group with a friend. Initially, it was okay, but then I had to sit with a leader, who tried teaching me the motto. Somehow, I didn't get it right, no matter how hard I tried. He was increasingly frustrated with my failed attempts. The exasperating experience for the man, and me, meant that although Mum encouraged me to return the next week, I would not go. That was my first, and last, experience of the Cubs.

Public baths

We children often went to swim at the public baths. Having your own swimming pool in a garden was unheard of in our community. We went to Margaret Street swimming baths (opened in 1863),[30] a short walk from home. Sessions were designated: "men's swimming", "women's swimming", and "mixed". These baths also had "private baths", for those wanting a private wash in hot, soapy water.

We also went swimming at Lister Drive Baths, where I

---

[30] Baths and Wash Houses, Historical Archive, 'Liverpool'. Undated. Accessed 10 August 2022 at Liverpool | Baths and Wash Houses Historical Archive

taught my cousin Alf to float. But it was a long walk via Newsham Park, although it made for a good Saturday morning out. It was next to the electricity-generating Lister Drive Power Station. Often, we walked home along Green Lane, joining West Derby Road in Tuebrook. It was a healthier way to spend time than watching TV or cinema. Alf also recalls swimming in Cornwallis Street baths, which had salt water.

Libraries

On Saturdays, we walked to local libraries. This was a chance to go with friends. One library was along Breck Road, near the end of Walton Breck Road (Liverpool's ground was nearby). Another, in the opposite direction, was on Kensington. I often read books on conjuring tricks, and fiction, e.g. *Jennings and Derbyshire* and the *Just William* series. As I played chess, I read books on that, too. We were allowed to borrow books for two weeks.

Pier Head

Going to the Pier Head on the Mersey was a short bus ride from home. We saw ferries, boats and larger ships. Liverpool had extensive docks. Alf recalls: 'Getting [the] bus to Pier Head on a Sunday, having a cup of tea and a hot Eccles cake before getting on the Birkenhead Ferry to New Brighton.' At the floating landing stages, we caught ferries to Birkenhead, Wallasey or New Brighton (for a day trip up the Mersey). Cycling was popular and many cyclists (including me) took early Sunday morning ferries to Birkenhead before cycling through the Wirral to Wales, for exercise and scenery. If we hiked in north Wales, we also used ferries. Returning to Liverpool's Pier Head, we heard street preachers enthusiastically engaging listeners.

Democracy and freedom of speech in action!

At the Pier Head ran the Liverpool Overhead Railway – the first electric railway in Britain, operating from 1893 until its demise in 1956. I can just recall it.[31]

Specific jobs: trades

What specific jobs did people do in our community? Kelly's 1938 Street Directory gives the jobs of people living in Harewood Street (just across Whitefield Road from Grey Rock Street).[32] Going up the left side of the street (from Nos. 1-63), we find the heads of households listed with the trades: railway checker, labourer, labourer, French polisher, engineer, silk worker, jobber, dock labourer, plumber (No. 33), ship's cook, bricklayer, cotton porter, shopkeeper, shopkeeper, sheet metal worker, tailor, and labourer. On the right side (Nos. 2-70), a similar range of manual workers' occupations are identified. Noticeably, even when women were heads of households, no trade is shown. That was 1938. When war broke out in 1939, women workers were needed. Before we were born, Stanley Dutch (our dad) lived at 33 Harewood Street and in 1936 he joined the Royal Navy.

---

[31] *The Liverpool Overhead Railway 1950's*, video. Accessed 11 August 2022 at The Liverpool Overhead Railway - 1950's (Facebook Search: "The Four Squares") - YouTube

[32] Kelly's Street Directory (1938), p.385. For trades in 1900 Harewood St, see 'Gore's Directory of Liverpool & Birkenhead, 1900. [Part 1_ Street List & Street Directory] - Part 306 (street directory pages 256-257) - Historical Directories of England & Wales - Special Collections Online'. University of Leicester. Accessed 11 August 2022 at Gore's Directory of Liverpool & Birkenhead, 1900. [Part 1: Street List & Street Directory] - Historical Directories of England & Wales - Special Collections For Grey Rock St in 1900 see Part 294 (p.244). Accessed 11 August 2022 at Gore's Directory of Liverpool & Birkenhead, 1900. [Part 1: Street List & Street Directory] - Historical Directories of England & Wales - Special Collections

Working-class communities

Over time, the perception of working-class communities in Britain has changed. Where we grew up, our working-class community worked hard. During the Second World War, men and women made considerable contributions to the war effort. Those people who didn't leave the British Isles worked long hours at normal jobs or munitions work, for example. But many made further contributions in voluntary organisations after their regular work, e.g. ARP (Air Raid Precautions, which changed its title later to Civil Defence Service) wardens, Auxiliary Fire Service (later amalgamated into the National Fire Service), and LDV (Local Defence Volunteers, becoming the Home Guard in August 1940). From 1st September 1939, ARP wardens enforced the "blackout".

After the war, considerable efforts and sacrifices were made to rebuild Britain. Our community had men that toiled in building trades (e.g. bricklayers, plasterers, plumbers, carpenters, labourers), and were trade union members. They married, had children, and earned respect in their community. Anne recalls that we would run down the street to meet Dad coming home from work. But barriers existed between middle class and working class. Kynaston reports that a 1946 survey of 400 building workers showed forty-nine per cent definitely disapproved of their sons entering the industry. Their replies showed they often resented the inferior status modern society gave to manual workers (skilled and unskilled).[33] Over time, the term "working class" has changed, and communities still face problems in modern Britain.[34]

More might be said on our working-class community, but I have introduced topics which I will develop as my story unfolds. For an interesting list of what British people did, and

---

[33] Kynaston, *Smoke*, pp.138-140.

[34] Stewart Lansley and Joanna Mack, *Breadline Britain: The Rise of Mass Poverty* (London: Oneworld, 2015).

didn't, have in 1945, see David Kynaston's *A World to Build*.[35] Our streets were demolished in the late 1960s under Liverpool's "slum clearance" and new homes and streets were built (e.g. New Grey Rock Close), so we cannot return to walk my original streets. Also, sadly, Sheil Park was built over, and children can no longer enjoy the fun we had there.

---

[35] David Kynaston, *A World to Build* (London: Bloomsbury, 2008), p.19. He covers 'Austerity Britain 1945-48'.

CHAPTER 3

Grandparents, Parents and Other Relatives

Maternal grandparents

Mum and Dad's families include Irish, Scottish, Welsh, Yorkshire and Liverpool origins. There is a family tree for Mum after chapter 12, to assist readers.

Mum's parents were born in Liverpool at the end of the 19th century, when Queen Victoria ruled. Gran, Elizabeth Mary Thompson (née Thomas), was born on 10th June 1892 and lived in the First Court, second house, Cranmer Street. Courts were an important part of Liverpool's housing.[36]

Liverpool's 'courts' were high-density brick-built houses prevalent from the 18th-20th centuries. They were easily and economically built, and met the needs of the city's increasing population. They were let to the poor for low rents. Courts were usually accessed through passageways from the main streets or roads. Inside the courts, the number of houses varied from two to twenty, but typically there were four to ten. Houses were built "back-to-back", with the back wall forming the back of another house in a nearby court.

---

[36] See Elizabeth J. Stewart, *Courts and Alleys: A history of Liverpool's courtyard housing* (Liverpool: Liverpool University Press, 2019). Accessed 24 August 2022 at A History of Liverpool's Courtyard Housing with Elizabeth Stewart | Liverpool University Press Blog For a review see: Martin Greaney, 'Courts and Alleys by Elizabeth J. Stewart', 31 July 2020. Accessed 24 August 2022 at https://historic-liverpool.co.uk/courts-alleys-elizabeth-j-stewart/ Also see Catherine Jones, 'Liverpool's court housing that were once home to half the city's population', *Liverpool Echo* 19 December 2013. Accessed 24 August 2022 at Liverpool's court housing that were once home to half the city's population - Liverpool Echo

Thus, they had no back door or windows. The front door opened on to the paved courtyard, which was overlooked by windows. The buildings ranged in height up to four storeys, and often had cellars. Courts typically shared two toilets built around the court. Water was supplied to a shared central standpipe. Houses and cellars were sometimes sub-let, resulting in overcrowding and unhealthy conditions with high mortality. Irish migrants particularly (but not exclusively) lived in courts.[37]

Oral history through Gran recounts that her dad left Ireland for Liverpool as a result of the Irish Potato Famine or Great Hunger (1845-51), and their farm being burnt down.[38] Gran's father, Charles Thomas (my great-grandfather), was born in 1855 in Cork, Ireland. His father, also called Charles, lived in Cork (born c.1821).

By 1871, my great-grandfather Charles, aged fifteen, was living with his sister Catherine in 181 Bond Street, Liverpool. Aged nineteen, he married Ellen Gardiner in 1875, but she died young, and in 1881 he married Elizabeth Ellen (née Renkin, born 1862 in Liverpool) – my great-grandmother – at St Mary's Anglican Church, Kirkdale, Walton on the Hill. Sadly, Elizabeth – Gran's mum – died in 1907, aged forty-four. By 1911, Gran had moved to Rochdale, Lancashire, to work in a cotton mill, while living with her brother James and his family.[39] By 1913, she had returned to Liverpool. On 22nd March 1914, she married Alfred Thompson at St Mary's Church, Kirkdale, where her parents had married in 1881.[40]

---

[37] For memories of court life see: Maggie Clarke and Cathryn Kemp, *Jam Butties and a Pan of Scouse: Hardship and happiness in the Liverpool docks* (London: Trapeze, 2016).

[38] We consider this accurate because Gran told Anne that her brother William was killed on the *Thracia* and later we confirmed the loss of the ship with few survivors.

[39] On mills, see Tracy Johnson, *The Mill Girls: Moving true stories of love and loss from Lancashire's cotton mills* (London: Ebury Press, 2014).

[40] St Mary's church (Archer Street): opened August 1836, closed 1973, demolished 1979. Canon Thomas Major Lester (1829-1903), an

Her dad died c. 1917 (aged about sixty).

Gran's husband Alfred was born in Liverpool, but his family was Scottish. His mum, Jane Carrie (née Millar, born 1847), was married in 1868 to James Thompson (born 1847 in Dundee). Their parents were Scottish. They moved to Liverpool before 1880 and had thirteen children (with twelve surviving). In 1911, James (my great-grandfather, aged sixty-four) was a retired joiner, living in 267 Fountains Road with Jane (aged sixty-three) and five single children, including their son Alfred (my grandad, then aged twenty-three and born 1887) a bricklayer/contractor.[41] But sadly Jane died in April 1912, two years before Alfred married Elizabeth Thomas at St Mary's Church. In September 1914, the First World War started. James Thompson died in 1915 (aged sixty-eight).

Liverpool was a fast-growing port city in the 19th century and job opportunities with higher pay than elsewhere probably made it attractive to some of my relatives. However, it was particularly attractive to Irish migrants (until 1921, Ireland was part of Britain). Until the late 1840s, migration was slow, but the Great Famine accelerated the numbers of Irish people leaving the country for Britain and overseas. Some people reached Liverpool and didn't travel further. Laura Kelly notes the high percentage of Irish-born people living in Liverpool as a percentage of the total population: 17.3 (1841), 22.3 (1851), over 15 (1871).[42]

---

education visionary, was its vicar (for about fifty years) and the church grew under him. See Ken Rogers, 'In tribute to Canon Thomas Major Lester'. Undated. Accessed 24 August 2022 at Education visionary Canon Thomas Major Lester - The Lost Tribe of Everton

[41] The 1911 England Census.

[42] Laura Kelly, 'Irish Migration to Liverpool and Lancashire in the Nineteenth Century', University of Warwick, last revised 18 June 2014. Accessed 24 August 2022 at Irish Migration to Liverpool and Lancashire in the Nineteenth Century by Laura Kelly (warwick.ac.uk) Also 'Great Irish Famine', Skibbereen Heritage Centre. Accessed 24 August 2022 at Great Irish Famine - Skibbereen Heritage Centre (skibbheritage.com)

Tragically, on 7th May 1915 the German submarine U-20 sank the Cunard passenger liner RMS *Lusitania* off the coast of County Cork, Ireland, en route from New York to Liverpool. Deaths were 1,191 men, women and children. Liverpudlians were heartbroken.[43] Then Gran sadly lost her older brother William (my great uncle), a waiter, when his Merchant Navy ship the *Thracia* was torpedoed by the German submarine UC-69 on 27th March 1917.

After the First World War, Spanish Flu swept the world and without vaccines an estimated fifty million people died (although this could have been as high as 100 million). Fortunately, Alf and Elizabeth survived. But in the 1930s they experienced the Great Depression, and then the Second World War. Gran and Grandad had two children: Alfred William (born 23rd September 1914), our Uncle Alf, and Lilian (Mum - born 10th June 1921). As mentioned earlier, Alfred William married Edith May Connor on 5th August 1939 and lived at 62 Grey Rock Street.[44]

Gran, Grandad and our mum and dad experienced trying times being working-class and war-weary – but they had a determination to improve their lives, their children's lives, and their communities.

Mum (Lilian Dutch, née Thompson)

Moving

British Prime Minister Neville Chamberlain made a radio broadcast on 3rd September 1939, stating 'this country is at war with Germany.' Lil, a single woman, was eighteen and

---

[43] See J. Kent Layton, *Lusitania: 7 May 1915*. Undated. Accessed 24 August 2022 at https://www.liverpoolmuseums.org.uk/stories/lusitania-7-may-1915 And J. Kent Layton, *Lusitania 100 years later: never forget*. Undated. Accessed 24 August 2022 at Lusitania 100 years later: never forget | National Museums Liverpool (liverpoolmuseums.org.uk)
[44] The 1939 Register.

living at home with her parents in 57 Grey Rock Street. They had moved from 33 Barry Street in 1934, when Lil was about thirteen. Compulsory school leaving age was fourteen, so she went to her new school, "Newsham" Council school Sheil Road Girls, which was walking distance from home. She left in midsummer 1935 with a very good "Scholar's Report and Testimonial". By then, ominous clouds had appeared above Europe, with the rise of the Nazis. Although Neville Chamberlain reached an agreement with Adolf Hitler in September 1938 for 'peace in our time', this agreement did not hold after Germany attacked and occupied Poland (Britain's ally).

War and munitions work

Many men were conscripted into the armed forces, so women took on their roles. At the start of the war, it was generally believed that men would resent their wives and daughters being required to do any war work, but it turned out that women were willing to be involved even before the war started. They made major contributions.[45]

As far as we know, Lil never put on a uniform, although single women aged twenty to thirty were being conscripted as the war progressed. By January 1940, Winston Churchill (First Lord of the Admiralty) called for women to do war work, especially on munitions. Maureen Hill notes that there were many such calls until December 1941, when "mobile" women (those without home responsibilities) who were aged twenty to thirty were conscripted for essential work.[46]

In June 1941, Lil was twenty. When she started is unknown, but she became a munitions worker at the Kirkby Royal Ordinance Factory, six miles from Liverpool. This was

---

[45] Jacky Hyams, *Bomb Girls, Britain's Secret Army: The Munitions Women of World War II* (London: John Blake, 2014), p.29.
[46] Maureen Hill, *Britain at War: Unseen Archives* (Bath: Parragon, 2006), p.219.

her job in 1944 when she met Stan, her future husband.

Again, Hill clearly explains the vital role of munitions workers: they made bombs, bullets, mines, shells, casings, etc. Casings were sent to factories, usually located outside towns and cities, for filling. This was a risky business, and women working with explosives wore special clothing and had to remember to remove any metal items that could cause a spark and start an explosion.[47]

It was extremely hazardous at Kirkby; one of the nation's filling factories. Thirty-seven awards were made for acts of bravery related to accidents and fires.[48] Lil worked shifts, including nights, and Kirkby was some distance to travel in blackouts. Minimising lights made it difficult for enemy aircraft to spot targets, but some people died in road accidents as a result.

Tony Graham and Paul Wright record that a railway station was opened for the Kirkby factory on 9th December 1940; a branch line off the Liverpool to Wigan line. The factory was linked with trams (from December 1943). However, the first shells were finished in September 1940, with around 50-100 workers on site. They note that eventually Kirkby had 1,000 buildings, eighteen miles of roadway and twenty-three miles of railway! In summer 1941, the workforce was 10,000, rising to a maximum of 23,000. For secrecy, the railway station was not known as the Kirkby Royal Ordinance Factory, but Simonswood.[49]

---

[47] Hill, *Britain*, p.220. See chapter five 'Women in the Workforce' with photographs. For male munitions workers see chapter six 'Don't You Know There's a War On!'

[48] See 'Spirit of the Blitz: Exhibition - Munitions factories: The Royal Ordnance factory Kirkby'. National Museums Liverpool. Accessed 24 August 2022 at Spirit of the Blitz | National Museums Liverpool (liverpoolmuseums.org.uk)

[49] Tony Graham and Paul Wright, *Disused Stations Site Record. Station Name: Kirkby Royal Ordinance Factory*. Last updated 21 May 2017. Accessed 24 August 2022 at http://www.disused-stations.org.uk/k/kirkby_royal_ordnance_factory/ Also see *Kirkby Royal*

Women were Britain's "secret army" in the munitions factories. Hyams, speaking of single women, notes ninety per cent were employed in such factories.[50] Her informative book charts the "munitions women", including their memories. Without them, the Spitfires in the Battle of Britain, North Atlantic convoys, D-Day landing forces, etc., would have lacked ammunition. Yet, she observes, it was not until Remembrance Sunday in 2012 London that a small group of elderly "Bomb Girls" walked with other veterans. Mum kept silent about her secret war work.[51]

The Kirkby Factory closed in March 1946. Six months later, Lil married Stan, on 14th September 1946, at St Margaret's Anglican Church, Anfield.

Rationing

January 1940 saw the first food rationing and ration books issued to attempt a fair distribution of limited resources. As 57 Grey Rock was a small terraced house, with no front garden and only a tiny backyard for access to the outside toilet, there was virtually nowhere to grow food in the "Dig for Victory" programme. In a patch of soil next to the small privet tree, they could grow a few vegetables, or use window boxes. Perhaps they had a local allotment to grow food (in Sheil Park?). Some people kept chickens for their eggs.

People with large gardens, or who lived in the country, generally had more to eat, and a better selection of food.

Ordinance Factory known as Simonswood (1940-1946). Undated. Accessed 24 August 2022 at Kirkby Royal Ordnance (oldrailways.uk)
[50] Hyams, *Bomb Girls*, p.29.
[51] Further, see Lauren Potts and Monica Rimmer, 'The Canary Girls: The workers the war turned yellow', BBC News 20 May 2017. Accessed 24 August 2022 at The Canary Girls: The workers the war turned yellow - BBC News And BBC News, 'Memorial fund for WWII munitions workers', 29 April 2013. Accessed 24 August 2022 at Memorial fund for WWII munitions workers - BBC News

June 1941 brought the rationing of clothing using a points system (sixty points per year initially, and then reduced to forty-eight points). Queuing ("waiting in a line") and long waits became common. Further rationing followed and remained in Britain after the war. Cigarettes were in short supply. Of course, items were bought and sold on the black market through spivs (as illustrated by the character "Walker" in the TV series *Dad's Army*).

Nationwide, people struggled. Besides normal work and overtime, they were expected to volunteer for other duties, or cover for people to give them a day off work. Hall remarks that life for all, irrespective of age, wealth and gender, was very demanding, taking time and energy in paid work, voluntary commitments and running homes.[52]

Uncle Alf was a bricklayer and an ARP warden before joining the army. Wardens patrolled the streets and enforced the blackout requirements so no lights could be seen – "Put that light out!" as Hodges shouted in *Dad's Army*.

The Blitz and Mill Road Maternity Hospital

As a "munitions worker", Lil faced many dangers. But there were also dangers back home. She wondered if her home might be bombed and her parents killed or injured while she was at work. Liverpool, like London and other cities, experienced the Blitz, and so Lil would have gone through the horror of sheltering in the cellar in their house, or using a public air raid shelter. Sometimes these were in the centre of narrow streets. Sadly, they could not withstand direct hits, and my parents mentioned occupants being killed.

The docks at Liverpool suffered heavy overnight bombing during a "Christmas Blitz" on 20th and 21st December 1940,

---

[52] Hill, *Britain*, p.247. For a boy living near Sheil Rd see: K.H. Bayley, 'Memories of the War 1939-1945', BBC Home 11 November 2003. Accessed 24 August 2022 at BBC - WW2 People's War - Memories of Growing Up in Liverpool during WW2

with more than 200 people killed and many injured. A previous raid occurred on 12th December. The *Index of Liverpool Civilian War Dead* December 1940 records six people in 40 Grey Rock Street killed that month (five on 21st December and one died on 24th from injuries), including a Mrs Jones and her three sons. Eileen Knight provides eyewitness testimony of her father William Hunt helping Mr Jones to dig out his dead family.[53] Mr and Mrs Morris also died. As children, we played on the cleared debris from the site.

People who had homes destroyed had to rescue their possessions and find other accommodation. Some people ("trekkers"), mainly made homeless by bombs, put their belongings on prams, carts etc., and walked to the edge of cities for safety. Sadly, looters targeted people's homes before folk could recover their possessions.

Mill Road Hospital (not far from Grey Rock), where I was born, was hit during the 2nd May 1941 Blitz (called the May Blitz, lasting from 1st to 7th May). In this period, National Museums Liverpool report that enormous damage occurred from 870 tons of high explosives and more than 112,000 firebombs. Joseph Domingo, who was born in Mill Road, remarks that during the bombing he was separated from his mother and in the confusion, they were in different hospitals for two days.[54] He records seventy-eight named people

---

[53] 'Index of Liverpool Civilian War Dead, December 1940' (Information supplied by the Commonwealth War Graves Commission). Accessed 24 August 2022 at Index of Liverpool Civilian War - December 1940 (liverpoolmonuments.co.uk) See Kay Jones, 'Sharing the human stories behind the Blitz: Eileen Knight'. Undated. Accessed 24 August 2022 at Sharing the human stories behind the Blitz | National Museums Liverpool (liverpoolmuseums.org.uk)

[54] Mark Duell, 'Blitz survivor, 78, who was just one-week-old when a Nazi bomb smashed into hospital tells new documentary how her mother picked her up and fled maternity ward as it crumbled', *MailOnline*, updated 24 May 2019. Accessed 24 August 2022 at Blitz survivor reveals how her mother fled maternity hospital during bombing | Daily Mail Online

killed in the attack (noting the true number was probably far higher). These included mums with babies, children, men and women. One lady (seventy-six years old), the widow of James Robinson, and a neighbour who lived at 31 Grey Rock Street, died on 3rd May.

The dead included hospital patients, students, doctors, nurses and ambulance drivers. People injured elsewhere during the bombing were waiting for treatment when the bomb struck. Domingo adds that Gertrude Riding worked at the hospital from 1910, becoming a Matron in 1927. In the bombing, she lost an eye, and was later awarded the OBE. She was still working there when I was born, and she retired in 1948. Dr Leonard Findlay was awarded the George Medal for bravery. The hospital closed in the 1990s. People listened to wirelesses or cinema newsreels to learn what was happening – there were no TVs then.[55] In summer 2019, Channel 5 showed three captivating, but horrific, episodes on Liverpool called *The Blitz: Britain on Fire*.[56]

Our cousin Edna Elizabeth Thompson was born 22nd January 1941, before the May Blitz. Many parents evacuated their children to the countryside for safety, in 1939/40. Around 130,000 Liverpool children were evacuated. Again, with the 2nd May 1941 bombings, parents packed Lime Street Station to evacuate their children.[57] Perhaps Auntie Edie left with baby Edna – we do not know. In 1942-43, Auntie Edie gave birth to Barbara Thompson, but sadly Barbara died in this period. Billy Butler's mum was

---

[55] For insights, see Joshua Levine, *The Secret History of the Blitz* (London: Simon & Schuster, 2015).
[56] Michael Buerk, Angellica Bell and Rob Bell (presenters), *The Blitz: Britain on Fire*, Channel 5 TV, Episodes 1-3, 2019. Accessed 24 August 2022 at The Blitz: Britain On Fire - Channel 5. Also: 'Spirit of the Blitz', National Museums Liverpool. Accessed 24 August 2022 at Spirit of the Blitz | National Museums Liverpool (liverpoolmuseums.org.uk)
[57] See 'Liverpool and the May Blitz of 1941', National Museums Liverpool. Accessed 24 August 2022 at Liverpool and the May Blitz of 1941 | National Museums Liverpool (liverpoolmuseums.org.uk)

evacuated to Amlwch, Anglesey in Wales, where he was born in January 1942.

National Museums Liverpool notes the city suffered terribly with the second-highest number of civilian deaths from bombings. Also, press reports at the time often didn't tell the complete story because of necessary censorship.[58]

Later, my cousin Pauline E. Thompson was born in 1947 (the same year as me), but sadly died in 1949, at two years old. Apparently, we played together and shared a pram, but I was too young to be able to remember this. However, we visited the family grave with Pauline's next to it. In 1950, my cousin Alfred was born, and we became great friends as we grew up.

Dad (Stanley Dutch)

Shop assistant to sailor

Stan was aged eleven when his mum Florence Dutch (born 1878 in Lancashire, née Woodhead) died in November 1929. He went to live with Auntie Bel (Isabella Hoban, born 1908) and her dad, "Pop" John Thomas Hoban (1875-1955) at 33 Harewood Street. In June 1901, John had married Elizabeth Ann Siddall at a Roman Catholic Church, but we children cannot recall ever meeting her. John's father, John Blake Hoban, was born in Cork, Ireland, while his mother Anne Jane (née Owen) was born in Liverpool in 1850 and she had a Welsh dad and grandad.

However, Pop's daughter, our Auntie Bel, was christened in a Protestant church and attended an Anglican church. Further, she marched in Liverpool's Orange Lodge parades, a Protestant organisation with roots in the Reformation.

---

[58] 'Blitzed: Liverpool lives', National Museums Liverpool Exhibition 14 Jun 2019—Summer 2022. Accessed 24 August 2022 at Blitzed: Liverpool lives | National Museums Liverpool (liverpoolmuseums.org.uk)

Dad's family tree is not as straightforward as Mum's. John Dutch (of 9 Severs Street) married Florence (living at 65 Boundary Lane) on 16th June 1902 at Emmanuel Anglican Church, West Derby Road, Everton. Florence's family came from Yorkshire. She had three children and then Stan was born in 78 Casterton Street. The 1921 census records four family members living together: Florence (aged forty-two), son John (almost twelve), daughter Lilian (nine years and six months) and Stan (two years, nine months). Eventually, they moved to 39 Harewood Street. We were told for very many years that Stan's father (John Dutch) had died from war wounds before Dad was born. But later we found he died in 1915. Decades later, Auntie Bel told Stan that he was her half-brother, which meant her dad, John Thomas Hoban, was his father. It was a revelation to us! His father was John Blake Holborn, born c.1847, in Cork, Ireland.

Florence Dutch's mum, Emma Woodhead (née Hardington) – my great-grandmother – was born in 1850 in Sheffield, where her father Robert J. Hardington was also born, c.1827. They knew about 11th March 1864 (the Great Sheffield Flood), when a dam catastrophically ruptured, pouring water into Sheffield as people slept. Dan Snow notes drownings included almost 250 people and 700 animals. Fifteen bridges were also destroyed and hundreds of buildings were ruined or damaged. For civilian lives lost, it was Victorian Britain's worst non-maritime disaster.[59] Tourists came to see the aftermath.

In 1860, Emma married George in Worksop (Nottinghamshire), and later moved to Liverpool. But Stan wouldn't have known his grandparents, as they died in Liverpool in 1901 (George) and 1906 (Emma), well before Stan was born (1918).

Sometimes Stan didn't have shoes and went barefoot, and

---

[59] Dan Snow, *On This Day in History* (London: John Murray, 2018), p.79, 11 March.

he was involved in fights with other children that would leave him with grazed knuckles. He attended Whitefield Road School for infants and juniors, but attended the Steers Street council school Senior Boys (off Spencer Street), built in 1885. He left in October 1932 (aged fourteen, the compulsory school leaving age) with a very good report. His first job was as a shop assistant in Minton's, which sold paint, wallpaper, varnish etc., in Prescott Road and later in Manchester Street. Minton's was a family business and old photos (1947 and 1960) show the shop at the junction of Manchester Street and Dale Street, just behind the entrance/exit to the Queensway Mersey Tunnel (opened 1934). A massive advertisement on the side of Minton's stated: 'Minton's The Paint and Wallpaper People. STOCKISTS OF GAYMEL the PROFESSIONAL PAINT'.[60] Stan stayed for about three years and then made the important decision in January 1936 to join the Royal Navy, aged seventeen-and-a-half He was 5' 3¼" tall, with brown hair, blue eyes and a "fresh" complexion.

After a long engagement, Auntie Bel married Uncle Jim Doran between April and June 1936, but from 6th May 1936, Stan started training at Portsmouth. Back then, the Royal Navy was the largest navy in the world, and respected as the "senior service" for its long history. As a radio operator, Stan learnt Morse code, to send and receive messages. During his career, he would receive coded messages originating in Britain's Bletchley Park, the secret codebreaking base where accomplishments made helped to shorten the war.[61] By July 1937, Stan had passed his Ordinary Telephonist exams and

---

[60] *Memories of Liverpool* (Halifax: True North Books, 1998). See Section Three 'Around the city centre'. There are no authors and pages are not numbered. But Minton's photos are inside section three counting the pages: 4 (1947), 11 (c.1960 with the side wall advert) and 16 (1960).
[61] See Sinclair McKay, *The Secret Life of Bletchley Park: The WWII Codebreaking Centre and the Men and Women Who Worked There* (London: Arum Press, 2011). I visited it for my 70th birthday.

would become a Leading Telephonist in September 1942. Dad played his part in the Second World War.

Atlantic, Norway, Mediterranean & Hellenic Medal for Outstanding Acts

Dad's naval records show that his first ship was HMS *Glasgow* (from May 1938 to November 1940). In 1939, before war broke out, HMS *Glasgow* escorted the liner RMS *Empress of Australia* with HM King George VI and Queen Elizabeth to Canada and the United States. We have photos of Dad in New York. G. D. Oliver *In Peace and War: The Story of HMS Glasgow 1937 – 1958* records the ship's history.

Stan was serving on HMS *Glasgow* when Britain declared war on Germany, on 3rd September 1939. Before the end of September, the aircraft carrier HMS *Courageous* was sunk by a torpedo from a German U-boat. It sank in around fifteen minutes, with 518 men lost. Glyn Prysor in *Citizen Sailors* calls it 'the first major warship loss of the war'. In October, the battleship *Royal Oak* was sunk at Scapa Flow, after the submarine U-47 cleverly crept through the defences and torpedoed it. Able Seaman I.G. Hall, who was serving on HMS *Glasgow*, noted in his diary that 800 hands were lost, and thought that something was wrong somehow, for this to have occurred so early in the war.

Such a loss would impact psychologically on HMS *Glasgow's* crew, including Stan. During October, HMS *Glasgow* was in the Atlantic, escorting and protecting ships.

In April 1940, German troops invaded Norway. The port of Narvik saw fighting involving French, British and Norwegian troops, navy vessels and aircraft, but Narvik could not be retaken. While under attack, HMS *Glasgow* evacuated King Haakon and his government, plus Crown Prince Olav and gold reserves from Molde town, which was on fire. In May 1940, HMS *Glasgow* took part in the Icelandic Offensive

(Operation Fork), landing marines to capture Iceland, thus preventing a German occupation. Then in November 1940, HMS *Glasgow* escorted the aircraft carrier HMS *Illustrious*, with other ships supporting the British air attack on the Italian navy based at Taranto (in southern Italy). This attack seriously weakened Italy's navy.

Prysor notes the importance of naval identity, with its friendship and community founded on both its history and tradition. HMS *Glasgow* had as its motto 'Memor es tuorum': 'Be mindful of your ancestors'.[62]

Later (February to November 1941), Stan served on the fast battleship HMS *Queen Elizabeth.* He spent three and a half years in Egypt for the Mediterranean War. Egypt held an important tactical position for the allies in the North Africa campaign against the Italians and Hitler's forces led by Erwin Rommel, as Tom Bower states. The Royal Navy had to control the Mediterranean Sea to ensure victory in the desert with the 8th Army, and keep open supply lines to India. Moreover, the Royal Navy had to disrupt the German ships delivering weapons etc., to Rommel's German army. It was a long, hard-fought campaign.[63]

From 22nd November 1942, Stan was assigned to HMS *Nile* (Command and Control). This was at the Royal Naval base in Alexandria, Egypt. In this period, he served on the Greek destroyer the *Queen Olga* (*Vasilissa Olga*), from 8th March 1942, and also from 15th September 1942 to 23rd July 1943.

Lt Cdr Geoffrey B. Mason RN (Rtd) recorded that on 25th March 1942 the *Queen Olga* was deployed with the destroyer HMS *Jervis* to take supplies to Tobruk. Then on 16th February 1943, HMS *Jervis*, with other HM destroyers, and the *Queen Olga* escorted a convoy at Tripoli to Alexandria. Next, on June 2nd it was 'Deployed with Greek destroyer VASILISSA OLGA and sank Italian torpedo boat

[62] Glyn Prysor, *Citizen Sailors: The Royal Navy in the Second World War* (London: Viking, 2011), p.138.
[63] Tom Bower, *Heroes of World War II* (London: BCA, 1995), p.66.

CASTORE and two mercantiles being escorted off Cape Spartivento on passage from Taranto to Messina.'[64] The *Naval Review* records this battle when Stan was present on the *Queen Olga*.[65]

Stan was cited in the *Supplement to the London Gazette* 17th October 1944 as he was awarded the Hellenic Medal for Outstanding Acts in this battle. It was conferred by 'the King of the Hellenes for services to the Greek Navy: *Medal for Outstanding Acts:* Leading Telegraphist, Stanley Dutch.'[66]

However, no more details are available. Dad spoke with affection about serving with his Greek friends, and his personal loss when they were killed. He kept their letters, which were discovered after his death. I recall the sadness sometimes when he spoke of them. Presumably, this was the attack on the *Queen Olga* after Stan was reassigned. I mentioned this in my unpublished family notes:

> While anchored in Lakki Bay, on the Greek island of Leros (Dodecanese between Samos and Cos, not far from the Turkish coast) the *Queen Olga* was sunk by

---

[64] Lt Cdr Geoffrey B Mason RN (Rtd), *Service Histories of Royal Navy Warships in World War 2: HMS Jervis (F.00) – J-class Flotilla Leader including Convoy Escort Movements,* 2004. Accessed 24 August 2022 at HMS Jervis, destroyer (naval-history.net) HMS *Jervis's* captain, Anthony Follett Pugsley, was awarded a Bar to the Distinguished Service Order (DSO) for his 'courage, resolution and skill in a successful attack on an enemy convoy while serving in H.M.S. Jervis', in the same battle alongside HHMS *Queen Olga*. See 'Second Supplement to the London Gazette', 3785, 20 August 1943, with 24 August approved reward and honours. Accessed 13 April 2023 at data.pdf (thegazette.co.uk)

[65] *The Naval Review*, 'The Royal Hellenic Navy, 1822 to 1949, Part 11', Vol. XXXVII (3) August 1949, pp.274-278 (274). Tom Bower, *Heroes*, p.64 calls Admiral Sir Andrew Cunningham the 'mastermind of the Battle of the Mediterranean'.

[66] His Majesty's Stationery Office, *Supplement to the London Gazette* 17th October 1944, p.4746. Accessed 15 July 2023 at Page 4746 | Issue 36749, 13 October 1944 | London Gazette | The Gazette)

German aircraft on 26 September 1943. Commander Blessas fell first, before six officers; sixty-five sailors and other crew members were killed. The attack was made by 25 Ju 88 bomber aircraft (a twin-engine multirole aircraft with more than 16,000 built during the war).

A war memorial stands on Lakki's waterfront, and an annual three-day service commemorates her sinking.

As a radio operator, Stan did not fire the ship's guns, but he told me a brief story. Once, while having a break on deck, resting, they were attacked by an enemy plane. Stan ran to mount a gun and fire at the plane, but by the time he reached it the plane had fired its shots and flown on. He was unhurt and I think everyone was safe. Worries of attacks from enemy planes (with machine guns, cannon, bombs and torpedoes), ships, U-boats and minefields, as well as stormy seas, were a daily reality. Physical and psychological strains existed side-by-side.

D-Day landings and escort duty

Stan returned from the Mediterranean and was assigned before D-Day to HMS *Attack* (shore establishment), which was a Coastal Forces base at Portland, near Weymouth. By D-Day on Tuesday 6th June 1944, he was on board ship working as a radio operator. He told me that during D-Day he was on HMS *Grey Fox* (a steam gunboat) in Operation Neptune, escorting American troops that landed on Omaha Beach.[67] Enemy resistance was fierce, and losses were very high, so it was called "Bloody Omaha". The Royal Navy's contribution to the American landings was recognised with an inscription on the American Memorial,

_____

[67] Stan's ship was one of six steam gunboats (SGBs) as escorts on D-Day. For the naval Task Organisation, see *Omaha Beach: American Troops*, TOP SECRET – NEPTUNE 20 May 1944. Accessed 24 August 2022 at D-Day : Normandy 1944 - OMAHA BEACH : U.S. Troops (6juin1944.com)

Weymouth, Dorset on the Esplanade, which was unveiled at a ceremony on 3rd December 1947.

Unhurt, Stan survived D-Day and subsequent escort duties across the channel, where ships transported the wounded, fresh troops with their equipment and ammunition, plus prisoners. From 1st February 1945, he was a leading telegraphist on HMS *Stork* and from 25th September 1945 at HMS *Mercury* (shore establishment), a base for the Royal Navy Signals School and Combined Signals School. Eventually, he was "demobbed" on 19th December 1945, after almost ten years' service; but immediately enrolled as a reservist. Sadly, so many people never returned home.

Meeting and marriage

In 1944, Stan met Lilian Thompson. He was on leave and by 1944 he'd been to the Mediterranean twice. Stan was coming up Grey Rock after swimming and he met Edie Thompson (our future Auntie Edie) and Owen Doran (Jim Doran's brother). Owen introduced Edie to Stan as his mate Alf Thompson's wife. Then Lilian came down the stairs in 57 Grey Rock and met Stan, who invited the family (Alf, Elizabeth, Alf, Edie and Lilian) out for a drink, which they accepted. After that, Stan and Lilian kept in touch by writing: each hoping (and probably praying) that they would survive the war.

When demobbed, Stan's address was 33 Harewood Street, (where Auntie Bel, Uncle Jim and Pop Hoban lived). He trained as a bricklayer and worked with Pop Hoban. I recall Dad talking about his "demob" suit for life back in "civvy street". Once, I went with him to buy himself a new coat, and he paid for it with an old type of £5 note, which was worth much more back then than it is now. After being in the navy for almost ten years' service, this was indeed a new life, though many struggles lay ahead.

Births, baptisms, beginnings

After their marriage, Lil and Stan settled into 57 Grey Rock with our maternal grandparents. Their first winter together was desperately cold and snowy. It has been called "the big freeze of forty-seven", "In the bleakest midwinter", and the "snowiest winter". Snow fell from Friday 24th January until March 1947. Massive drifts affected roads and railways. North-eastern ports were frozen, as was the River Thames. Britain relied heavily on coal for homes, industry and power stations. But when coal could not be delivered, there were power cuts in industry and electricity cuts to homes. Frozen ground meant vegetables could not be easily unearthed (picks and pneumatic drills were used), and the dead could not be buried. When the March thaw came, melting snow caused floods.[68] This showed the problem of relying on one main fuel source for the nation. No work and no warmth – people struggled.

I was born in summer 1947, in the previously bombed Mill Road Hospital. I had my first gift through a letter to Mum: cousin Edna (aged six) had written to Mum in hospital. She hoped Mum was getting better and asked 'are you glad that you have got a little Baby boy?' followed by 'I am sending a three pence [piece] to little robert for sweet' signed 'Love from Edna' with lots of kisses. The letter and old three-penny piece Mum kept, as they were so touching. I still have the coin and letter. Also, I still have my National ID card.

Anne was born in 1949, under the free National Health Service. She was also christened at St Margaret's, as I had been. Some years later Christina was born at home.

When we were growing up, in the mornings, at 7.55am and 8.55am, loud hooters sounded from Ogden's Tobacco

---

[68] Jonathan Bastable (ed.), *Reader's Digest Yesterday's Britain: The Illustrated Story of How We Lived, Worked and Played* (1st edition reprinted with amendments; London: The Reader's Digest Association Ltd, 2003) pp.176-175 in the section 'In the bleakest midwinter'.

factory, summoning the workers. Auntie Edie worked there. In the evenings, men wearing work clothes and flat caps trailed home, tired at the end of long days of manual work. Thursdays were pay days. The cash had to last until the following Thursday, because credit and loans were difficult to obtain. Dad worked as a bricklayer usually Monday to Friday, and Saturday mornings, but on some rainy days he was sent home early without earning a full day's pay. Clearly, this was bad for the family.

Women scrubbed their front steps and cleaned the brass front doors fittings (e.g. knocker and letterbox) with Brasso metal polish. Window cleaners with their ladders and buckets washed the house windows. Children walked to and from local schools. Adults who wanted a "natter" stood outside their front doors and chatted to passers-by. Women often wore their hair in curlers under a hair net. Looking good in the evenings was all-important, so curlers in the day was okay. These were our streets. But they were ear-marked for demolition under "slum clearance".

The year I was born was one of Britain's worst winters. Ian McCaskill and Paul Hudson in *Frozen Britain* devote Part III 'The Snowiest Winter – 1947' to what was the snowiest winter since records began – forty-five pages explain the desperate situation with cold and snow.[69] As mentioned earlier, our house had no central heating, no double glazing, and no insulation. My parents and grandparents suffered! They relied upon coal for the fires and gas for cooking and heating hot water in a large tub for washing, as I recall. But people had the option of using 'washer women' who, for a fee, would take clothes to a washing house. The problem was that people did not have many changes of clothes. Children often relied on 'hand-me-downs' from older siblings or neighbours.

Kynaston reports the shock when, as the war finished,

---

[69] Ian McCaskill and Paul Hudson, *Frozen Britain* (Ilkley: Great Northern Books, 2011). First published as *Frozen in Time* (2006).

people realised the long-term hardships they had experienced in the Blitz had to continue now in a bankrupt peace. The "enormous economic blitz" was just starting.[70]

Even in 1948, when I was a toddler, rationing continued and two million people ate horse meat weekly. But not everyone realised it was horse if it was sold as 'steak'. Whale meat was also eaten, but not rationed. Bread was not rationed during the war but for two years, July 1946-48, it was.[71] Clothes rationing continued until March 1949. Petrol rationing continued, but our family could not afford a car.

Housing continued in short supply. New towns were built but, despite a million new homes by 1951, the crisis continued. New council houses were allocated to people on a points-based priority list. We were to stay in our rented terraced house for twenty years after I was born – no new council house or prefab for us.

In the 1918 Fisher Act, the school leaving age was raised to fourteen years. Prohibitions and restrictions were also placed on children's employment hours. Later, the 1944 Education Act established three stages of formal education: primary, secondary and further. Then in April 1947, the school leaving age was raised from fourteen to fifteen, which was when I would be able to finish schooling.

In all the setbacks and brutal changes there were two symbols of Liverpool's spirit of endurance. From 1903-1974, Liverpool's Anglican Cathedral was being built – the world's largest Anglican Cathedral. We were Anglicans, but the long building project started before my parents were born and was completed after we moved from Liverpool. The largest Roman Catholic cathedral in England, the Metropolitan Cathedral of Christ the King Liverpool, now stands at the opposite end of

---

[70] David Kynaston, *A World to Build* (London: Bloomsbury, 2008), p.103 in chapter 4 'We're so short of everything'. Quote from novelist Panter-Downes, who sent letters to *The New Yorker*.
[71] Jonathan Bastable (ed.), R*eader's Digest Yesterday's Britain*, pp.178-180.

Hope Street to the Anglican Cathedral. On the fourth attempt, building started in October 1962 and it was consecrated on 14th May 1967. Both cathedrals are magnificent, and I've enjoyed visiting them, most recently in 2018. In a class-conscious country, we were working class. Clothing was not abundant and daily changes of clothing and showers were not options.[72] And we didn't speak proper English – it was Liverpudlian. Yet we were to see our two new cathedrals.

---

[72] See Lynda Lee-Potter, *Class Act: How to Beat the British Class System* (London: Metro, 2000).

CHAPTER 4

Primary School Years

The day arrived when I started school: life was to be "enhanced" by education. This chapter explains my life around Whitefield Road Primary School (infants and juniors). Our church, St Margaret's, had a primary school but that was further away, so I went to Whitefield Road. Paying for private education wasn't a remote possibility.

First day at school

My clearest memory is the first day at Whitefield Road School – a short walk from home. I started in late August 1951, shortly after my fourth birthday; 9-4 every day, but I went home for dinner (what some now call lunch). I guess my family felt I was ready for school.

Whitefield Road Infants' entrance had a gate into the concrete playground, which was surrounded by a wall and railings. Mum and Gran took me on my first day and my sister Anne remembers it. This was my earliest experience of education as I recall – no pre-school nursery. As the older child, I had no siblings to explain school to me. I can't recall even having a visiting day as a "settling-in" experience.

Our ground-floor classroom overlooked the playground. Miss May was the teacher. It was a warm, dry day, and the large concertina window was open onto the playground. I was given a desk and seat near the centre of the classroom. Classes had large numbers of boys and girls, but I don't recall knowing anyone.

Anyway, I decided against attending school, and looked for an escape route. Chance quickly came my way. Miss May asked the children to line up at the door by the corridor.

As children moved right towards Miss May, I stayed in my seat, and when the window side of the classroom was clear, I quickly moved left to the window. I stepped on the window sill and looked out – the way was clear. It was now or never, as nobody in the room appeared to notice me, so I jumped from the window into the playground. I landed safely on the concrete and the route to the school gate on my right was clear – so I ran for it. 'Freedom at last,' I thought.

Unfortunately, when I looked to my left, I saw Mum, Gran and Anne coming out of the main door into the playground. No doubt they were pleased that I was safely inside, and they were off home. However, they spotted me. This was no time to hesitate. I ran for the gate as fast as my little legs could go, with Mum in hot pursuit. But I was no match for her, and she caught me before I made the gate. I cannot recall her words, but I was swiftly taken back to begin "the best days of your life".

I never attempted another escape (and my schooling would be much longer than I imagined). Vague memories include riding that lovely rocking horse (with Miss May's encouragement), a sandpit, water and toys. One day, my cousin Edna (from Red Rock) spoke to me through the open classroom window. She was born in January 1941, so was ten years old, and I think we only exchanged a few words, but it meant so much to me that I still remember. There was a large gap in our ages, but we kept in touch as adults, even after she moved with her family to America.

At one edge of the playground, opposite the school gate stood a brick Second World War air-raid shelter with a concrete roof. It was rectangular, with two entrances facing the playground. The doors were missing, so we ran through it during playtimes, especially if I was being chased by someone. Mind you, debris (bricks and rubbish) on the floor created a tripping hazard. There were no lights, but sunlight shining through the entrances made it light enough.

My younger sisters Anne and Christina also attended

Whitefield Road, but never jumped out of windows. During our time there, we knew if we were going to be late. Firstly, Ogden's Imperial Tobacco factory in Boundary Lane had a large tower clock, so we could see the time. Secondly, and more importantly, its works' hooter/buzzer sounded at 7.55am and 8.55am, reminding workers to clock in. The 8.55am hooter told schoolchildren we had five minutes left to get to school – time to run.

Whitefield Road (Juniors)

Worship with warnings

After a while, I moved to the Juniors. It occupied the common site with the Infants but the separate entrance on Boundary Lane was slightly nearer home. It was "mixed", as it had girls and boys. Both schools were built with red bricks and joined, but with separate concrete playgrounds and entrances (although a narrow passageway connected them near the air raid shelter). The Junior School entrance was set in brick walls on the pavement's edge. Once inside, we were in the playground. The school had no grassed areas, unlike the modern Whitefield Primary School. Also, it lacked a gymnasium (the hall doubled as one), a swimming pool, sports fields, and similar facilities.

The hall was used for daily morning assemblies. We stood or sat on the floor in our class groups and sang Christian hymns, and said prayers. Although a state school, during the war years people believed that Christian faith could renew education and society. John Lawson and Harold Silver note that many called for Christian education in schools. In fact, the 1943 Norwood Report mentioned 'the present genuine demand that there shall be an opportunity for religious education in all schools'. It was recognised that homes provided little in the way of religious education, and even churches often had low attendance. Therefore, schools should supply instruction. Indeed, the National Union of Teachers recognised the situation and accepted state schools should provide religious instruction.[73]

In the school assembly, our head teacher, Mr J. Cain, gave talks and warnings. He was an older, smartly-dressed man, with grey hair, plenty of energy, and he was funny. In particular, his vivid warnings about the dangers of Bonfire Night still stick with me. This celebration recalls how the 1605 Gunpowder Plot by Guy Fawkes and co-conspirators to blow up King James I and the Houses of Parliament was foiled. Thereafter, people set off fireworks and build bonfires to burn "the guy" on 5th November each year. The event is widely celebrated, even now; yet I can't recall seeing formal firework displays.

We pupils laughed as Mr Cain warned us not to jump over lit bonfires, and then before the school assembly he proceeded to jump over an imaginary bonfire. He demonstrated spectacularly **not** to play dangerous games of sitting on seats on the top of burning bonfires. Brave (foolhardy?) children did run up a wooden door or pieces of wood and sit on a seat (e.g. an old armchair) above the flames. After showing their bravery, they ran down, daring another child to copy the dangerous display. Mr Cain imitated this before us while warning us **not** to do it. I listened, and took his warning very seriously.

However, I saw boys in our street doing this very thing on our nearest bonfire in Grey Rock. They ran up individually and sat above the hot flames. Eventually, they stopped, when they thought that the flames were too high, or the armchair was likely to collapse. Young and old boys joined in. You may ask, 'Where were their parents?'.

Dad arranged safe firework displays in our small backyard. We watched through the window while he lit them, and

[73] John Lawson and Harold Silver, *A Social History of Education in England* (London: Methuen, 1973), p.417 in chapter XI 'Education and social ideals 1939-1972'.

enjoyed spectacular colours, Catherine wheels, crackles, Roman candles, volcanoes, sparks and shooting rockets. Sparklers were safer for children to handle, and this was fun. As we got older, we bought our fireworks in shops (but had to be thirteen to do so). To raise money for fireworks, we dressed up around Hallowe'en (31st October) and went in groups from house to house, seeing people we mainly knew with our simple effigy of Guy Fawkes, made from old clothes stuffed with newspaper or rags. We would request 'Penny for the guy, please!'. Money collected was shared out later. Cousin Alf recalls asking 'Penny for the Guy' outside the pub on the corner of Red Rock and West Derby Road.

I recall "penny bangers" (then an old penny, not the modern decimal coinage) that we lit while still holding them, and either threw them or dropped them quietly near someone. The bangs startled people. We also had "jumping jacks"; these would bang and jump a few times. However, once I held one to light it and it went bang before I let go. Luckily, no harm was done – all fingers intact, and no burns. These fireworks were far less powerful than the modern ones.

Each street collected wood etc., for bonfires, and made sure nobody tried stealing it. Grey Rock, Red Rock and White Rock Streets had their bonfires, as did many other streets (often building them on the cleared Second World War bombsites). At the end of the night, the fires were left to smoulder and go out. Sometimes, bonfires were lit in the road, but this wasn't good because the tar caught fire. Occasionally, fire brigades came to extinguish fires. I think Mr Cain's humorous talks were valuable in keeping children safe. I certainly listened. No child, as far as I know, was burnt in our street through silly behaviour, although we were aware that accidents happened.

Fireworks nights were great fun, but our dog Trixie was terrified by loud bangs. She hid behind an armchair in our backroom, trembling and refusing to come out. Uncle Alf would come from his house to calm her. I grew up with Trixie (and our cat) and it was sad years later when Trixie had to be "put down" through illness.

Hallowe'en was a calmer night than Bonfire Night, also called "duck apple", from the games of being blindfolded and using our teeth to catch apples floating in a bowl of water. Also, we had a line in the kitchen with apples hanging down on string. Children had to catch them with their teeth, without using hands. We also had toffee apples and hot roasted horse chestnuts with salt. Mum and Gran encouraged the fun, and friends visited. Of course, not everyone celebrated Hallowe'en, because of its sinister associations. It was nothing like the modern commercial version, with sales of children's outfits and decorated homes.

In the summer, Mr Cain gave talks about not making "tar bombs", done with a wooden lolly-ice stick and tar from roads. Children sat at the side of roads where tar bubbled up under the hot sun. We would roll some into a heavy ball on the end of the stick, which could be thrown, but we didn't light them. However, it wasn't good for clothes, hands, or road surfaces. During one talk, he asked for a show of hands if we made them. I didn't put my hand up (although that didn't mean I never made any!).

School swimming

With no pool at school, pupils used Margaret Street Swimming Baths (built 1863, opening with its first gala in 1864 but demolished 1985). Supervised by a teacher, we walked in pairs, clutching towels and costumes, along Whitefield Road to the end of Margaret Street. Sometimes we took the route: Boundary Lane along Dawber Street to Kelshaw Street, then Spencer Street into Margaret Street.

It had a large swimming pool for public use and individual bath rooms, where people paid to wash in hot water. We pupils used the large pool with its double changing rooms arranged around the sides, with hanging curtains providing privacy. We left our clothes on the bench while swimming, as no lockers were available. The tiled pool was twenty or twenty-five-yards long, with a shallow end (three feet) and a deep end (six feet six inches). Water was chlorinated, to kill bugs. A smallish warm foot bath and shower were near the shallow end, so we washed before entering the pool and after getting out.

In the pool, we were largely left to our own devices – no coaches teaching us to swim, except for one instructor who taught me to dive (probably in secondary school). Some pupils were afraid of water and non-swimmers mainly splashed around in the shallow end. Some children could dive/swim, and did okay in school swimming galas. Getting dressed was a hassle, with teacher(s) shouting 'Hurry up!' and threatening to pull the curtains back!

Two events spring to mind. I could not swim, but wanted to enter the deep end so, tightly holding the side bar around the pool's edge, I carefully made my way there. I made good progress but was ultimately spotted by a teacher who told me to get out. He wasn't pleased! Which I guess was fair, as if I'd slipped, I might have drowned. Taking back a drowned pupil would be bad. On our way back to school, he stopped the class, and I was publicly reprimanded for my stupid act. But it didn't stop me going again. Sadly, there weren't swimming classes outside school, or none that I was aware of.

Another time, Dad took us swimming. He dived and swam confidently. He first met Mum when he was on leave from the Royal Navy and was returning from swimming. He also swam for the Navy. As he worked long days, I don't recall us swimming often as a family. Although Margaret Street was also open in evenings and Saturdays, sessions were restricted: male only, female only and mixed ("mixie").

It was not until July 1960 that I was awarded my Swimming Certificate "Beginners 50 Yards" from the Liverpool Association of Schoolmasters.

School tests and reports

We had periodic school tests. In one class, after a test, the teacher said I did well and that I was "a dark horse". Yet, I did not know what that meant – was it good or bad? So, I asked, 'What's a "dark horse"?'. She had to explain it meant that I was quiet and not easily noticed but I understood the material taught. A compliment! It impressed me so much that I remember it more than sixty years later.

School reports were issued for pupils at Christmas and summer, and Mum kept hold of them. They showed aptitude, attendance and conduct.

When I was seven, my Christmas 1954 report stated that I was in Class 9, which had a "roll" of forty-two pupils. Attendance and conduct were good and very good. The subjects studied included: scripture; reading; history; geography; arithmetic; art; and handwork. These were marked as fair, satisfactory, f(airly) good or good. The remarks (signed by Class Teacher M.J. Higgins and Head Teacher J. Cain) said my reading was improving. In mid-summer 1956, I came second in a class of forty, but my spelling was only "fair". In July 1957, I was tenth in a class of forty-eight but spelling was "weak". My final report for mid-summer 1958 (when I was ten), recorded that I was in Standard 4.B with a roll of forty-seven pupils and came sixth. It is difficult to imagine such large classes today.

The range of subjects had widened to: scripture; general English; history; geography; arithmetic; science; art; physical training and games; handwork; music; reading; writing: comprehension; spelling. Subjects were graded out of ten, twenty or sixty marks. Most subjects were fine, but spelling was still a struggle. Music was a miserable "Fail". However, the remarks (signed by Class Teacher B. Egginton and Head Teacher J. Cain) said: 'An excellent result. Robert has worked really hard and is an alert and intelligent pupil.' Nevertheless, I wasn't in the top A stream but the B class.

Was I good enough to pass the 11-plus exam?

Learning was often by rote. For our "times table" the class "sang" loud: 'One six is six, two sixes are twelve, three sixes are eighteen,' etc. Money was tricky before decimalisation in 1971. We used pounds, shillings (twenty shillings made one pound) and pence (twelve old pence made one shilling). Halfpennies (pronounced 'hay-pennies') also came in and farthings (one quarter of a penny) were legal until 1960. No calculators back then. All sums were done longhand, and fortunately I was good at arithmetic. To be honest, "spelling" was a long-term struggle and my sister Anne beat me here. Eventually, I was called a "late developer". Nowadays, research has indicated that summer-born babies have disadvantages.

School milk, dentists and nit nurses

One of my jobs at school was a "milk monitor". Governments provided us pupils with free school milk (a third of a pint each) stored in glass bottles in crates. Milk monitors distributed the milk and paper drinking-straws. In the winter, the milk would be cold and, in the summer, warm (there were no refrigerators at school). Regular milk provided children with nutrition. I certainly enjoyed my bottle, but not everyone did.

We first had teaching on dental hygiene in the Juniors. The teacher explained the design of teeth, protection and cleaning. After this, I took a more informed view of caring for them. Like many people, Gran used to leave her false teeth overnight in a glass at the bedside. Our parents' teeth weren't in good condition, but that was considered "normal". Anyway, schools ran a free dental service for pupils, which might mean extractions. Gas was used to put me to sleep before pulling my teeth. Unfortunately, bits of teeth were left in after one procedure, and I had to wait for these to drop out in due course. Although free, treatment was feared, and frankly not appreciated. Schools also had nit nurses, to see what living things we pupils had in our hair besides "tats" (knots). At home Gran would comb my hair to remove the tats; the term "tatty head" was often used disrespectfully of children – not just about me.

Home

Our 1950s home life was happy. Mum stayed home and looked after Anne and me, with Gran's assistance. Grandad and Dad were bricklayers, and went to work wherever they found it. We got the usual childhood illnesses (e.g. chickenpox, measles, mumps), but Mum was keen to get us vaccinated with the latest the NHS had. When we were young, polio (poliomyelitis), which particularly affects the young, was a potential killer, with no vaccines available. Survivors were often paralysed (temporarily or permanently) and had damaged legs; some were isolated for months. I recall seeing on TV rows of children in "iron lungs" to help them breathe. It struck fear into the population. Thankfully, in 1956 a polio vaccine was rolled out in Britain, and Mum sensibly made sure we had our injections; in 1962, an oral vaccine became available.[74] (Sadly, there's still no cure, and polio is a significant risk in some countries.)

For meals, we had a range of food, including: toast; breakfast cereals; eggs; mashed potatoes with corned beef or spam; bacon; liver; kidney; faggots; black puddings (their main ingredients were pork blood and fat, but I didn't realise that as a child!); fish; spaghetti on toast; Sunday roast (meat, potatoes and vegetables); or "scouse", a traditional

---

[74] See Nuala McCann, 'Polio: memories of self-isolation in the 1950s', BBC News NI 29 March 2020. Accessed 26 August 2022 at Polio: memories of self-isolation in the 1950s - BBC News Also, see NHS, 'Polio', page last reviewed 10 August 2022. Accessed 26 August 2022 at https://www.nhs.uk/conditions/polio

Liverpool stew made from leftovers that included lamb or beef, vegetables, potatoes, gravy, etc.[75] Dad finished his off with a piece of bread laid flat on the plate to soak up the gravy, and then cut up the bread with his knife and fork. Some adults ate tripe (edible muscles from the stomach lining of cattle, pigs or sheep), but this white stuff looked so disgusting I didn't eat it. If we bought a chicken at the butcher's, this was plucked by Gran or Mum. On Shrove Tuesdays, the day before Ash Wednesday and the start of Lent, we had delicious home-made pancakes, often with lemon juice, sugar or jam. Mum would toss them into the air, flipping them forward from the frying pan and catching them after they turned over and before they fell on the floor! On Good Friday, we had salt fish instead of meat, but Roman Catholic families always had fish on Fridays.

For snacks, we had a "jam butty" or "sugar butty", which was white bread spread with butter and then sprinkled with sugar. Sometimes, we had the meat juices/fat on bread (dripping is not considered too healthy these days because of saturated fats). Anne and I didn't like eating the bread crusts, so we hid them behind the tea cosy (on the tea pot). Dad and Mum weren't fooled, and found them: 'Eat them – it will make your hair curl!'. One of my hates was sprouts. Once, when I refused to eat them, Mum and Gran had a tactic. One shouted, 'Grab his nose!' – which is what happened. I could not escape, and they just waited until I opened my mouth to breathe. Then the ghastly sprout was put in and I had to eat it. I am still not keen on sprouts but, as they are "good for you", I eat them at Christmas.

For puddings, we enjoyed hot rice pudding with a dollop of jam – eating the skin was the best part; also semolina, roly-poly (suet with a jam filling) or tapioca. If we had ice cream, Dad often spelt it 'I-C-E' as a code with Mum, so we children

---

[75] For a recipe see IZZYM, 'How to Make Scouse, the Traditional Liverpool Stew', *Delishably* 7 January 2020. Accessed 26 August 2022 at How to Make Scouse, the Traditional Liverpool Stew - Delishably

didn't understand what he said, but in time we responded, 'We know that's ice cream!' For treats, we had plain Smith's crisps, which had a small blue bag inside the packet containing the salt to pour in (flavoured crisps were still to come). Perhaps we had a spoon of malt syrup (sold under the name 'Virol'), as it was considered good for us; I can recall having it when I was a little older as I tried to put on some weight.

When Gran and Mum knitted, wool needed to be rewound from being in a loop into a ball. I held out both arms to support the loop, and they wound off the wool to make a ball. With the number of home-knitted jumpers, this was a regular occurrence. To ensure clocks and watches were correct, people listened to the sound of the One O'clock Gun firing.[76] And this reminds me of Christmastime, with the sound of festive carol singers and church bells, and adorning rooms with lovely decorations.

Christmas

Christmases were always fun, with a Christmas tree, food, family and presents. Our parents put presents in pillowcases, which they placed at the foot of the bed when we were asleep. However, we often woke up around 2-3am when it was still dark, and started opening them. We ran along the landing to our parents' room. One Christmas, I was sleeping in the middle room with Gran and woke up to look in my pillowcase. Inside, I was amazed to see a large wrapped box – it was a Tri-ang American Sherman tank. Gran had written on the box 'Lots of Love From Gran xxxx.' It was a beautifully-made scale model in green plastic with rubber tracks which worked by clockwork with a large key.

---

[76] See 'Maritime Tales: the One O'Clock Gun', National Museums Liverpool, 2021. Accessed 26 August 2022 at Maritime Tales : the One O'Clock Gun | National Museums Liverpool (liverpoolmuseums.org.uk)

As it moved, the turret rotated, and a soldier popped his head out the top. If I filled the turret with talcum powder, it fired this out like smoke; it scaled obstacles and flashed its machine gun. I had so much fun with that tank, and looked after it carefully. I still have it in the box. For Christmas 1951, I had the large-print *Mother Goose's Book of Nursery Stories, Rhymes and Fables*, which had plenty of illustrations with some in colour (I still have it). One year, I had a battery-operated train set and another year I had a beautiful red pedal car, which I loved riding along the pavement.

We read books and played with our toys from Christmas and board games such as Snakes and Ladders and Ludo were popular. I liked Meccano construction sets and played with marbles and conkers when they were around in autumn.

Before Christmas lunch, we dressed up and visited Auntie Bel and Uncle Jim in Harewood Street and her dad John "Pop" Hoban while he was alive (he died in 1955). Then we would have a lovely Christmas dinner; probably chicken, roast potatoes and vegetables, followed by Christmas pudding.

After Christmas and Boxing Day, people returned to work and we looked forward to New Year's Eve celebrations in parties or local streets. Mum put lovely spreads on the table, believing that if the table was full on New Year's Eve, then it would be all year. People often gathered and celebrated at the West Derby Road and Boundary Lane junction. There was one drawback to the midnight celebrations – work the following day. A national holiday on New Year's Day was years away.

Sadness: Grandad Alf dies

In my first school year, Grandad Alf ('Dadda') died at our home in February 1952, when I was four-and-a-half years old. He had lived through terribly trying times. After a tough life, sadly he didn't enjoy the benefits of a long, happy retirement.

Unfortunately, unlike Anne, I only have vague memories of our front room, where he lived with Gran, and where I had an accident falling from a chair. The thin scar is still on my lip. But I recall he kept racing pigeons in the shed, and Mum told Anne that when Grandad went to the barber's shop, he took his dog too. We have lovely black-and-white photographs of him. A heart and lung condition killed him, and Uncle Alf was present at his death. I was given Grandad Alf's penknife. He was buried in a nice grave in Anfield Cemetery, with a white marble headstone and surround. Not only was his death at sixty-four years a tragic loss to all, but it meant that without his income, life was harsher, with more struggles, including paying rent. Gran too had a tough life, including the early deaths of her mum, dad, older brother William ("Will") Henry Thomas (my great-uncle) and two nieces (Barbara and Pauline, Uncle Alf and Auntie Edie's children). Now she had lost her husband. Fortunately, Gran had us at home, so she was not alone. But in a few months, Dad was conscripted for the Korean War and went overseas.

King George VI dies –

Princess Elizabeth becomes Queen

Also in February 1952, King George VI died. He had broadcast on radio to the British people for VE Day on 8th May 1945. He had become King in 1936, when his older brother King Edward VIII abdicated to marry the American divorcee Mrs Wallis Simpson. George VI reigned during 1936-1952 throughout the war years, and was popular. Moreover, George, along with Queen Elizabeth, was the first reigning monarch to visit North America, in summer 1939, accompanied by Dad's ship HMS *Glasgow*. The visit included Canada. Following George's death, young Princess Elizabeth became Queen. She was abroad on safari in Kenya (Africa) with her husband Prince Phillip when news reached them of the King's death.

Coronation Day, when Elizabeth was crowned, was 2nd June 1953. It was the first coronation to be shown live on TV (although few homes had TVs then). I was five, and Anne was three. We dressed up in our best clothes and had photographs taken, including a lovely street group photo with us children holding flags. I wore sandals and recall that the new NHS was keen on treating children with "flat feet", so I had tests and restrictions on my footwear for a while. The children in our street went off to a hall for a celebratory meal (possibly in Tuebrook). We had a coach or charabanc to take us. We also received our commemorative gold-coloured crown moneyboxes. We used them for years. Decades later, on Wednesday 9th September 2015, the nation celebrated Queen Elizabeth II as the longest reigning British monarch ever (sixty-three years and seven months then) – exceeding her great-great-grandmother Queen Victoria. But sadly, on Friday 9th April 2021 we heard that Prince Philip, the Duke of Edinburgh, had died (from old age, at ninety-nine). I watched the funeral service, which was held at Windsor Castle, where Covid-19 restrictions limited the number of guests. Many remembered him for introducing the Duke of Edinburgh's Award Scheme (see chapter 7).

In June 2022, the Queen celebrated seventy years on the throne – her platinum jubilee – longer than any other British monarch! However, on 8th September 2022, sadly the Queen too died (aged ninety-six), while at Balmoral Castle in Scotland. She lay in state at Westminster Hall, and her spectacular funeral happened on Monday 19th September. Millions of us across the world watched it live. Then on 6th May 2023, millions worldwide watched the Coronation of King Charles III – for me, precisely seventy years after celebrating the Queen's Coronation.

We had our first TV set when I was about six, but I don't

know if it was bought, or rented, possibly to see the Coronation. It was a small (fourteen-inch) black-and-white set with limited channels and programmes, but we enjoyed it. There were programmes for children to watch (e.g. *Andy Pandy, Bill and Ben –The Flowerpot Men, Billy Bunter of Greyfriars School, Crackerjack!*), and for the family. Many were American, e.g. *Champion the Wonder Horse, Cheyenne, Highway Patrol, I Love Lucy, Lassie, Maverick, Rawhide, Roy Rogers* and *Wagon Train* but also British ones such as *The Army Game, Dixon of Dock Green,* and *Emergency Ward 10* (one of the early soap operas).

Another war? Called-up: Korea (1952-53)

In 1952, after losing Grandad, Dad was called up, and left home. The Second World War was barely over when another war began in Korea. Dad, a naval reservist, was mobilised on 4th June 1952. I was four, Anne was two. Marr astutely observes that Korea is a largely forgotten war, but it was very dangerous and long. Britain played its role, including its troops fighting the Chinese People's Liberation Army.[77]

On 25th June 1950, the Communist North Korean People's Army invaded the South. The United Nations (UN) stood against the aggressor. The British government provided soldiers and the Royal Navy to assist the Americans. As Marr notes, many in Korea were British National Service conscripts. But Dad was a former Royal Navy sailor with Second World War experience when he was called up. He was based in Ceylon (now Sri Lanka) at HMS *Highflyer.* We have photos of him in Ceylon.

It was difficult for Mum: she had lost her dad, and now her husband was off across the world. We didn't go to Ceylon with him, as I couldn't cope with heat, and was afraid of

---

[77] Andrew Marr, *A History of Modern Britain* (London: Pan Books, 2008), p.101.

insects (also, Gran would be left alone). Fortunately, Gran could help Mum. Auntie Edie and Uncle Alf lived in the next street. Dear Auntie Edie often collected Anne and me from school. Dad returned with presents at least once during his long time away (nineteen months). But from 10th October 1953, he was sent to serve at HMS *Mercury* back in England. An armistice occurred in July 1953 and Dad was released on 30th December 1953, when his reservist status expired.

When Dad returned, he had completed his many service years and didn't volunteer again. He went to Ceylon with brown hair and came back with it white. 'Because of the snakes,' he said. He encountered snakes on dark roads, hanging from trees, and even water snakes. For him, and us, life back in England was far better.

Hospital

As well as flat feet, the NHS was interested in children's tonsils for those with recurrent sore throats, and that was me. Eventually, I went to hospital and had them removed. I was about six years old, and remember Mum taking me in with a supply of comics, e.g. *The Dandy* and *Beano*. I was in a children's ward where the beds were close enough for boys to enjoy jumping from one to the next. We settled in the first day after a bath (I had never seen such a small amount of water in a bath!) and the next day we had an injection before being issued with woolly socks to wear.

I entered the operating theatre on a trolley, saw items on another trolley, and passed out under the anaesthetic. When I awoke in bed, blood covered the pillow and, as expected, my throat was sore. Later, one of the treats was to eat lovely ice cream and jelly, being easy to swallow and painless. I probably stayed another night before being discharged. Dressed and ready to go, I heard my name called and went to identify myself. However, as my throat hurt, trying to speak to the nurse was a struggle. But I managed it and went home with Mum. The operation was a success. I didn't need further hospitalisation, and sore throats were no longer a problem.

Accidents

Besides my operation, I recall three accidents: outside and indoors. The one in the street happened when I went to the corner dairy to buy a pint of milk. It was nearby and I was walking with a friend. When I came out, I held the glass milk bottle in my right hand and started a gentle game of football with him. Unfortunately, I tripped, falling over backwards, and the glass bottle broke, spilling the milk and cutting my right palm near my third finger. When I got home, shaken, Mum and Gran put my hand in warm water to get out any glass lodged in the cut. The water turned red, but that sight didn't make me faint. The treatment worked fine when at least one chunk of glass came out of the cut. Thankfully, I did not need stitches, and the cut healed well; although I still have a faint scar.

My next accident, when I was six, also involved glass, but it was more serious. One fine day, Anne and I were playing in our small backyard. Dad had put a glass window in our dog Trixie's kennel roof so that Trixie had some daylight, but this turned out to be risky. I liked climbing and decided to climb on to the roof of Trixie's kennel. This window (or skylight) interested me so much, I wondered how strong it was. It was just plain glass; not safety glass or glass with wire mesh inside it. I manoeuvred myself onto the centre of the glass and then moved my arms down by my sides. All went well in this "test" for a split second, and then there was a mighty crash of broken glass, and I started falling backwards. Quickly, I grabbed the kennel's sides and stopped myself. I pulled myself up on the roof, got down and hurried into the kitchen very shaken, not knowing how bad my injuries were. Mum and Gran both saw that I had a deep cut on the back of my left thigh and another on my left shoulder blade. I needed immediate hospital attention.

We didn't own a car but, fortunately, a neighbour had a van. So, wrapped in a blanket and being reassured, I sat on Mum's knee (there were no seatbelt laws then) in the front passenger seat. The man drove us quickly to Liverpool Infirmary's Accident and Emergency. I was truly scared and repeatedly I said, 'I hope I don't get the needle!' (I didn't like injections). Mum had worse thoughts for sure, and getting "the needle" was nothing compared to what happened.

I was treated quickly. My left leg was stitched up rapidly with about six stitches, but they didn't give me anaesthetics or painkillers! They stitched, and I really screamed with the pain. I am sure my loud screams carried a long way, and disturbed others in the hospital. When they examined my back, they decided it wasn't possible to stitch it, because the large cut was above the bone. It was simply treated and dressed. We were sent home with instructions to return every other day for new dressings, even having to travel back from our holiday in Meols.

At home, I was sleeping in a single bed in the smallest bedroom, and it was difficult sleeping with the pain, especially lying on my back. Thankfully, everything healed well with support from medics, parents and Gran. I still have the scars, and remain cautious with glass. Later in my life, I did risk-assessments and looked ahead to consequences and preventions; something I was unable to do as a little boy.

Finally, I had a third accident in Auntie Edie's house. I wasn't injured, but it caused damage. By their backroom wall they had a large kitchen storage unit with three sections. The bottom section had double doors where food was kept, the centre section had storage space and a pulldown door that made a working surface, while the top section (sliding glass doors) provided storage for crockery. It was a well-designed unit. For some reason, I decided to grab hold of the bottom section's door handles and swung backwards on them. As the unit was not fixed to the wall, it moved under my weight and eventually fell forward onto me! Aaargh! As it fell, crockery, cutlery and food came shooting towards me and into the room. I couldn't stop it, but I guess one of the adults caught the cabinet before I was crushed. I was shaken but not injured. I felt bad about it, as it was rather tough on Auntie Edie: money was short, and some items were likely broken. Perhaps my parents paid for the damages? I don't remember anyone scolding me for this accident; perhaps it was accepted as one hazard of bringing up boys, another accident by "Our Robert".

Gran dies and Christina is born:

March 1956

Grandad had died on 1st February 1952, aged only sixty-four. Gran died a little over four years later, on 12th March 1956, aged sixty-three. We loved her, and I cannot recall knowing she was ill. She looked after Anne and me at home and on holidays in Meols. Gran had a distinct scar on the top inside of one arm, from an accident with a spike (perhaps on railings). My last memory of her, though, was when the ambulance pulled up outside our home in Grey Rock and she went in. I stood looking, the ambulance drove off, and I never saw her again. I was just eight-and-a-half. Cancer killed her. Such sadness! Who was going to help Mum now that both her parents had died? Especially as her baby was due to arrive soon. Thankfully, Uncle Alf and Auntie Edie lived nearby, and Dad was there. Gran was buried in the same grave as Grandad in Anfield. I can't recall attending her funeral, but I wear her gold wedding ring.

Our sister Christina was born at home (in the downstairs backroom), later. Auntie Edie arrived in the morning and told Anne and me that the baby was being born that day and we should go to her house, which we did. Auntie Edie was always around to help, and was very nice to be with. Later, we went back to see the new baby – our Christina! We had waited a while for her, after asking Mum and Dad a few times if we could have a new baby. Now she was safely with us, and healthy. Mum was fine. We were keen to help if possible. That month had many mixed emotions. However, Christina recalls that Mum told her that having a baby to look after helped her cope with the sad loss of her mum.

Sometime after my grandparents died, the landlord (Mr Burrows) tried to either put up our rent or evict us (I don't recall which). Mum had to go to court with the rent book, and Mr Burrows lost. Thankfully, we were okay, and stayed in No. 57. However, I also recall Mr Burrows for kindly giving me occasional lifts to school, in his furniture van.

Cinemas

We regularly attended cinemas in the 1950s, especially matinees. They were usually eye-catching, luxurious, comfortable places of entertainment, so different from many homes. Our local was the Palladium, and I saw many films there. As "baby boomers" (born 1946-1964) we were fascinated with the "King of the Wild Frontier" American frontiersman Davy Crockett, played by the young and handsome actor Fess Parker. This Disney Film (*Davy Crockett: King of the Wild Frontier*) was released in May 1955 in glorious colour. It was shown at the Hippodrome cinema at West Derby Road.[78] As we paid, we met cousin Edna on the

---

[78] The Hippodrome was originally a circus, then theatre, and from 20th July 1931 a cinema. After almost forty years it closed in May 1970 before demolition in 1980/81. See 'The Royal Hippodrome Theatre, West Derby Road, Liverpool'. Undated. Accessed 26 August 2022 at The Royal Hippodrome Theatre, West Derby Road, Liverpool (arthurlloyd.co.uk)

way out (she had enjoyed the film), holding a nice photograph of Fess Parker. As mentioned previously, Davy Crockett wore a coonskin cap and this was latest craze for boys to wear. I wore mine with pride. It was an exciting "American history" film.

One main event etched in my memory was a mixture of joy, pain, and trouble with our parents. Again, it was at the Hippodrome. Cousin Alf and I went to the matinee showing around 2pm one pleasant day, to see the Walt Disney Technicolour films *The Story of Robin Hood and His Merrie Men* (released in 1952; filmed in England, with Richard Todd as Robin) which, as I mentioned earlier, was paired with the animated musical *Lady and the Tramp* (released June 1955). We sat at the front of the cinema. After seeing the films once, we decided to see them again, so we stayed on. There was no long break between showings. When it changed from the matinee to the evening showing, we simply moved back from the front, crossing a marked line, and mingled with the adults. There was a scene in *Lady and the Tramp* with singing dogs which was rather long and loud. Eventually, I had a painful headache. Nevertheless, we decided to stay on for the third viewing. By then it was late, and we had no way of contacting our parents (there were no mobile phones), but we weren't worried – it was fun.

However, much to our surprise, we saw Uncle Alf was in the cinema, and he found us sitting still enjoying the film. Apparently, he'd been looking for us for hours and a notice had appeared on the screen about us (which we somehow missed!).[79] We were taken from the cinema and promptly marched home. The clock on the spire of Emmanuel

---

[79] Then cinemas had one large screen, not multiple screens. So, Uncle Alf only had to look in the one area, but it was dark. How we lasted for seven hours without food and drink I don't know, although they sold snacks, drinks and ice cream from the usherettes during the break between films.

Anglican Church (West Derby Road) showed 9.15pm.[80] We had been watching for seven hours! Our parents were worried – hence the search – in case we'd been abducted or something else. Still, we returned safely, were reprimanded, and didn't repeat our mistake. But the films were great, even with a headache, and we only paid once.

Near the Hippodrome on West Derby Road and Baker Street was the Savoy Cinema. Here, I saw Judy Garland as Dorothy Gale in the spectacular MGM American musical fantasy *The Wizard of Oz*. I got there a little late with friends, but when we walked inside, we were stunned by the film's amazing colour. And Dorothy sang *Over the Rainbow*. It's been listed among the greatest films of all time. Made in 1939, I saw a re-release from around 1955, I think.

A short distance away on Boaler Street, I visited the Cosy Cinema on Saturdays to see *Superman*, and similar series adventures for children, but had to come back the following week to see what happened! It's now a church. The Lido (Nos. 33-35 Belmont Road) in Anfield was a favourite for matinees. I queued with friends under the outdoor roofed area by the wall to pay my 6d (that's six old pence) for matinees. It was here, while waiting and talking, I discovered to my surprise that they didn't believe in Father Christmas! So, was I wrong or what?

---

[80] Founded 1867, closed 1973. Demolished 1974. Dad's mum Florence was married there on 16th June 1902.

CHAPTER 5

Weekends in the Wirral

Liverpool was a smoky city and it was good to get away for some fresh air. Our family often spent spring and summer weekends in the 1950s and early 1960s at Burbo Camp, Meols, between Hoylake and Moreton on the Wirral coastline. It was named after the nearby Burbo Bank (a sandbank). Meols was an ancient settlement before Roman times.[81] For us, Meols was in Cheshire, and Liverpool in Lancashire.

Our earliest black-and-white photograph, probably from 1950/51, shows our family by the marquee. The back row has Auntie Edie, Edna and Uncle Alf Thompson, and the front shows Dad (Stan) Dutch, me, Mum, little Anne, Gran and Grandad Alf Thompson. We holidayed at Burbo Camp annually from when I was at least three years old, for over ten years. This was a major element of my early life into my teenage years. When we started going to Meols, our family had a marquee (a large tent), and later the site changed to caravans.

Travelling from Liverpool to Meols

Visiting Burbo Camp was a welcome break from Liverpool. Meols had a sandy shore, sea, fresh air, spacious countryside, and panoramic views across Liverpool Bay. In the summer holidays and when we were pre-school age, we often stayed on with Gran, while Mum returned to Liverpool with Dad.

Our normal means of travelling from home to Meols was public transport. We walked down Grey Rock to West Derby

---

[81] See 'The Guide to Cheshire, Derbyshire, Lancashire and the Wirral', 2005-2006. Accessed 27 August 2022 at Meols (cheshirenow.co.uk)

Road, crossed using the zebra crossing at Boundary Lane, and walked the short distance to the bus stop. The green double-decker buses were regular and reliable. The early buses did not have two closing doors for the passengers to enter/exit, but just an open platform at the rear corner of the bus. It had a central upright pole to hold for safety, but adults needed to watch that their children did not fall off. Once on the bus, we had the option of going upstairs or staying downstairs. Typically, women and young children stayed downstairs, which was a non-smoking area. Men and older children went upstairs into what could be a smoky area. The bus driver had a separate small driver's cab, entered from outside the bus while the conductor stood on the access platform. He took your cash and gave you a paper ticket with change. Young children travelled free of charge.

Once we got to Liverpool's Central Station (next to Lewis's), we left the bus and took the electric train to Meols. This used the railway tunnel under the River Mersey and after some stops arrived at Meols village before travelling on to Hoylake and West Kirby (in Cheshire but now in Merseyside).[82] We enjoyed these train journeys as the trains were pleasant, not too crowded, and did not take too long to reach Meols. Anne and I loved to sing 'Choo choo to Meols' as we travelled along. Mum and Dad joined in, and sometimes cousin Alfie, and Christina when she was older. Once in Meols village, we walked to Burbo Camp down the rough road called Park Lane. This was a countryside walk with ditches on either side of the lane and trees/bushes. Beside pedestrians, we would see cars, cyclists, and farmers' tractors. It was perhaps not a road by modern standards, but it did the job. Some way along, at a right-hand bend, there was an option of taking a left path that led along the beach, but this tended to take longer. When we

---

[82] Note the different spelling between Kirkby, just outside Liverpool, where Mum was a munitions worker, and West Kirby in the Wirral.

arrived at the camp's main entrance, we went left, and the road continued towards farmers' fields.

Another route to Meols we really enjoyed was via bus to the Liverpool Pier Head, from where we took the ferry across the Mersey to Birkenhead. When we came up the landing stage, the bus station was just outside. From there, we got on the lovely blue bus to take us to the front at Moreton shore. Then we walked along the seafront to Meols. I particularly liked this route. However, as a small child I often suffered travel sickness and buses did affect me, but I just had to endure it. Sometimes, Moreton had small fairgrounds. Once we passed when a young man was being carried out with his arms around two men (one on either side). He looked semi-conscious and had blood trickling down his nose. He had either had an accident or been in a fight. We didn't feel we should stop and ask.

In the 1950s and 1960s, the concrete anti-invasion defences were still in position along the sea front, having been constructed to stop Hitler's forces coming ashore if he invaded Britain. There was a vast concrete slope up from the sand/sea, with huge concrete cubes and pyramids (dragon's teeth) standing on it to prevent German tanks and vehicles coming ashore. Also, there were two concrete pillboxes along the section from Moreton with one right at the Meols end of the defences. The doors were locked and the guns no longer present, but I could imagine soldiers staying there day and night on lookout. It was a constant reminder of when Britain had stood alone in the Second World War, under the threat of the Nazi invasion. The concrete defences had a flat walkway on the top to Meols, with the sea on the right and sand hills on the left. Soon after the concrete path passed the second pillbox, we turned left and walked a short distance through little sand hills to come into Burbo Camp at the beach entrance by the camp's house, including its only shop. We had arrived! My youngest sister Christina recalls the walk as a long way. Once, she was so tired and crying so much that Dad kindly carried her on his shoulders.

Later, as a teenager, I cycled a similar route, using the ferry across the Mersey. My parents had travelled ahead but when I worked as a paperboy, I had to deliver newspapers on Saturday evenings, so I arrived later. Once in Birkenhead, I used major and minor roads to reach the camp. This involved a country lane (Carr Lane), where there was an unmanned railway crossing over the electric train line. I recall cautiously crossing the line without incident – "stop, look, listen". Cycling was fine in daylight. It was a pleasant ride in the quiet countryside, without congested roads. However, unmanned railway crossings have resulted in many deaths over the decades.[83]

Dad once had a photo of us taken (in 1954) with him standing by a van near our marquee, while Anne and I sat on the bonnet. He said: 'One day we will be able to have a car!' and that came true. For the time being, we dreamt, and just took a photo. Whose van it was, I don't know. Eventually, we had a car for trips to Meols, but owning one in the 1950s was not affordable.

Burbo Camp life

When we were at Meols, with Mum and Dad or when we had stayed on with Gran, relatives, friends and neighbours regularly visited, often for a day out. When Dad returned to Liverpool for work, we sometimes remained in Meols. For us children, it seemed a long walk from Burbo Camp to Meols railway station, along the country road, and we worried, asking Dad, 'What if you get attacked?'. But Dad reassured us: 'Don't worry! If I am attacked, I'll batter them with my bag.' He had a strong brown grip bag with leather handles.

---

[83] As *The Times* (1st December 2015) article explained: 'Most rail crossings "still too dangerous"'.

His words reassured us, and he was never attacked, as far as we know.

Initially, Burbo Camp only had marquees. These were large canvas tents with two tall vertical poles located centrally at each end of the tent as supports. Guy ropes secured them, with pegs hammered into the ground. Further side guy ropes supported the tent. Over the main tent was a flysheet to give extra protection from the weather. Again, the flysheet had guy ropes. The flooring was wood. Also, the tent was high enough for adults to stand easily, and it usually had a wooden door.

It was equipped with a rear section to make a large bedroom with just two double beds. At the front of the tent there were storage and cooking facilities, together with a table and chairs. We had a battery-operated wireless but no TV. There was no installed gas supply, so we used primus stoves for cooking and possibly, years later, Calor gas bottles. There was mains electricity onsite, but no installed electricity was supplied for the site tents. For lighting, we used Tilley lamps, which had a mantle and paraffin fuel in the base. The gas mantle gave a bright white light for our tent, and other tents had them, too. Running water was not available; it had to be collected from site standpipes. I would fill up an empty container with water and take it back to the tent. Water was put into a bowl for any hand-washing, and for washing dishes. There were no toilets or showers/baths in the tents. We used the site's lavatory (toilet) block. If it rained, I put on a coat to make the trip. If it was night, folk used the site lights or torches, and the glow from the marquees, to walk safely. We were often grateful for the glow!

Marquees were not used all year round. At the end of the season, everyone had to take theirs down and store it, with its furniture, in the site's corrugated iron shed. At the beginning of the season, we returned and put up our own marquee – nobody else on the site was responsible for this. I clearly recall one year when I was small, and too little to help. Mum and Dad tried putting up the marquee by themselves. Unfortunately, Mum was holding up one of the long wooden central poles when it fell and hit her on the head. She was in tears. Thankfully, the accident only caused distress to us, and no physical damage to her. I felt the powerlessness of being too small to save the situation. Then Mum and Dad managed to get some assistance from other people, and everything went smoothly; finally, the tent was erected okay. Then we had to put in our furniture. At the end of the season, we repeated the procedure in reverse. Taking out horizontal support poles from the tent one year, I recall they were covered with scores of earwigs. They would get into the tent and into our paper sweet bags, e.g. onto the toffee pieces, which then very regretfully had to be thrown away.

Once the giant storage shed was emptied for the season, the site residents used it for entertainment. Housey-housey (or bingo but with no electronic equipment) was popular. Here, for a small payment, you got your card for the game and listened as the person called out the numbers. When your number was called, you crossed that out on the card. Cash was awarded for getting a line of numbers, and more cash if someone got all the numbers on their card. I can't recall us winning, but I guess we must have, considering the years we were there!

Further, in the shed there was music and dancing, using a basic record-player with 45 rpm vinyl records (no cassettes or CDs then). One popular song was Ricky Valance's *Tell Laura I Love Her*, a hit in 1960 when I started becoming interested in music. Paul Feeney called it a "one hit wonder" but I still recall it.[84] In 1961, young Helen Shapiro was singing the hit record *Walking Back to Happiness*. People would jive, and once I had a brave go at a little dancing, including doing "the twist" to Chubby Checker's *Let's Twist*

---

[84] Paul Feeney, *A 1960s Childhood: From Thunderbirds to Beatlemania* (Stroud: The History Press, 2010), p.109.

Again, 1961 (followed in 1962 by other records, e.g. Sam Cooke *Twistin' the Night Away*). "The twist" became a popular dance at the start of the Sixties. The shed was open freely to all (children and adults).

Racing games were put on at least annually by camp organisers, using the empty grass field at the entrance to the site and later, when static caravans had replaced canvas tents, using the large rectangular grass space between caravans. Bunting was put up and races were run in age groups. I remember running one length of the enclosed area between the caravans. I was good at sprinting and did well, coming first one year. This sports day was great fun for children and adults, with small prizes. One year, Uncle John (Mum's uncle; Grandad Alf's younger brother) from Warrington visited us and enthusiastically participated in the races; he may have even had a go at running, although by then he was no longer young). He laughed a lot and was friendly, so we enjoyed his visits. I think he came a few times, since we have a photograph with him, Gran and an unknown lady (possibly John's wife) taken in 1952 (probably the summer) at Meols, when I was about five. Also, I recall us visiting him in Warrington, where we met his daughter.

Near the camp's exit to the beach there was just one small shop to buy our food and milk. The exit, like the entrance to the site, had no security, so anyone could freely walk in and out of the site unchallenged. The site was surrounded by hedges, ditches and farmers' fields, giving life a contrast to living in Liverpool. Also, Meols had a large Railway Inn, which is still there. Other shops and services were in Meols village, including a doctor's surgery that I attended when my back was cut and infected after my accident falling through the dog kennel skylight (see chapter 4). When we stayed in Meols after my accident, we initially travelled on alternate days into Liverpool on the train to visit the Royal Infirmary for fresh dressings and checks.

Camp surroundings

Countryside is what I remember surrounding the camp – great green spaces. There were ditches with water rats and fields with rabbits, hares, horses and cows. Birds and ducks flew overhead. Fields were used for growing crops such as lettuce. There was an overgrown area (a bit like an overgrown quarry) a little walk away, where we could find plenty of blackberries to pick. It made a good adventure to climb down by the bushes, watching our steps and picking fruit to eat or possibly make into jam. One year I went shooting in the fields with an older friend who had a shotgun (licensed!). He taught me how to walk safely with it, and how it should be used. I don't recall getting much when we went together but once he came back with a huge hare he'd shot. It was to be skinned and eaten. I had an air pistol when I was thirteen (later an air rifle), but these could not kill anything to eat.

Then there was the beach. Leaving Burbo Camp via the entrance near the shop took us the short distance to the beach, across small sand hills. There was a considerable concrete structure running along the front (stretching off left towards Hoylake and right to Moreton) and going down to the beach. First, there was the top concrete walkway, which had a small wall on the seaward side. Some steps led down from this top section to the lower broad concrete walkway. Finally, some more steps led down from this section to the beach. When the tide was in, the deep water would reach to the top of these steps. When the tide was out, the long, sandy beach stretched for miles. On the right at the top section was the Second World War pillbox next to a children's sandpit, surrounded by a low concrete wall. Sometimes there was a small kiosk shop there selling local cockles and the like, which Gran liked to eat.

When it was stormy, the waves came over the lower walkway and hit the sloping wall leading to the top walkway.

White spray went everywhere. Standing safely on the top walkway, I watched the pounding waves come over and break against the wall, and I quickly moved back before I got soaked. It was great fun on a stormy day, but we learnt to be attentive.

As we grew older and our legs became stronger, we enjoyed running up the sloping wall from the lower walkway to the top one. However, we didn't do this when the tide was in and the sea was fierce, for fear of being swept away and drowned. Circular lifebelts were hung on posts by the beach, but nobody wanted to be dragged into the fierce sea during those rough, dangerous days. Meols had its beach, but lifeguards never patrolled it, even in summertime. We have a lovely picture (from the 1950s) of cousin Edna with our friend Joyce O'Brien swimming in the sea with the deep water at the top of the steps; the tide was in, but the sea stayed calm.

When the tide was out, we accessed the beach from the steps. The beach was an expanse of yellow sand, and then there were some mud banks before we reached the water channel. Across the water channel lay a large sandbank which some people ventured to reach. To the right of the beach (towards Moreton), there was a large section of various sized rocks and a small pool for paddling. Crabs lived under the rocks. To the left of the beach (towards Hoylake) there was another, larger pool for paddling and catching crabs. Next to this pool there was a wide slope leading off the beach to the walkways. It thus provided access for those not using the steps. We have a wonderful c.1955 photo of Gran coming up the slope, holding my sister Anne with her right hand, and me with her left. Mum took the picture and I vividly recall wanting to have a different pose to normal. So, I decided to stand on my left leg and held my right leg horizontal but bent at the knee. The picture was good. It was a warm, dry summer day. Oh, those long, carefree summer days we had as children!

We had to be careful with crabs. I recall one incident when cousin Alfie picked up a largeish crab, incorrectly handling it from the front near its eyes (instead of from the back to hold the top and bottom of its shell, or its sides). The crab just used its claws to grab hold of Alfie's finger, and pain followed! How could we persuade it to release its hold without having to kill it? It was a puzzle until one adult saw us and helped. The crab, holding Alf with its claws, was lowered into the large pool, where it released its grip and swam away to safety. What a relief! (Although another time he was stung by a jellyfish!) This crab experience was such a contrast to a sad incident I witnessed once, where a gang of older boys turned over the large rocks at the other end of the beach. Crabs of assorted shapes, sizes and colours scattered, but the boys smashed them by throwing stones. They laughed at the carnage. It was a sorry spectacle. We expected older boys to behave better. I don't remember challenging them, for fear of being attacked verbally, and possibly physically. Today, it reminds me of the current concerns over the loss of biodiversity in our world, e.g. through greed, destruction of habitats and climate change.

Playing with my boats in little pools was safe, although one year I was distressed at losing a favourite new toy in a pool. However, I learnt that when the tide came in, we had to be careful when standing on the large sandbank that was across mud banks and the channel. We risked being cut off unawares. We could watch the incoming tide and paddle, but there was a hidden danger. The tide swept around to the right of the sandbank and the gentle, shallow water channel started to change. It rapidly grew with the rising tide, in depth, width and speed. Getting safely back across the channel could be an unnerving challenge, so it was important to remember this risk. I can't recall anyone needing rescuing but, as I said, there were no lifeguards. Anyone who saw someone in trouble had to fetch a lifebelt mounted by the concrete walkway and throw it. There were no mobile phones for calling help (they were decades in the future). But the Hoylake Lifeboat Station was nearby (founded by the Liverpool Docks Trustees in 1803).

A treat for us children was to walk to the beach front at night. 'Can we go and see the lights?' we would request. Then Gran, Mum or Dad took us for a short visit before bed. From the top walkway, there were lights as far as we could see towards Hoylake, Moreton and beyond. What a wonder! I particularly remember orange colours – a contrast to what we saw at night in Liverpool's confined streets.

On 20th July 1962, when I was nearly fifteen, I watched the launch of the hovercraft from the wide, flat beach at Moreton to Rhyl in North Wales. It was a British United Airways Hovercraft (Vickers Type VA3) and a world first: the first passenger and mail service hovercraft, attaining a cruising speed of sixty mph around eight inches above the water. It weighed two tons and took twenty-four passengers. It was celebrated in major papers, including the *Liverpool Echo* (with a colour supplement). Websites mark the historic event with photographs.[85] Since I viewed the event from a distance at Meols, I am not in any photos. However, it had problems, including engine failures and storm damage. Sadly, the service's last trip was Friday 14th September 1962.

Fishing

One year, when we still had our marquee, I went night fishing along the coast with a young married man whose tent

---

[85] See: *World's First Passenger & Mail Hovercraft Service Between Moreton, Wirral and Rhyl, North Wales 20th July 1962*, updated 23 January 2020. Accessed 27 August 2022 at Worlds First Hovercraft Passenger and Mail Service 1962 from Moreton to Rhyl (wirralhistory.uk) The 50th Anniversary was celebrated in July 2012 and reported in BBC Wales History: James Roberts, 'The world's first passenger hovercraft', 19 July 2012. Accessed 27 August 2022 at BBC – Wales History: The world's first passenger hovercraft

was just behind ours. He didn't use rods but walked out along the sand to his night lines. Short wooden stakes were driven into the sand and a line connected each pair; attached to them were shorter lines with fish-hooks on the end. I was invited to go along with him and have a line. For bait, we dug in the sand to find large sandworms and then threaded them live on the hooks. As a child, I didn't like that part; not at all. We covered them with sand to stop seagulls eating them.

The tide came in and washed off the sand, leaving the bait for fish (e.g. plaice and whiting). We returned as the tide went out (sometimes quite early in the morning), to collect our fish before the seagulls ate them. Usually, we had a few fish each. Then we repeated the process of putting bait on the lines and covering it. Once the early morning catch was brought to the tent, Mum was pleased to cook the fresh fish for breakfast. They tasted good.

That year, we also took our tiny tortoises to Meols, and let them walk on the grass. Unfortunately, they didn't live long – a common problem then with imported tortoises. It wasn't until my wife Sue and I were given a large tortoise when our children were small that we managed to have one survive hibernation and live for decades.

Day trips to Hoylake and West Kirby

As children, we loved visiting Hoylake and West Kirby. As we didn't own a car, we walked or used public transport from Meols. Hoylake was a nice relaxing place to go, where we saw many shops – I especially liked toy shops with soldiers. As money wasn't plentiful, I can't recall buying many, but enjoyed window shopping.

At West Kirby, I remember walking out on the wide, flat sands to the little Hilbre Islands in the River Dee, when the tide was out. The wide estuary and the distant North Wales coastline spoke of extensiveness, unlike our little streets at home. As a child, it seemed a long way to go, and we had to make sure we were back safely before the tide started coming in. During one trip to West Kirby, our family was on the sand with our hired deckchairs by the large outdoor boating lake, which had flat concrete sides but no railings. I had gone along the beach and when I returned, I saw my sister Anne sitting in a deck chair wrapped in a towel but rather wet, distressed and crying. It had been a near tragedy. She was walking along the side of the marine lake and somehow fell into the deep water. Very fortunately, a man saw this happen, and rescued her. A shocking incident that shows how a charming day at the seaside can become a nightmare. Mum had to buy Anne new clothes. Thankfully, Anne was fine afterwards and enjoyed a full life. We needed to learn how to swim! The lake still had no railings when I visited in 2018.

Canvas to caravans

With our marquees, we had different locations over the years, with perhaps the best one facing a large hedge with nearby trees at the edge of the site towards fields. There was plenty of space to play ball and it was more private than being surrounded by other tents. A tall wooden boundary fence (with gaps between thin uprights) kept us safely outside the hedge and inside the site. Our tent doorway faced the hedge, and on the left of the tent there was another hedge. So, it was a private space for Gran and us children, including cousin Alfie and our friend Harold, to play with water or fight with bows and arrows and shields.

But after about ten happy years under canvas, Burbo Camp changed to caravans. We had our first one in about 1959. Now we were nearer the site entrance. When the site road came in, it headed straight to the beach end by the shop, but a new "road" was laid on the right. Caravans were situated on either side of the road. We were a couple of caravans up on the left. Across the road on the bend was the caravan of our friends Ossie and Joyce O'Brien, with their son Harold. We also knew other owners. We had a reasonably-sized caravan, as did Ossie and Joyce, but there were smaller caravans on site as well. Caravans didn't have surrounding decking – such luxury was in the future. The site was modest in size, and facilities compared with modern ones. Many people were from the Liverpool area and working-class, I guess. Dad was a bricklayer and Ossie (who had also served in the navy) was a Liverpool docker.

There was a tragic accident one year in a family who had a small caravan near Ossie and Joyce. We did not know them particularly well, but the family included a young, engaged woman. Sadly, we heard that her fiancé was killed in a road accident somewhere off site. What could one say in such crushing circumstances? Caravan residents would offer support.

The site owners did not sell caravans; we had to buy our own. Mum and Dad found one they liked (and could afford) at Maghull, north of Liverpool. We travelled there and sometimes stored items we needed in Meols before the caravan was moved.

Our first caravan in 1959ish was two-tone: white, with a lower, light blue section (shown in an early coloured photo – most photos then were black-and-white) and one entrance door. By 29th March 1960, we expected the delivery of our "new" two-tone caravan with two doors. It had a kitchen, lounge area and storage facilities. There were no separate bedrooms, no toilet or shower; we still had to use the site's lavatory block. A double bed was folded down from the wall at night, and a screen provided privacy. The lounge's long sofa-type seats converted into single beds. Making up beds each night and putting them away in the morning was an effort. But my parents gladly did this for us. There was a small fire to keep us warm. Two doors on the same side (a precaution perhaps against fire) gave easy access to the caravan. Calor gas bottles provided fuel for cooking. However, we still had no running water. This was collected (often by me) from a site standpipe and then I poured the water into the caravan's tank, ready for pumping into the kitchen basin. When the tank ran dry, I returned to the standpipe. There was still no electricity for lighting. Calor Gas mantles were used to give bright illumination.

Despite some restrictions, caravans provided a much easier life than marquees. They didn't need to be erected, restocked with furniture, or dismantled for winter storage. Also, the lounge seats were comfortable. Mum cooked for us as there were no on-site cafés or takeaways. Later, when we had a car (a four-door Austin Cambridge with a stick gear change on the steering wheel shaft), we were able to travel quickly to Meols and park it near the caravan on the grass or at the car park.

Visitors

Mum and Dad often had visitors at Meols, as their photos from the 1950s show. Early cameras were far more basic than today's high-quality digital and phone cameras. First, they used short rolls of photographic film, giving about a dozen black-and-white pictures that we took to a chemist's shop for developing and printing. All pictures had to be paid for and any bad ones were just wasted. Second, early cameras were held at waist height, and the person taking the picture looked down into the camera and tried to locate the shot in the small viewer. Eventually, we had cameras with a viewer at eye level; coloured film appeared years later.

We have photographs of Uncle Alf and Auntie Edie, Edna and Alfie. Uncle Jim and Auntie Bel visited (September 1961). Another shows Mr and Mrs Winer, our next-door neighbours, with their family.

My photo album has pictures from 1960 taken with my first camera. These include a lovely picture (1960) of Mum standing alone on the steps by the caravan, then one with Anne and also in a group. Dad is with me in one photo. There is a small white wigwam outside the caravan, with three children. In 1961, my friends David Kent and Alan Magee are visiting lying on a canvas bed outside the caravan, aiming my air rifle and pistol, but just in a posed position.

Over the years, other friends visited (e.g. Stephen Butler, Rodney, Ritchie) and Anne brought friends, too. Edna brought her girlfriends and her boyfriend Rob (later to be her husband). They were content to sit outside the caravan or lie on the grass in the sun having discussions, jokes and drinks. They added sparkle, interest and humour to our times together. It was good to be on the Wirral coast by the sea.

Farewell to Meols

After so many happy years at Meols, the time came to say 'farewell'. The last time I recall going to Meols was when I cycled as a teenager; by then, it was easy to cycle in and out of the camp. I also recall sitting on the electric train travelling there wearing my jacket proudly displaying my 'Prefect' badge from Newsham Secondary Modern School, so that was probably around 1962 when I was fifteen. By July 1962, when I watched the hovercraft, it was the end of my compulsory secondary education and we had decided what should be my next steps. Also, before we said 'farewell' to Meols, I was proudly wearing a Beatles' haircut with longish hair, the fringe over my forehead, to emulate the famous Liverpool group.

Eventually, Mum and Dad had to decide whether we should continue going to Burbo Camp. We could take holidays elsewhere. Dad asked us all what we thought. It was very considerate to involve us children in the decision. My response? 'We have had a good time there but perhaps it is now time to stop going.' After all, we were growing up and had many other things to do at weekends. So, a decision was made to leave Burbo Camp, after about a dozen very happy years.

Meols' countryside and seaside provided a contrast to life in Liverpool. Visiting Burbo Camp was a very welcome break. Meols had a shore, sand, sea, clean air, and spacious green countryside. We could see right to the horizon, and ships making their way to and from Liverpool. They were long, happy days for our family, friends and relatives, as photos show. We are immensely grateful to our parents and grandparents for having the foresight to give us such ongoing holiday opportunities, and providing the money and effort needed. What we as children learnt and enjoyed on the Wirral coast was beneficial both physically and psychologically.

When I returned in 2018 with my wife Susan, we enjoyed visiting West Kirby, Hoylake and Meols and their lovely stations on the clean electric trains. Walking from Hoylake to Meols' beach front was both familiar and different, with the Second World War concrete structures and pillboxes long since demolished. Even the way the tide flowed in had changed, and the mud bank and sandbanks were gone – my experiences in the 1950s and 1960s were now just part of history. But we enjoyed walking through the more modern Wirral Beach Caravan Park, the replacement for Burbo Camp, on our way to lovely Meols station, next to its large lake. In an age of international travel for holidays, we need to recall that back then some people didn't have holidays at all. In May 2021, West Kirby was among the UK's top 20 beaches.[86]

---

[86] Lisa Rand, 'West Kirby and Formby named in UK top 20 beaches', *Liverpool Echo* 4 May 2021. Accessed 27 August 2022 at West Kirby and Formby named in UK top 20 beaches – Liverpool Echo Formby was another beach I visited when my cousin Edna lived there (see chapter 8).

CHAPTER 6

Secondary Modern School Years

Selection for secondary education:

trials with the 11-plus

The 1944 Butler Act made secondary education free, but whether you attended a grammar school or a secondary modern was determined by the 11-plus. David Kynaston identifies this crucial selection, since children who attended grammar schools were more likely to have a middle-class future.[87]

In my last year at Whitefield Road Junior School (1957-1958), children nationwide were tested to determine which secondary schools they should attend. This was the 11-plus exam. Our school streamed us with top pupils (the 'most able') in the "A" class, next was the "B" class (where I was), and then at least a "C" class. Class 4B recognised that virtually all pupils in 4A would "pass" the 11-plus but in 4B most would "fail". That was the way, apparently, that the system worked. We probably had preparation for the exam at school, trialling the papers.

The state secondary school system was tripartite: grammar, technical, and secondary modern schools. In fact, few technical schools existed, and the number of grammar schools varied considerably across the country. The 11-plus covered English language, arithmetic/maths, and intelligence (IQ). Pupils who passed went to state grammar schools. Failures went to secondary moderns. Private education was not a financial option that our family, or most

---

[87] David Kynaston, *Smoke in the Valley* (London: Bloomsbury, 2008), p.276. It covers 'Austerity Britain 1948-51'.

families in our working-class community, could contemplate. I have a friend who failed his 11-plus, but his wealthy family sent him to a prestigious fee-paying independent school.

I can't recall how I heard the news – possibly by letter. But it wasn't good: I had failed – pure and simple – that was it! Government sources explained that the selection process was to match pupils with the most suitable schools. But parents and pupils weren't convinced by the rhetoric: it was "failing the 11-plus". That was our general perception. The accuracy of the test was taken for granted. At a young age, we were labelled publicly as "failures", and given an education appropriately non-academic, assuming that we would be employed as skilled, semi-skilled or unskilled workers when we left school, i.e. we'd be manual workers. Children who passed were seen as more able – successes. My cousin Edna had previously passed and was attending Holly Lodge Girls' School, and a few years after me, my cousin Alf passed for Liverpool Collegiate. My parents never made me feel bad, and offered their support with my education. I'd go in September 1958 to Newsham Secondary Modern (pronounced Newsh-am). It had the 13-plus to retry for grammar schools, but no guarantees. The shadow of failure hung over me.

Flawed selection system

It is now widely recognised that the 11-plus was a flawed system. Even at the time, there were doubts. Andrew Marr notes school selection systems have problems and unfairness in places, with necessary child failures and successes. However, in the late 1950s, the IQ tests were shown to be unreliable and annually up to 60,000 children were allocated to the "wrong" schools.[88]

---

[88] Andrew Marr, *A History of Modern Britain* (London: Pan Books, 2008), p.247.

Kynaston provides an analysis of the selection and school systems.[89] In particular, he mentions "testing intelligence" as advocated by the influential Sir Cyril Burt, a prominent educational psychologist. Burt believed in 'the scientific validity of intelligence testing' and that intelligence was primarily hereditary, not environmentally, determined. Kynaston, though, notes that after Burt died in 1971, evidence emerged that he had invented at least some data.[90] Presented as scientific, the system was flawed. I was a failure, but if I tried hard could I triumph over adversity?

Further, I started school in 1951, barely four years old. Now it's widely recognised that in England summer-born children are disadvantaged compared with those born in September. Of course, this research was unavailable back then. But later on, I was called a "late developer".

Newsham Secondary Modern

School for Boys

Newsham Secondary Modern (also called Sheil Road) was on Sheil Road, surrounded by three other roads: Romer, Bigham and Phillimore. The premises, largely unchanged externally, were in use – but not as a state school – when I visited them with my wife Sue in 2014.

I often walked to school with my friend Reggie from Red Rock. From Grey Rock, we crossed West Derby Road, went up Berwick Street, and crossed Boaler Street. After a couple more streets, we reached Romer Road and school. I went home (perhaps Reggie did – I can't recall) for dinner (12pm-1.30pm) and returned for afternoon classes.[91]

---

[89] Kynaston, *Smoke*, chapter 12 'A Kind of Measuring Rod'.
[90] Kynaston, *Smoke*, pp.275-276.
[91] We called this dinner but nowadays many call it lunch and dinner is the evening meal.

The main building's ground floor was the girls' school; boys were on the first floor. Separate entrance gates led into respective concrete playgrounds, on opposite sides of the building. Girls didn't normally mix with the boys, although we saw them walking to and from school.

At each end of the boys' playground were two small toilet blocks (lavatories) – sometimes smelly and smoky (from secret smokers or, as we said, someone having a "quick drag"). Near these were entrances upstairs to small cloakrooms and washrooms with coat hooks, basins and towels. A main corridor was the school's spine, with an assembly hall cutting across the centre. When the whistle went, we lined up in classes before going inside. Prefects policed the gates, recording latecomers' names.

The hall was used daily for morning assemblies: Bible readings, prayers and hymns. We stood or sat on the floor. Sometimes older boys altered the hymn's words. For example, 'Oft in danger, oft in woe' was sung enthusiastically as 'Toft in danger. Toft in woe,' about Mr Toft, the headmaster. Announcements were made, perhaps mentioning visits of Sergeant Wardale: 'Who's in trouble with the police?' we wondered.

Our hall was also the gym and film theatre. There were no changing rooms, and no showers for PT (Physical Training or, as the pupils said, 'Physical Torture'). Sometimes after school, we sat on rows of low benches to see black-and-white films. The funniest was the 1950-60s British comedy series set in the fictional St Trinian's boarding school for "young ladies" who behaved badly. We probably saw *The Belles of St. Trinian's* (released 1954) – hilarious.

At the end of the corridor, nearest Sheil Road, was our one science laboratory, the Prefects' Room, cloakroom/washroom, and headmaster's office. At ninety degrees to this corridor ran a shorter corridor parallel to Sheil Road, leading to classrooms and woodwork workshops, where an external staircase descended to the girls' playground and small single-storey classroom buildings with patches of grass at the front. We had onsite facilities for dinnertime meals, but I only stayed a couple of times while Mum had hospital tests. Meals were cooked elsewhere and delivered. Once, not knowing the protocol, I sat at an empty table already "reserved" by the big boys; when they arrived, I was promptly told 'Move or else!' – which I did.

We weren't required to wear school uniforms, although there was at least a red tie. Just as well; many families would find it difficult to afford full uniforms. We normally started secondary school wearing shorts and long grey woolly socks to our knees. Socks were always falling down and had holes in the heels (needing darning). At around thirteen, we started wearing long trousers with turn-ups. As boys grew, these were let down to delay buying new pairs.

Selection tests and early subjects

Once we arrived, we took selection tests. Would I be in the A class (top class) or the B class?

Miss Olga Myddleton invigilated. She was a young, attractive teacher; tall and slim, well-dressed, and with a beehive hair style. When she walked through the playground, heads turned, and not just the boys'! But she was excellent with discipline and wouldn't stand nonsense. Anyway, I was in the "A" stream – good news for me.

No foreign languages were taught (although the girls learnt French). Metalwork was excluded, as facilities didn't exist. Subjects were: art; drama; English language; English literature; geography; geometrical and engineering drawing; history; maths; physical education; religious education; science and woodwork. Pupils left four years later with a "school testimonial" on character, conduct, attendance and exam results (assessed by our school). Grammar schools, by contrast, had external exams, with publicly-recognised

General Certificate of Education O-Levels, where O = ordinary level standard.

Football (a winter sport) and cricket (a summer sport) happened in the public Newsham Park. I had an accident during cricket (either with the school or Life Boys). While I was in batting, the ball bounced high and hit my left cheek. I dropped the bat and collapsed, with an adult trying to catch me. Fortunately, there was no broken nose, nor broken teeth (we had no protective head/face gear then), but it left me disenchanted with cricket.

First two years (1958-1960)

Mr Norman Bryden was our teacher for two years (usually teachers kept classes for one year). We had an end classroom in the main corridor, with large group tables. Mr Bryden was pleasant, friendly, and an able teacher in many subjects.

I liked him and we got on. One morning, the class was involved in a deep subject (about life, meaning and spiritual issues), and I nervously noted that the time was passing and we should leave to go swimming at Lister Drive Baths. Eventually, I became so uneasy that I raised my hand while he was still in full flow. When he saw it, he asked, 'What is your question?' I replied, 'Sir, can we go swimming now?' It caught him off-guard and, rather amused, he replied: 'I thought you were going to ask some deep question about the important issue I am discussing.' The boys roared with laughter. Thankfully, he assured me that we would be going swimming soon, and we did.

Now, I wasn't much good at swimming, but I liked to go weekly, even if we missed some morning classes. This didn't help academically, though. Unfortunately, there weren't proper swimming lessons. We just muddled along. It was exercise.

Another time, Mr Bryden had a word with me because I had a growth spurt. Calling me to his desk, he said: 'When you started my class, I could hardly see your head over the desk. What has happened? Has someone put horse manure in your shoes?' I was one of the smallest boys. This growth did help me to be seen more easily, but I never grew tall. I stopped growing at fifteen.

His aim was to prepare us for the 13-plus – another chance of reaching grammar schools. Mr Bryden worked hard preparing us for English language, maths and IQ tests. We had weekly homework, which I did and handed in. It was good teaching and preparation. But when it came to the day of the exam, we had to travel to another school by public bus. This unsettled some of us, I reckon. When the results came through, I desperately wondered, 'Have I passed? Have I?' Then I was devastated – I learned that I had failed again.

First the 11-plus and now 13-plus. Trying, trials and failures! No further opportunities remained to reach a grammar school – that was it. The system gave two formal chances, so I remained in the secondary modern system. Marr states "secondary modern" spoke of sub-standard and lower status schools.[92] Struggles seemed fruitless.

Let's face it, I had to settle down for two more years there, and get a job at fifteen. 'Just work at what you've got,' I thought. I imagine my parents were disappointed. Nevertheless, thankfully, they still supported my education.

One glimmer of hope, before the 13-plus, had been the Liverpool Schools Savings Committee essay competition, in the Spring Term of 1959, when I was eleven. Our school participated in the "Essay Completion for ages 11 years to 13 years". We had to write an essay on "saving", and the best ones were sent in to the competition. Apparently, the committee found it quite stiff to determine the winner because of the high standard of essay-writing. Surprisingly, I won first prize, with an award of one pound. Three other children from different schools received second, third and fourth prizes. I

---

[92] Marr, *History*, pp.246-247.

was the only child in our school to receive a prize. My parents and I attended the "prizegiving" by Liverpool Schools Savings Committee at the Radiant House Theatre, Bold Street, Liverpool, on Monday May 4th 1959. Light refreshments were provided and Vernon S. Maxwell, Esq. J.P., Chairman of the Liverpool Savings Bank, presented prizes. My name was in the *Liverpool Echo* under 'Savings Champions', showing Mr Maxwell presenting certificates.

I still have the newspaper cutting, list of prize-winners, and the programme for the prizegiving, with a copy of the booklet *What you should know about Trustee Savings Banks (and all they can do for you!)* (April 1958). This listed my bank at 14 West Derby Road, Liverpool 6 (Tel. ANFIeld 2179). Sadly, I don't have a copy of my essay, but recall its closing remarks. After addressing the merits of saving money, I concluded with a realistic comment that went something like: 'Unfortunately, some people will never save, and my sister is one of them!' I reckon that realistic assessment with the example of my sister won me the competition. I attended the ceremony, smartly dressed in my shorts, where I had my photograph taken. The school and my parents were pleased with my achievement. I was pretty pleased, too.

1960-1962

After two years with Mr Bryden, we had a new teacher. Another leaver was in my class: David Kent was a 13-plus success, so he left. However, surprisingly, he returned because he found that grammar school homework gave him insufficient time to continue his music studies. I don't know if anyone else replaced him, but nobody from our school did – I would have gone. Anyway, we became good friends.

Geography, history, and art

We had classes in geography and history. To be honest, I remember little about them, except that the geography teacher gave very similar written tests each time, but the test still seemed difficult. For history, I remember nothing.

Mr Paul taught art. He was a friendly older teacher and the first to call me "Bob", a name which I used afterwards. Once, we were asked to draw a man walking, and I did my best. However, when I showed it to Mr Paul, he gently asked: 'Don't you think it looks a bit stiff, a bit wooden?' It was more like a matchstick man than a realistic human figure. 'Yes, I agree.' Frankly, art was not my subject (or drama, which was sometimes fun). But years later, imagine my surprise when I visited the Art Gallery at Salford on The Crescent (near Manchester), where pictures of the industrial North of England by the artist L.S. Lowry (1887-1976) were proudly displayed – smoky streets, industrial scenes, and matchstick people. So, my matchstick figure was not that far off after all.

Music, English language

and English literature

Music was another subject I struggled with. Mr Bill Sharpe was a good teacher but had a disciplinarian approach. We sat as a class group (30-40+) for choir singing. I couldn't sing, but that made no difference, I had to try: music – miserable or melodious. We were individually tested to follow notes on Mr Sharpe's piano, to see if we were musically able – I failed. Though I guess Mr Sharpe found the class singing joyous as we began: 'Some talk of Alexander, and some of Hercules, of Hector and Lysander, and such great names as these...' The worst thing was his strictness. We had to sit on wooden chairs throughout the whole class, with hands behind our backs. Bodily wishes were subdued. 'No talking and no itching.' If we had itchy noses, we couldn't bring out a finger and scratch. If caught, the penalty was caning on your hand. So, pupils tried to rub their nose on a shoulder, to ease the itchiness or take the risk of using a finger, being caught and caned. Corporal punishment ruled. Music for the gifted and unmusical meant discomfort, discipline and dread. It wasn't just Mr Sharpe: other teachers frequently threw pieces of chalk or board dusters at boys to "get your attention" while asking 'Are you listening, boy?' The reply, 'Yes, sir.'

Mr Sharpe also taught us English language and literature; how to write formal letters and adverts. One advert I wrote, he liked: 'You can write for miles and miles without refilling your pen.' It broadcast the merits of biros versus the disadvantages of fountain pens and nib pens that we dipped into ink in the desk's inkwell. We were permitted fountain pens, but Mr Sharpe didn't allow biros – unless it was school policy.

He had his hair combed down the middle, and liked jumping into the air, clicking his shoe heels, usually without any support, but sometimes by resting one hand on a desk. As he went up and down, his hair on either side of the parting flopped up and down. We lined up outside his classroom and as we entered, he stood at the door and made witty remarks like: 'Abandon hope all ye who enter here.' Over the blackboard (which was truly black) was a sign that said 'Manners maketh man'. He taught us English language, which was quite a challenge for us Liverpudlian boys and also for Mr Sharpe. One able student ("Hutch") once spelt "dangerous" in an essay as "dangrous". After that Mr Sharpe called him publicly and in a humorous way "Dan Grouse". We had little on English grammar. Learning to write sentences, spellings and apostrophes was challenging enough. Although we spoke about "me dad" (my dad) or "me 'ead" (my head), this was unacceptable. Queen's English was Mr Sharpe's rule.

English literature included: *Animal Farm* (George Orwell, 1945); the thriller *The Thirty-Nine Steps* (John Buchan, 1915); *The Cruel Sea* (Nicholas Monserrat, 1951) – a novel based on the author's experience about Royal Navy sailors in the Battle of the Atlantic; and the comic novel *The History of Mr Polly* (H.G. Wells, 1910).[93] Once, our class visited a cinema in Birkenhead or Wallasey (across the Mersey), where Shakespeare's *Macbeth* was shown in colour. An enjoyable learning experience. Besides class readings, we read individually. I read *The Wooden Horse* (Eric Williams, 1949), perhaps in the children's 1956 edition. It told the true story of three British officers' successful Second World War escape from a German Prisoner of War Camp (Stalag-Luft III). About sixty years later, during England's first 2020 lockdown for Covid-19, I read the new and revised thirtieth anniversary 1979 edition. Reading books and comics about the Second World War was popular with boys.

One year, I entered the school's elocution competition. Standing in the crowded hall before teachers and pupils, I recited "Abou Ben Adhem (may his tribe increase!)" from memory in my best Liverpudlian accent. Surprisingly, after repeating it, I won third prize. I chose the book *Tales of Terror* from Mr Sharpe.

PT and sports

Weekly PT was compulsory. Boys hated it so much that excuses not to exercise were expected. Some pupils

---

[93] These books were adapted into films, often with later remakes. *The History of Mr Polly* (a comedy of an Englishman's midlife crisis; he is an antihero) was voted no. 39 in the 100 Best Novels in *The Guardian*. Wells wrote fifty novels but Robert McCrum considers this his best. See Robert McCrum, 'The 100 best novels: No 39 – The History of Mr Polly by HG Wells (1910)', *The Guardian*, 16 June 2014. Accessed 28 August 2022 at The 100 best novels: No 39 – The History of Mr Polly by HG Wells (1910) | HG Wells | The Guardian

falsified letters in their parents' names, giving reasons for missing PT (for example, a cold). Once, Mr Ken Morton said to one boy: 'This doesn't look like your parent's signature.' Nevertheless, he gave him "the benefit of the doubt", and he was excused. Later, I learnt it was a forgery.

Without changing rooms, we changed in the classroom with its clear windows into the corridor (there was no privacy); some boys came to school wearing shorts under their trousers. When lessons finished, there were no showers – clothes went back on sweaty bodies. Often, we ran around the hall and then along the corridor, downstairs, across the playground, upstairs, along the corridor, and back into the hall. Running with boys shoving was tricky – it was a wonder nobody was injured. If the teacher thought boys were slacking when running in the hall, he'd hit them with a cane across their legs. This was distressing for boys who found PT difficult. I was small, but a speedy sprinter.

In one exercise, pairs of boys faced each other, squatting with their hands on their partner's shoulders. Then we bounced up and down. I bounced high and enjoyed it. In fact, I did so well that Mr Morton shouted with amusement, 'Give that boy a carrot!' A nice compliment, even if I was being compared with a rabbit.

PT had vaulting "horse" and springboard exercises. I tried hard. We were expected to vault with our legs wide open, or manage a forward roll across the top. Once, when PT teacher Mr Sargent was standing to the left of the box helping boys vault its length, one long-legged boy vaulted and kicked Mr Sargent's face. Although a shocking moment, he remained calm and told the boy he considered it an accident. So, the boy wasn't caned, but was it really an accident? Possibly not.

Mr Morton spent weeks teaching us how to do handsprings. Mats on the hall's hard wooden floor helped us avoid injuries. We were split into ability groups and tried pretty hard to be successful. Eventually, some became so confident at doing handsprings that one day they did a display, under their own volition, in the playground. They ran, a few together, throwing their hands into the air and then placing them firmly on the concrete to give a substantial push that sent them head-over-heels into the air and landing on their feet. This was repeated, including boys making two lines and running towards each line crossing between for handsprings. It was impressive enough to gather a crowd. However, handsprings on concrete had safety implications. But nobody worried. At that stage, I couldn't do them, but my confidence grew, and later on a family holiday in Cemaes Bay, Anglesey, I did them on concrete without fear or accident.

Of course, sometimes accidents did happen. One summer, we did athletics in the playground and during high jump practice a friend ("Hutch" again) landed badly on the mats. They weren't thick enough to break his fall, and he broke his wrist. The most frequent accident was damaging scabs, as I'll explain. Liverpool wisely operated a schools' vaccination programme for prevention of TB (tuberculosis). We had a simple test to see if we needed the injection, and most boys did. This was later given as an injection in the arm – my BCG vaccination was on 23rd June 1960. Problems arose when the injection sites turned into scabs. These scabs were frequently knocked off during PT, with blood streaming out and medical help needed. It was an unpleasant sight we often saw, but it didn't happen to me.[94]

Sheil Road lacked swimming baths and sports fields. For football and cricket, we walked down Sheil Road to Newsham Park. For swimming, we walked for about twenty minutes along the edge of Newsham Park to Lister Drive

---

[94] Tuberculosis (TB) seems distant in 21st century Britain, but its destructive nature often resulted in multiple deaths in families. Its horrors are narrated by Jennifer Worth, *Farewell to the East End* (London: Phoenix, 2009) in chapters 'The Master's Arms' (a family destroyed by TB) and 'Tuberculosis'. She draws upon her experience in London as a midwife in the 1950s-1960s. I recall seeing the film *Twice Round the Daffodils* (1962), where new TB patients arrive at a sanatorium.

public swimming baths, which was much like Margaret Street baths. In July 1960 (aged twelve), I received my "Beginners 50 Yards" certificate. I don't think that we had school football or cricket teams in leagues, but we had a summer athletics team.

Athletics happened in the playgrounds, and I was good at sprinting. We had our Annual Inter House Sports Day in the girls' playground, as it was larger than ours, allowing us to run 75-yard sprints and longer races, such as 220 yards on a central marked oval. Houses were: Faraday, Livingstone, Nelson and Scott. Points were awarded as follows: 1st place (four points); 2nd (three points); 3rd (two points) and 4th (one point). Relay teams earned double points. I still have the programme for July 1960.

We competed in the schools' annual district athletics (the District Championships). I represented our school more than once. We travelled by public bus to the outdoor athletics area across the city (there was no school coach). I don't recall us having school shirts and shorts, but the school held a stock of spiked running shoes. We found the correct size and borrowed them. In July 1961, I ran in both the 100 yards (no metres used then) and 220 yards individual events and received a merit certificate in the Central District Age Group 13/14 years. I also ran the 220 yards in our four-boy relay team, reaching the finals, where we triumphed in fourth place. We were presented our certificates before the whole school. The aching legs were worth it.

Further, on 26th May 1961, I passed my National Cycling Proficiency Test in our school playground. The certificate was signed by the president of the RSPA (Royal Society for the Prevention of Accidents).

Sheil Road Evening Institute

(City of Liverpool Education Committee)

Besides being a state school, Sheil Road provided community evening classes. Older boys were encouraged to take some additional studies. When I was in class 4T (1961-62), I took evening classes in: English; maths; practical drawing, and science. I clearly recall the first evening in September 1961, after walking, for the third time that day, from home to school. The whole school was illuminated like a Christmas tree. Previously, I hadn't seen the school "shine" like this. A memorable part of the evenings was gathering for our short "tea break", when we talked over important issues such as the cost of taking girls to the cinema – was it ten shillings (then a paper note, now just 50p)? Science classes were held in our science lab. All went well with classes and homework until summer 1962, when the science exam papers were distributed. We read the questions with considerable concern – they were too difficult.

Fortunately, we knew the teacher, and he calmly addressed our fears, pointing out questions that we could attempt. So, listening to his wise advice, we stayed and wrote answers as best we could. Clearly, we had learnt enough, but in an anxious situation it was difficult for us to assess our own abilities – his help was crucial.

In July 1962, I concluded my last compulsory school year and did well in 4T. In fact, that month I received the school book prize from Mr Toft for 'excellent conduct and very good work'. It was *North Wales (Northern Section)* by Ward Lock.

But what about my evening class exams? Well, I received my "Record of Work Certificate" (31st July 1962), showing attendance (seventy-two per cent) and marks being '% Combined Classwork and Homework Marks' and '% Examination Marks'. In English, maths and practical drawing all marks were seventy-four per cent or higher. My science

'% Combined Classwork and Homework Marks' was sixty-seven per cent and the exam mark fifty-one per cent (a pass – yes). My science marks were the lowest but, nevertheless, a pleasing overall result for one year's evening studies.

Towards 7th September 1962, a letter arrived from the City of Liverpool Director of Education (H.S. Magnay) entitled 'Award of Studentships for Session 1962/63'. It offered me a free scholarship. Very nice! But with me starting in the new 5T class (see below), I focused on that and didn't attend another year. Nevertheless, evening studies had strengthened me in those subjects.

Dinnertime Cavern Club,

missing the Beatles

Many boys stayed for school dinners but as my friends grew older, they discovered a fabulous group was playing in Liverpool's Cavern Club in Mathew Street. It was in an arched cellar below a warehouse. They had previously played in Hamburg, but they were a Liverpool group regularly on over lunchtimes. So, some friends (Reggie included) often caught buses in Kensington and went to the original Cavern Club. They had great times, but then rushed back to school by 1.30pm. The group was the Beatles. I had heard of them previously in a conversation that went: 'Look at the Beatles. They are the best group in Liverpool and have never got anywhere.'[95] Little did we know the future. My friends tried to get me there but somehow, I never made the effort (a massive mistake in retrospect).

My sister Anne was a Beatles fan. One Friday evening, on 10th July 1964, the Beatles had a civic reception with the Lord Mayor and other dignitaries at the Town Hall in Water

---

[95] Possibly outside No. 52 Grey Rock between Billy Butler and Billy Kinsley.

Street. The Beatles had arrived at Speke Airport and vast crowds of fans cheered them on their journey to the city centre. Anne was among them and recalls being fortunate enough to be in the right place when the car with John Lennon passed nearby and she saw him. Anne also went to the Beatles' concerts, but recalls that there was so much screaming and shouting that you couldn't hear them sing – which rather defeated the object of buying tickets and seeing them in person.

In March 1966, John Lennon made an infamous comment about the Beatles being 'more popular than Jesus'. Months later, this remark was picked up in America and produced a major reaction, or backlash, with protests. John had to clarify his position many times and later apologised. UK TV showed crowds of young people in America bringing out their Beatles' records and burning them publicly on bonfires. Anne recalls giving away her records.

In their early days, the Beatles wore leather jackets and jumpers (including polo necks); later, their manager Brian Epstein persuaded them to wear suits. When I started university, I bought myself a smart leather jacket, which I liked to wear with a polo neck.

I have had the advantage of walking Liverpool's streets and landmarks in the Sixties. And I've enjoyed visiting the current Cavern Club, but my memory of the atmosphere of the original Cavern Club and Mathew Street still outshines the reproduction.

Back in the early days, working in the Cavern cloakroom was a young woman from Scottie Road, who became the famous singer and entertainer, Cilla Black. On TV, I sadly watched her funeral at St Mary's RC Church in Woolton, Liverpool, on 20th August 2015.[96]

Chris Ingram outlines the Cavern's history, noting that in

---

[96] See 'Cilla Black funeral: Fans and stars say farewell in Liverpool', BBC News 20 August 2015. Accessed 28 August 2022 at Cilla Black funeral: Fans and stars say farewell in Liverpool – BBC News

the two years from August 1961-63, when we were in our final two years at Sheil Road and "me mates" went to the Cavern, the Beatles performed there almost 300 times.[97] Later, I enjoyed going to all-night sessions in that amazing musical atmosphere, even if it was hot and sweaty. It closed briefly in 1965, before reopening under new management, but closed in 1973. Ingram observed it was demolished for 'an underground ventilation duct'. A new Cavern Club opened briefly across the street from the original. However, after John Lennon's death (8th December 1980), the Cavern was authentically re-created at 10 Mathew Street (opening in April 1984). It occupied seventy-five per cent of the old site and used 15,000 bricks from the Beatles' Cavern. I have visited it a few times since (last time in 2018). Each time, it brings back vivid memories of the original, including when I was short of change for the cloakroom and a lad I didn't know gave me enough money – thanks. Coming out of all-night sessions into the morning sun was an experience, and once a spiritual experience when I felt like attending church.

School camps

During summer holidays, school staff ran camps on the Isle of Man. It was reached by ferry from Liverpool into Douglas Harbour. Our school corridor proudly displayed black-and-white photographs of the camp. Round white tents provided accommodation for boys and teachers (seen wearing their shorts). The camp ran for up to two weeks and pupils paid weekly over the year towards their holiday. It looked good and the teachers were clearly committed in giving up their holidays for the boys. However, I heard sad stories about how some smaller boys were mistreated by bigger boys. I thought: 'I don't wish to be at school with some boys

---

[97] Chris Ingram, *The Rough Guide to the Beatles* (2nd ed.; London: Rough Guides, 2006), pp.253-254.

because of their bad behaviour. So why should I pay to go on holiday with them?' I thought it a fair point. One year, however, I decided to give it a go and began paying. But, for a reason I can't recall, the school cancelled that year, and I never went afterwards.

Nevertheless, I did holiday on the Isle of Man in August 1961 (as my tiny photos show) with family friends, staying at a bed and breakfast in Douglas. We bought "runabout" tickets on the trains and travelled the island for a lovely week. Two things stand out. First, I was surprised that when the tide was in at Douglas, I could see from the promenade right through the deep water (eight feet or so?) to the bottom. 'So, water is transparent, just as science teachers say it is,' I thought. The Mersey was brown (coffee-coloured) and even at Meols it was that colour. Before then, the deepest clearest water I recall was the six-feet deep end in the swimming baths. Second, the return ferry trip to Liverpool was rough once we left the harbour. Waves went up and down and the ferry rolled. People were sick; seasickness tablets stopped me throwing up – fortunately. I was so glad when we sailed up the Mersey, but it still took about thirty minutes to dock the short distance. Land at last! Dad was a sailor in the Royal Navy, but that ferry trip put me off the sea. Perhaps science would be a better vocation?

New studies: 5T (1962-63)

In class 4T, I looked ahead and tried joining Liverpool's police cadets. One school captain joined the police and Mr Toft shared this news in school assemblies, no doubt to inspire us. I had an interview at the police cadets' college in Mather Avenue (the road where John Lennon lived, 1945-1963, with his Aunt Mimi). It went well except for the physical. Liverpool's minimum height requirement was five feet eight inches. Sadly, I was five feet five-and-a-half inches – not tall enough. The officer kindly suggested that I continued studying and return if I reached five feet seven inches (assuming I'd grow more). Sadly, I never did. Decades later, the minimum height was abolished, but by then I was too old. However, I had other opportunities thanks to 5T.

Mr Toft was innovative and saw more in us than we could. He decided to introduce a fifth form 5T (T for technical) for boys who wanted to stay beyond age fifteen and obtain public qualifications. Many families wanted boys to leave and earn wages to help their family finances.

My parents wisely thought differently. Mum often said: 'We will support you in your education if you want to stay on.' Dad asked: 'What would you like to be when you are older?' I didn't say 'A bricklayer like you, Dad,' but 'A boss!' He smiled. I had heard him speaking about 'the boss said this and the boss did that', so it sounded like a good job. Anyway, my parents agreed that I join 5T. Mr Toft convinced our teachers to follow his vision, accept extra teaching and administrative responsibilities, and follow set curricula for external exams. So, in September 1962 the first small 5T class started (with fourteen pupils). I began with friends Reggie and George Tully. This decision completely changed my life.

What exams would we take? Sensibly, Mr Toft arranged for us to sit the local Union of Lancashire and Cheshire Institutes Examinations (ULCIs). They were demanding, but easier than the Ordinary Level (O-Level) exams taken in grammar schools. Perhaps the ULCIs were comparable with the later externally set Certificate of Secondary Education (CSEs), which ran from 1965-1987 for secondary modern schools.

I studied: chemistry; English language; English literature (with *The History of Mr Polly* and Shakespeare's *Macbeth*); geometrical and engineering drawing; maths; physics; and woodwork. Plus, I took O-Levels in: English language; geometrical and engineering drawing; maths; and physics-with-chemistry. Teachers supported us in a direction requiring effort, energy and endurance until summer 1963.

Mr Toft held two degrees and was an able teacher in maths and science. School finished at 4pm, but he arranged after-school classes till 5-5.30pm on two or three evenings a week. For example, he taught physics in both the lab and the classroom (using chalk, talk and blackboard – no overhead projectors, calculators, or computers then). Without calculators, maths classes often required working out arithmetic problems using logarithm tables (logs). It was a complicated and tedious process, which I won't attempt to describe. Previously, Mr Eric Turner had taught us science, and spent weary weeks teaching us log tables in maths classes. Learning about science (including Archimedes' principle related to objects in fluids) and doing relevant experiments interested me. Weirdly, I found physics enjoyable.

So committed was Mr Toft that he arranged for 5T to come into school even in the 1962-63 winter holidays, with snow on the ground. Once dates were chosen in advance, we just turned up; it wasn't easy to change arrangements without someone typing letters and posting them to us. Remember: there were no mobile phones nor emails then.

I mention the snow because this was serious stuff. Ian McCaskill and Paul Hudson called 1947 'The Snowiest Winter'.[98] However, winter 1962-63 they termed 'The Coldest Winter'.[99] It was Britain's coldest winter of the twentieth century and right back to 1740! (Only 1739-40 was colder.) Bitterly cold. Snow was accompanied with smoke, fog and smog (smoke mixed with sulphur dioxide). Disruption, delays, death, disease, and destruction followed. There were electricity cuts. Our main heating was from coal fires, with some paraffin or electric heaters, and

---

[98] Ian McCaskill and Paul Hudson, *Frozen Britain* (Ilkley: Great Northern Books, 2011), 'Part III The Snowiest Winter – 1947', pp.47-92 with illustrations.
[99] McCaskill and Hudson, *Frozen Britain*, 'Part IV The Coldest Winter – 1962-63', pp.93-127.

no central heating. Huge icicles hung from the roof of our outside toilet.

But in January we walked in the snow to our lab for Mr Toft's classes. How he made it, I don't know, but he did, so teaching went ahead even in the chilly building. I don't recall if Dad went to work; bricklayers travelled and worked outdoors, so I guess he didn't. January 1963 was, according to McCaskill and Hudson, 'one of the most miserable in British history – the coldest month of the entire twentieth century'.[100]

We looked forward to spring, and summer exams. Back then, there was no coursework and no modules. Everything was by final written exam. As I took seven ULCIs and four GCEs, I had many exams but, thankfully, they were in school. No need to travel. By and large, the preparation and exams went well, with only two hiccups. First, in my ULCI English literature exam, I mistakenly turned over two pages and missed one question on *Macbeth* that I could have easily answered. What a shock to find out after the exam! I thought desperately, 'would I pass with this omission?' Also, in the GCE geometrical and engineering drawing, I misread a question and it was too late to correct it before we were told, 'Put your pencils down.' Again, I thought, 'would I pass with this mistake?' I waited nervous months.

Summer 1963 finished with the Leavers' Service in the hall. I had attended many and now it was my turn. This was a Christian service, with prayers and hymns such as *God be with you 'til we meet again*. Mr Toft spoke encouraging words. I received my individual "Scholar's Reference Cards" (dated 18th July 1963), which favourably commented on character, conduct, attendance and any exams. Five years of education ended. I waited, hoping for good results. Would I transfer to a grammar school?

As a final celebration of our time at Newsham Secondary

---

[100] McCaskill and Hudson, *Frozen Britain*, p.120.

Modern, we had a "Distribution of Prizes and Certificates" ceremony, on Thursday 12th December 1963 at 7.30pm, in St Philip's Church Hall, Sheil Road, Liverpool 6.

Learning to learn

Somewhile into our studies, I learnt that Mr Toft and our teachers were committed to helping us, but they couldn't do it alone. We needed to work, too. This became evident in one class and was a turning point. One evening, Mr Toft was teaching us about "density" and different materials in physics. I was sat at a desk in the middle of the classroom, looking and listening, with "me mates", as he wrote on the blackboard. Then he turned and said, 'Define density!' I tried to see the board, but he stood in the way, with his arms outstretched and his hands gripping the sides of my desk. Try as I might, I couldn't see past him.

He became very animated, shaking his head and loudly repeating: 'You'll fail! You'll fail! You'll fail! If you don't learn, you'll fail!' My, he was forthright! But it made me think: 'Perhaps, I will fail if I continue as I am?' It was a wake-up call, a turning point. Mr Toft continued teaching, and I resolved to learn besides looking and listening. One technique he liked was to spot us in the corridor, stop and demand, 'Define density!' or similar. If we saw him coming, we changed direction or went into the prefects' room. But he simply followed us. He was so determined to do the best for us, and it worked – we learnt a "lorra stuff". I imagine my parents were pretty pleased with him.

Discipline and violence

In time, I became a prefect and eventually School Captain, while my friend Reggie became Vice-Captain. Prefects helped teachers maintain discipline in the school. Boys bullied boys. Teachers "disciplined" boys. One of the prefects' duties was to ensure safe use of the stairs as boys moved to and from the playground. They also closed the school gates at 9am, and 1.30pm, and recorded latecomers in the school late book. Before I was a prefect, one morning so many boys (about fifty?) were late that Mr Toft held a public interrogation in the school hall, followed by a brutal public caning for those without valid excuses. It was still many years before the government made corporal punishment illegal in state schools. Parliament outlawed the practice in 1986, and it came into effect in 1987.

In my years at Sheil Road, Frank (in my class) looked out for me, as I was rather small and susceptible to being bullied by bigger, taller, and stronger boys. Frank kindly decided to take me under his wing. I was grateful. He warned off boys threatening me. Later, I went to some classes in a large house midway along Sheil Road. Outside stood a large, impressive sign, 'Learn Jujitsu. Fear Nobody.' Some rooms were converted with mats into suitable dojos, and a good black-belt taught us (adults and me). He was a short cockney man, with thick glasses, who knew his stuff. We learnt various blocks, locks and throws to defend ourselves against punches, etc. However, I didn't go long enough for a grading. But what I learnt was good.

I also read books and watched self-defence moves on TV, or in films. Twice, I used techniques to protect myself. One boy tried a rear bear hug on me in the playground. I reached down and swiftly pulled his leg. He quickly fell backwards on the concrete – fortunately, he didn't crack his head open! Another boy I knew grabbed my throat/shoulder and threatened me on the way home. I used a wrist lock to free myself, and put him on the ground. Then I made a quick exit. Neither boy attempted attacks on me again. When I was a prefect, a boy with a knife threatened me after I told him off for sharpening the knife on the school wall. I couldn't let him get away with that, so off we went together to see Mr Toft. It never happened again.

At times, there were school fights with individuals or groups inside a semi-enclosed block of local garages. Women were out on their front doorsteps watching and when the police were called, I didn't wait any longer. On two occasions, I witnessed boys bringing air pistols to school and stupidly shooting at people (one friend was shot above his eye, as we walked to school – he could have been blinded – and a girl shot in her leg). The postman saw the boy shooting the girl and got involved with the boy, and school. Sometimes bigger boys "argued" with the teachers.

Violence was not restricted to schools, but arose on Liverpool's streets. Once there was a fight involving around fifty men. Another time, a boy I knew in our school was attacked by a gang who slashed his cheeks with a razor. When he returned to school, we saw his scars. It reminded us of bad things in the Teddy Boy era.

A fight occurred inside and outside our house one New Year's Day. Dad had a friend who was "a bit of a boxer" and he turned up with mates. Dad was at work (this was still before 1st January was a public holiday). The friends had been celebrating and were, frankly, the worse for wear. One man declined a cup of tea from Mum, and that started an argument, then a fight, with a punch to his jaw. It spilled into the street before they eventually moved on. I was young enough to watch the fight, but unable to intervene. Mum tried calming them. I don't think Dad was too pleased when he returned home.

TV showed violence. We watched the Civil Rights demonstrations in the US, horrified. People protested peacefully, yet police attacked them with considerable violence. In April 1963, Rev Martin Luther King Jr., US Civil Rights Campaigner and leader of the Southern Christian Leadership Conference (SCLC) was imprisoned in Birmingham, Alabama. And in May 1963, the "Children's Crusade" non-violent march was attacked with fire hoses and dogs by Birmingham police.[101]

We were in the Cold War. As a teenager, I visited a central police station in Liverpool. Wall maps showed how Russian nuclear bombs would bring death and destruction. Our streets would be obliterated! Living with the fear of nuclear war was an everyday reality. Important people had nuclear bunkers/shelters, while we foresaw death. In the Space Race (part of the Cold War), 13th April 1961 saw the first man in space: Soviet cosmonaut Yuri Gagarin orbited the world. Amazingly, the Soviets were ahead of the US. In August 1961, the Berlin Wall was erected to stop escapees to the West. On TV, we saw that many attempting escape were killed.

Life outside school:

Home, work and church

Home life continued as normal: Dad worked hard, and Mum looked after us. When I started at Sheil Road in 1958, Anne was attending Whitefield Road School and Christina, my little sister, was aged two. The first two years meant homework in preparation for the 13-plus. I had pocket money weekly, but then I started my paper round for the newsagent shop along the short block on West Derby Road between Grey Rock and Red Rock Streets. This was an early morning and evening paper round, six days a week. Fortunately, Sunday papers were delivered by someone else; although occasionally I delivered them when the other boy was unavailable. I also supported my friend Billy Kinsley, who worked in another newsagent's shop on West Derby Road in the block between Grey Rock and Boundary Lane. When he asked, I did his evening round plus mine. In

---

[101] Clayborne Carson (ed.), *The Autobiography of Martin Luther King, Jr.* (London: Abacus, 2000), p.205.

1961, he was an original founder member of the Liverpool group the Merseybeats (then called the Mavericks).[102] They played at the Cavern Club with the Beatles and in summer 1963 released their first single.

My paper round initially paid six shillings and six pence weekly; doing a Sunday round or helping Billy brought in extra cash. Around early 1961, I bought a dark blue Carlton Capella Clubman racing bicycle with five gears for £23 19s 5d (more than I earned weekly as a building-site labourer years later). The bike shop on West Derby Road/Tweed Street arranged a hire purchase (HP) deal, where I paid weekly until I eventually bought it. Saturday evenings after I was paid, I crossed the road and paid around five shillings (5/-). Kynaston notes that children often got new bikes for passing the 11-plus; this option wasn't for me as: (1) I failed the exam and (2) my parents couldn't afford a new bike anyway.[103]

Dad woke me up around 6.30am to get me to my newsagent's, then he went to work. I delivered papers on streets off West Derby Road. The longest delivery was to the Catholic convent in Belmont Road. I couldn't arrive between 7.00-7.30am, as they had a morning service, so I arrived before 7am or after 7.30am. I often came down Grey Rock, collected my bike from home, and cycled to the convent for the final delivery. Evening deliveries started around 5.00-5.30pm. I waited outside the shop until the newspaper van arrived and unloaded the papers for delivery.

Most deliveries went okay, but one house had a dog outside that bit me. Sometimes I went to their back door (up the alley) rather than be bitten again! In another street, a dog shot down the hall barking but fortunately it was never outside, so I was safe. In the winter, with dark nights and smog, it was tricky crossing West Derby Road. I had a near miss with a car outside my newsagent's shop by the bus stop.

---

[102] 'Welcome to The Merseybeats official website'. Accessed 28 August 2022 at The Merseybeats Official Website
[103] Kynaston, *Smoke*, p.277.

Christmases were great. Folk expected me to knock and hand papers over, saying, 'Happy Christmas!' Often, they said, 'Wait there!' then went inside and returned with a tip: 'Have this and a Happy Christmas.' 'Thanks!' I replied. People were friendly and generous.

Unfortunately, newspaper headlines started reporting that babies were being born with disabilities. A terrible tragedy occurred with the drug thalidomide given to pregnant women; it caused some horrific birth defects. It was developed in Germany in 1954 and introduced to the UK in 1958. By late 1961, it was being withdrawn.[104]

One Christmas (1962), I worked Saturdays in the large department store T.J. Hughes on London Road in Liverpool's centre. I worked in two roles. In the food section, I collected and returned empty baskets from the checkout tills. In Santa's grotto, I issued children's toys in exchange for their tickets. Children and parents saw the shows and heard music, often *"Pinkie and Perky"* or *Z Cars* – the TV police series Z cars (pronounced 'zed cars'), filmed in Kirkby, which ran from 1962-1978. They came out happy to select gifts. The pay was good and we had a nice lunch break at 11.30am. I didn't know anyone there but some girls starting the same day were friendly. It was just a Christmas job, but fun.

We continued attending St Margaret's Sunday School and the outings, for example to Chester Zoo on 28th May 1961. Once, Alf and I were late for the bus and missed the trip. Disappointed, we went home and spoke to Auntie Edie (Alf's mum); she agreed that I was old enough for us to have our own outing (Alf was younger). So, we took the ferry up the Mersey to New Brighton and enjoyed its amusements, fair rides and beach. A wonderful day! Before the advent of package holidays, it was a popular place.

When I was too old for Sunday School, I went with Reggie

---

[104] See 'Thalidomide FAQs', Thalidomide Society 2022. Accessed 28 August 2022 at Thalidomide FAQs – The Thalidomide Society

to St Margaret's Sunday morning service, sitting in the pews of the original building. When it was communion, Reggie (who was confirmed) could participate but I couldn't – as I wasn't confirmed – but that was fine.

In mid-September 1961 when I left school for home, I went along Sheil Road. But something unusual seemed to be up. 'What is it? What is happening?'. We quickly saw a crowd gathered at the junction of Belmont Road and Rocky Lane by the church. It was on fire – our church! I joined the crowd and saw huge flames and smoke rising through the roof. A fireman on long extension ladders jetted water onto it. Other firemen with hoses tackled the flames. I'd never seen such a large fire.[105] (Apparently on 19th September *The Guardian* newspaper had a photo of the firemen in action.) We heard that an electrical fault caused it. Sadly, the original 1875 building was destroyed and demolished but rebuilt as a smaller structure. It opened in 1965, two years after I left Sheil Road School. Today, St Margaret's continues as a church.

Sadness: Uncle Alf dies

Uncle Alf survived the Second World War and worked hard as a bricklayer for his family: Auntie Edie, Edna and Alfred. It was brilliant for us having them living in the next street. We often visited and did things together. Once Alf appeared in the *Liverpool Echo* as he had carried on laying bricks despite a large local fire burning. But Uncle Alf had health problems and doctors discovered he had lung cancer. Thankfully, a successful operation removed the diseased lung, so he could walk, although he became breathless. He went to Sheil Park to play bowls. Once a boy stole an ice cream from a smaller child (possibly my sister Christina) and Alf, despite disability,

---

[105] For photos of the fine St Margaret's Church in 1875 and the devastating 1961 fire see: Colin Wilkinson, *The Streets of Liverpool Volume 2* (Liverpool: The Bluecoat Press, 2012), pp.36-37.

gave chase. He never caught the culprit but eventually the boy put the ice cream on the ground and scarpered. He never enjoyed it – some reward for Alf. Winters were difficult, still with no central heating. It was tough.

However, Alf's other lung was also affected. Doctors said: 'One day we will be able to do a lung transplant,' but that was decades away, and Alf was finally admitted to hospital. Mum asked: 'Do you want to visit him in hospital? He did not look good before but looks okay this week.' We knew that he wasn't coming out this time. However, I thought and said, 'No thanks,' as I didn't know if I could handle it. Mum understood and kindly replied: 'You want to remember him as he was, don't you?' 'Yes,' I said, and sadly I didn't see him again.

One evening on my paper round, I was called into our house. The family was in the back living room, 'Uncle Alf has died.' We were distressed and in tears, even though we had known his end was near. Alf was born in 1916 and died 12th February 1962, aged forty-six. I was fourteen. I wore a black armband to school, the usual way of showing a death, and the teacher Mr Morton asked, 'Who has died?' He looked sad after I told him Uncle Alf's age. In respect, neighbours drew their front curtains. Cousin Alf recalls that afterwards he got free school meals. Alf was buried with his parents in the family grave.

Edna and Rob

Cousin Edna was like a big sister to me and took me and Alf on days out such as to Southport's fairground, and the sandhills and sea at Freshfield. She left Holly Lodge school before going into the Sixth Form and became a nurse (back then, training was on-the-job). She worked with children and then left. I thought she'd left because the matrons were strict, but she told me years later it was because 'the suffering of the children' upset her so much. She moved into other employment. Edna was an intelligent, pleasant and attractive young lady.

She had a boyfriend called Rob Atkins (from Bootle in Liverpool), who was studying for his chemistry degree (BSc) at Manchester University. Rob often visited Edna and the family in Red Rock, and lived there for a while. He was young, humorous, intelligent and friendly. We became friends. He liked sports and we jogged together through Sheil Park to Newsham Park for laps. He also loaned me the "Charles Atlas" bodybuilding course, with exercises for improving size and strength, which I was happy to follow. Moreover, he encouraged me with my school studies.

Once, he wanted to see Liverpool Football Club play at Anfield, and asked if I wanted to go. When I hesitated, he said: 'Okay, I'll pay for you. Do you want to go?' With such a generous offer, I couldn't resist. 'Yes!' We walked there. I can't recall who was playing, or the score, but I remember standing behind the goal on the concrete steps (the Kop). It wasn't raining – so that was good. Supporters pushed and shoved, so we went up and down the steps, bumping against metal barriers. As a schoolboy, I was easily jostled. Cousin Alf recalls going regularly, but not me. Dad wasn't a football fan. Also, folk asked, 'Are you Everton or Liverpool (supporter)?'. My reply, 'Neither!' Frankly, I avoided arguments through neutrality.

Edna and Rob married in June 1962 at St Margaret's. Because Edna's dad had died, our dad gave her away. I didn't attend the wedding as my parents agreed a separate treat for us boys. We had a lovely meal (no doubt with chips) in the upstairs café of T.J. Hughes, then went to the pics to see *El Cid* in spectacular colour, probably at the Odeon cinema in London Road.[106] Edna and Rob lived in Red Rock before moving to a new semi-detached house in Formby. They would have three children: Andrew, Debbie and Steve.

---

[106] See: Alan Weston, 'Remembering the golden days of the Odeon cinema in Liverpool', *Liverpool Echo* 10 October 2020. Accessed 28 August 2022 at Remembering the golden days of the Odeon cinema in Liverpool – Liverpool Echo

Entertainment

Wireless/radio provided news and entertainment. I liked Radio Luxembourg for popular music, although it had more than music, including an infuriating advert on winning the football pools. Paul Feeney notes that until pirate radio stations appeared offshore in March 1964, Radio Luxembourg was the UK's only English-speaking commercial station.[107] Hard to imagine now, with current mass entertainment, but Radio Luxembourg was our lifeline.

We enjoyed TV programmes in black-and-white, on small screens, with few channels and for restricted hours. (We waited until April 1964 for our third British TV channel, BBC2.) Sometimes people stood outside shops such as Radio Rentals to watch the TVs through the windows. TVs were often rented and if you owned one then there was the constant fear of having to fork out for a new tube (they didn't seem to last long). There were no recordings then: if we missed a programme – tough! *Coronation Street*, the world's longest-running soap opera, began on 7th December 1960 and celebrated sixty years in 2020. I watched it at the beginning; it so resembled our streets that I said I lived in Coronation Street and gave up viewing, but others continued watching. In July 1962, satellite television's first broadcast occurred.

One important weekly Saturday TV programme we watched featured our neighbour, Billy Butler. He was our young Scouser on *Thank Your Lucky Stars* (shown 1961-1966), giving his valued views rating the latest records.

In 1960, Alfred Hitchcock's *Psycho* was released. I saw it at the Hippodrome – frightening. In 1962, I saw the first James Bond film (*Dr No*), newly released. What an enjoyable experience to see colourful exotic places, fast

---

[107] Paul Feeney, *A 1960s Childhood: From Thunderbirds to Beatlemania* (Stroud: The History Press, 2010), p.124.

cars, fancy gadgets, beautiful Bond girls and British intelligence fighting evil. The Cold War was in our minds, especially in October 1962 with the "Cuban Missile Crisis". The standoff between the USA and USSR over missiles in Cuba made nuclear war feel imminent. President John F. Kennedy and the UN secretary-general U Thant worked with Nikita Khrushchev (the well-known Soviet leader) on an agreement. We sighed in relief.

For me, the British music scene burst into life in the Sixties. In October 1962, the Beatles released *Love Me Do*. Their careers took off with a visit to the US. As well as the Beatles, and the US' Elvis Presley (*It's Now or Never*, 1960), many British singers and instrumentalists had hits in the early 1960s: Cliff Richard (*The Young Ones*, 1962), The Shadows (A*pache*, 1960; *Kon-Tiki*, 1961), Acker Bilk (*Stranger on the Shore*, 1962). I was a fan of Helen Shapiro (*Walking Back to Happiness*, 1961) and took the *New Musical Express*. "Beatlemania" was coined in 1963. My parents bought me a fashionable made-to-measure three-piece grey suit with cloth-coloured buttons, red lining, and narrow trousers. They also bought us an electric record player (not a wind-up one). Life felt great. Especially with a Beatles' haircut.

CHAPTER 7

Duke of Edinburgh's Award:

Struggles, Survival and Stickability

At Sheil Road school, we were expected to join the Duke of Edinburgh's (DofE) Award Scheme, launched in February 1956 by HRH Prince Philip as a "youth awards programme".[108] Boys aged thirteen to fourteen began the Bronze Award led by our teacher Mr J.K. Morton. I was thirteen, in Class 3A. The scheme was free to join.

The DofE offered adventures and achievements, particularly if we weren't in other youth activities such as Scouts, which I wasn't. Mr Morton's keyword was stickability (perseverance or staying power). We had to show commitment to succeed.

Bronze Award

Our scheme had four parts: (1) public service; (2) hobby/pursuit; (3) outdoor expedition; and (4) fitness. They were logged in our DofE Record Books.

For the public service, we took the St John's Ambulance first aid course, with its teaching and practical work applying bandages, slings and splints. Importantly, it included resuscitation, and we learnt the Holger Nielsen method of artificial respiration (resuscitation) for drowning. I can't recall mouth-to-mouth resuscitation being taught. We learnt loads and enjoyed "treating" classmates, who looked like lads in major accidents on the ITV soap opera *Emergency Ward 10*

---

[108] See: 'About the DofE'. Undated. Accessed 28 August 2022 at <u>About - The Duke of Edinburgh's Award (dofe.org)</u>

(shown from 1957-67).[109]

Learning first aid was valuable. The award required us to be retrained every three years, since procedures changed, and we forgot things. My St John's Ambulance Association certificates show that I passed in December 1961 and again in May 1964 (both at our school). What began as a DofE requirement interested me so much that I signalled my interest once I worked in industry, and took certificates in 1971 and 1973 as a first aider. Even when I retired, I was a first aider.

The second part was a hobby or pursuit. Some boys chose stamp collecting, but my interest in stamps lacked passion. Instead, I chose cycling – which had benefits. As explained in chapter 6, I bought my Carlton Capella Clubman racing bicycle from my earnings as a paperboy. It had Benelux five-speed gears. Another model had ten gears but at £25 19s 4d it was too expensive, so five had to do (Campagnolo gears were even more expensive). My bike had dropped handlebars, a racing saddle, a pump, and mudguards. I added: a water bottle and straw; lights; a bell; a saddlebag; and toe clips to the pedals. Eventually, I exchanged mudguards for half-guards. For cycle camping, I fixed a rear frame and pannier bags. In the rain, I wore a yellow cape and sou'wester (hat with a wide flap covering the neck). What was missing? A protective helmet! In the Sixties, these weren't available. Even professional cyclists had very limited head protection.

Mr Morton gave us sheets identifying the routes from home that we needed to be familiar with (within a set radius); including their road numbers and names (for example the A580 was the East Lancashire Road). I completed many cycle rides and recorded them in exercise books, which Mr

---

[109] Paul Feeney, *A 1960s Childhood: From Thunderbirds to Beatlemania* (Stroud: The History Press, 2010), p.152 remarks: 'One of British Televisions first soap operas, and the first hospital-based drama on British television.'

Morton marked. My first cycling trip for the DofE was to West Kirby on Wednesday 29th March 1961, with David Kent (who lived in nearby Farnworth Street). We went via Meols, where my parents' caravan was on site, to see if our new caravan had arrived – but it hadn't. My longest cycling trip to that point was completed with David on 30th April the same year, when we rode to Blackpool (about forty-eight miles there) virtually non-stop (but David had a puncture on the way). Blackpool is a northern seaside resort noted for its spectacular autumn promenade lights. (Dad worked there bricklaying one year, building a F.W. Woolworth's store, and as children we'd seen the spectacular illuminations.)

Riding into Wales was popular – weekends saw scores of cyclists. We mainly cycled along West Derby Road to busy Lime Street, and then the Pier Head for the ferry (e.g. the *Royal Iris*) to Birkenhead (Woodside). From there we cycled in the Wirral on the A41 and A550 into Queensferry and Wales. To get to the seaside at Rhyl, we used the A548 coast road (reasonably flat, thankfully) beyond Prestatyn's holiday caravans. The round trip was about eighty-five miles. Once, we cycled to Colwyn Bay via the A55 from Holywell through St Asaph, which was even longer.

My Rhyl photos on 11th May 1961 show me and two mates, David and his Schomberg Street neighbour, Alan Magee. I was thirteen and David fourteen. We are at the sea front in our shorts with the sand and pier behind us and the photo of David and Alan shows them eating ice-cream cones. It's a hot day. The same day, we visited Flint Castle by the River Dee. It's probably the trip when I got red legs from sunburn – we had no sun lotions then. We had plenty of exercise, no accidents, and no punctures. The open road and the scenery were wonderful. Thankfully, traffic was much lighter in 1961. After many rides, I passed my pursuit.

The third part of the award was an outdoor expedition. Our school chose hiking in Wales, around an area called Loggerheads, between the towns of Mold and Ruthin.

However, the expedition required team training and experience in hiking and camping. We did daytrips to Loggerheads. The route from Liverpool was straightforward: across to Woodside on the ferry (8d return fare), where we caught the double-decker bus (F10) through the Wirral to Loggerheads. It stopped frequently while we sat on the top deck, chatting and looking at the views. Once at Loggerheads, our first hike started up the local ascent (the Catwalk). It was quite exposed, I thought, and the stone made it a little slippery, so I took care not to lose my footing and fall – struggles and survival! We completed the circular hike, returning to Loggerheads for the bus back. The hilly countryside was lovely, and different from what I had enjoyed at Meols. We followed our leaders (our teachers), learnt map- and compass-reading, and kept the Country Code.

Sometimes we camped at Loggerheads; it had a permanent place for youth groups, near large fields, complete with dormitories, dining hall, proper toilets (ablutions), etc. It was called Colomendy and was first used in 1940 for Second World War evacuees, but later was acquired by Liverpool City Council as an outdoor education centre. Hundreds of thousands of schoolchildren, Scousers and others, enjoyed staying through the years.[110]

Mr Morton introduced us gently, arranging for us to pitch our tents and sleep in a field, but use many of the camp's facilities: we came to collect water and use the toilets. Our first camping trip, on 10th April 1961, was a washout with rain and not very successful; we returned home early. When I walked in, Mum was ironing in the backroom. She admitted to being worried and hadn't really wanted me to go. But she

---

[110] See Paul Coslett, 'Colomendy', BBC Home, last updated 4 July 2007. Accessed 28 August 2022 at BBC - Liverpool - Local History - Colomendy Also Ellen Kirwin, 'Things you will know if you used to go to Colomendy as a kid', *Liverpool Echo* 11 January 2020, updated 6 February 2020. Accessed 28 August 2022 at Things you will know if you used to go to Colomendy as a kid - Liverpool Echo

knew that I needed the freedom to grow up. I was grateful for her honesty. After that initial experience, we camped elsewhere, including using agreed farmers' fields.

Once, when camping at Colomendy (Loggerheads), 5-6th June 1961, Mr Morton and another teacher (Mr Yates) stayed in the permanent camp. Mr Toft came in his car. One important episode was our hike up Moel Famau (1,818ft or 554m) along a well-defined route.[111] We set off between 8-9pm as a large group (fourteen boys plus two teachers), via Cilcain village. As darkness arrived, we put on torches, and some boys sang songs. We could see Liverpool's lights in the distance. Later, Mr Morton made us turn off the torches so we could learn to walk in the dark. It was interesting and instructive. We saw glow-worms for the first time (there were not many in Liverpool). One boy was so fascinated that he blurted out: 'What would they do if we shined our torches at them, sir?' An interesting question for us city lads; however, this was rebutted. It ran something like: 'Don't be silly so-and-so [surname used]! How would you like a torch shone in your face?' Hmmm, we wondered, and moved on. Tired but safe, we returned, under the stars, to our sleeping bags for a night's sleep; at least what was left of it – it was 3am! In later days, we climbed Moel Famau many times.

Some miles from Loggerheads, near Cilcain, we used a hut/cabin set in woods. It had bunks (so no sleeping on the ground) and a basic living area/kitchen. Chemical toilets meant there was no need to find a secluded spot and dig a hole. However, emptying chemical toilets was hazardous if

---

[111] Moel Famau (also spelt Moel Fama and Moel Fammau) is situated along what is now called the Clwydian Range, previously called the Flintshire Range. It is the highest peak on the range which is situated between Flintshire and Denbighshire. Views from the summit on a clear day are spectacular over Wales and England, including Liverpool and beyond. Equally, from parts of Liverpool (e.g. near Quarry Bank High School) Moel Fama stood as a majestic, captivating shape, reminding me of our hikes there. It is located in an Area of Outstanding National Beauty (AONB).

one slipped. We cooked outdoors on the school's primus stoves. There was a nearby cabin where our instructors/teachers stayed.

We needed to use methylated spirits and paraffin to light the primus stove – not an easy task. What food did we cook? For breakfast, bacon or fried egg and Ready Brek cereal. Our evening menu options could include: bread, corned beef, fish fingers, kippers or sausages, with tea or coffee. Boiled eggs were popular, since they were quick, and we were not left tackling burnt food stuck to our aluminium cooking pans that needed washing and fitting together as a rectangular pair for compact storage. Sometimes we had powdered food reconstituted by adding boiling water. My most vivid memory is of Phil King preparing his meal. He was hungry, but couldn't face eating what looked grim; more like something unmentionable. It was unceremoniously dumped. We had to carry enough food. Plus, we needed "iron rations" (emergency supplies): Kendall mint cake, barley sugar sticks or glucose tablets. We obtained water from nearby fresh streams or farmers (who would also sometimes supply milk and bread). I can't recall adding sterilising tablets to the water or suffering bad guts – Liverpool lads were tough!

Where did we get our outdoor equipment? Fortunately, the school's store. There was a booking-out system to borrow maps, compasses, two-man tents, flysheets, groundsheets, sleeping bags, primus stoves, small spades, pans, and rucksacks. Typically, we paid 1s 6d (one shilling and six old pence), but anoraks were 1s extra. It was our responsibility to return them in good condition. We didn't always take flysheets because they were heavy, and our tents were waterproof. Unfortunately, groundsheets weren't sewn-in, so we laid them carefully to avoid streams inside. Although we had two-man tents, we often managed to squeeze three of us in. It meant that the tents were sometimes smelly, but lighter to carry than larger models! The tents were too small to stand in, so we knelt. Access flaps at the tent entrance were held together by simple tie strips – no zips or Velcro. Slugs and snails could sneak in as we slept.

For sleeping bags, we had to supply our own inner cotton-sheet sleeping bag, since it was too expensive and inconvenient for the school (or parents) to wash big sleeping bags. Drying them back home outdoors wasn't an option, prior to spin-driers being widely available. The cotton-sheet sleeping bag went inside the school sleeping bag. A weekly bath was the norm in those days, and after a day hiking, we had sweaty bodies. I hope staff arranged for the sleeping bags to get washed sometimes.

Anyway, my recurring memory is being cold, even with my inner sleeping bag and us boys packed together. Once, when I slept with a scarf around my neck, I actually felt warm for a change, and thankfully I didn't strangle myself. Woolly bobble hats kept us warm while walking. Mum made mine. I made the small bobble for the top with her help, and she sewed it on – partnership. A warm head in the wind was what we wanted. We bought other items: anorak, spare trousers, string vest, hiking boots, socks, whistle, etc.

Hikes and camping were recorded in exercise books; writing up our details and drawing maps was enjoyable, if time-consuming. Mr Morton often commented positively on the merits of my maps and sketches. Eventually, after map- and compass-reading, keeping the Country Code, and a mock expedition in mid-October, our team completed the two-day expedition from Saturday 4th to Sunday 5th November 1961. We stayed overnight in the hut. People monitored our progress at certain "check points", to ensure we were on time and on track. Without mobile phones then, making personal contact was a safety issue. Our team covered fifteen miles carrying our kit. Much to our delight, we passed. Struggles, stiff legs and sore shoulders were worth it. When I returned home exhausted, Mum gave me lovely hot meals, which I ate while trying not to fall asleep.

The fourth part was fitness. At school we had to complete a minimum number of press-ups (fifteen?), with our feet on low-level benches to add more weight on our shoulders. Another test was a timed race picking up beanbags; after picking up one beanbag, we returned it to the start line and ran to get the next, which was further away. A set number of beanbags laid out at fixed distances had to be collected within a time limit. Boys had to be quick and agile.

At Newsham Park, we took two tests. One was throwing a cricket ball. In turns, we took a short run-up to the start line and then threw the cricket ball as far as possible. With anticipation, we watched as it sailed through the air. Did we make the minimum distance? Some boys achieved this more easily than others. But we were allowed to have more than one try. The other test was the long-distance walk in a specified time (three miles, perhaps). Mr Morton knew how many laps around the edge of the park were needed and he had his stop clock. We were a large group. It was a walk, not a run, so no cheating. Someone kept an eye on us; probably Mr Morton on his bike. Boys passed this timed walk okay; after all, we regularly walked to and from school and other places. I walked on my paper round.

In conclusion, along with my mates, I passed all four parts and received my Bronze Award certificate and badge in November 1961 (the month I completed my expedition) when in class 4T. I was proud to wear my badge to show my achievements. When I worked at T.J. Hughes' department store (on London Road) one Christmas, a staff member noticed my award and commented favourably. So, thankfully, the public was becoming aware of the award.

Silver Award

After my Bronze, I began the Silver Award, along with "me mates", such as Reggie. Staying on the extra year in 5T (September 1962–July 1963) helped, since we continued the DofE uninterrupted by full-time jobs.

The same four parts were required, but to a higher standard. For the public service, we continued with first aid and grew in confidence. Also, I continued cycling. However, now the area I needed to cover had an increased radius (twenty-five miles). Of course, Liverpool was on the coast, and we couldn't radiate in all directions: the Mersey, the Dee and the sea made things easier in some respects. However, there was a downside; we couldn't go directly to Rhyl – we had to cycle to Queensferry and back up the Welsh coast, so a much longer ride than the journey that the crow flies.

Nevertheless, we enjoyed the experience of cycling, particularly in Wales and the Wirral. We tried cycling up hills in our lowest gear, but sometimes we just capitulated, dismounted, and pushed till we reached the top. It was a triumph either way.

The third part was our outdoor expedition, which again occurred near Moel Famau. We had numerous training days hiking, and weekends camping. Sometimes, we introduced younger boys to DofE hiking. Once, we attempted to climb Moel Famau in winter. Our team was doing well on the normal climbing route and then the snow started! It fell faster and thicker, and hit our eyes, and everything got colder. After a discussion, we decided it would be foolish to continue. Why put ourselves at risk? So, we chose an escape route, abandoning the climb, and arrived safely at our destination. We understood the risks of snow and wind, or of being cut off, of missing our arrival time, and the foolishness of involving the Mountain Rescue.

We continued using the cabin near Cilcain for training. For those boys who were bigger and older, there was a short walk to the local village pub. Although the legal drinking age was eighteen, some younger boys easily looked the part. This meant that sometimes they went drinking and returned in the dark after some pints. Distant singing signalled that they were making their way back through the woods feeling happy!

Fortunately, no accidents occurred, and nobody was lost.

The Silver expedition covered thirty miles, with camping in the area around Moel Famau for our team (Reggie, Tully and me). It took place from Good Friday to Easter Sunday (20th-22nd April 1962). At 7.30am, we caught the 74D bus to the Pier Head and took the ferry to Birkenhead, where we got the bus towards Loggerheads. My main memory is of big blisters. Previously, Reggie had sold me his hiking boots, but there was a problem as they were a large size, and my feet were smaller. However, buying new hiking boots was an expensive outlay, so I chose Reggie's. Even with two pairs of hiking socks and the laces tied tight, they were still too big, plus they were heavy. During the expedition, the rubbing produced big blisters. I finished the thirty miles, but by then they were enormous, each approaching half the size of a small egg! As we finished at the cabin and started to prepare to travel back to Liverpool, one leader (Mr Phillips) even took pictures of them with his camera (I was given copies), and I was given a piggy-back ride as walking was too difficult. Slowly, over the weeks, the blisters disappeared, and I walked normally again. We wrote our reports and passed, but I still remember the pain. Thankfully, I have never had blisters that blinkin' big again. Mr Morton's encouragement of "stickability" ensured that we finished the thirty-mile hike despite the pain. Trials and triumphs, but time to get better boots!

For our fourth part – the fitness – we had more demanding tests. However, there was some recognition that not all boys were likely to fulfil all the tests to the required standard. In this case, after a period of attempting to pass but being unsuccessful, we were offered another option: a timed, long-distance run. I recall doing this, and I think it was probably for the Silver Award rather than the Gold. The distance was six miles, in the girls' playground, which had a marked track. I hadn't put in much, if any, training. I wore normal PT shoes or pumps – there were no specially-designed running shoes then. Even if there had been, they'd have been too expensive, I guess. So, I ran round and round with Mr Morton counting the laps and keeping an eye on the stopwatch. I did it in the time! Another fitness test achieved! On reflection, that was the longest run of my life in school. Thankfully, there weren't blisters.

Eventually, I passed my Silver Award in April 1963. I had a much-welcomed letter (25th April) to our home from the City of Liverpool's Director of Education, informing me that the presentation ceremony in Liverpool's Town Hall was on Tuesday 30th April 1963. So, we arrived (Mum, Dad and me) for tea at 6.30pm before the 6.45pm presentation of my silver certificate and badge from the Lord Mayor (Alderman David Lewis J.P.). I was among the twenty-seven boys and girls present.

A report appeared in the *Liverpool Echo* headed: 'Britain's Youth: 99.5 Per Cent Decent People – Lord Mayor.' The *Echo* summarised the mayor's remarks: 'A young person needed parents who were interested in his activities and could set a correct standard of behaviour and ideals – ideals which youth could safely follow.' Then the Lord Mayor commented on how glad he was to see so many parents there. We were pleased with his remarks. Finally, the *Echo* recorded that he spoke to us, saying: 'You can be proud of your achievement. It is preparing you for the high task of citizenship.' He was spot-on: struggles, survival and stickability led to success. I was chuffed.

Gold Award

After the Silver Award, we began the more demanding Gold Award. By April 1963, I was in my final year at Sheil Road, in 5T. The important summer exams were fast approaching. After that, I had to either move schools, or get a job (see chapter 8).

During our DofE achievements, we were encouraged to

supervise younger boys. One occasion springs to mind. While our team were climbing in Wales, one boy was struggling up a hill with his rucksack and we weren't sure if he'd "make it". To help him, two of us decided to share carrying his rucksack on top of ours. So, his rucksack was balanced on top of mine, and I hiked with it until I needed a break, when another team member took on the task. Then it was my turn again to carry it. This was tough but worth it, as he completed the climb and was grateful.

I also completed "public service weekends". My second one was 13th-14th July 1963, at our usual hut in Coed-Nant Gain by Cilcain, with Phil, Reggie, and Dave Black. As Gold candidates, we were assisting other boys from different schools in their Bronze and Silver Schemes. We supervised, for example, pitching tents, and inspected kit.

I was learning to manage my time effectively: a paper round, cycling, study, the prospect of a new school. Somehow, I managed to be a paperboy both on weekdays and Saturdays, including on DofE weekends. Moreover, my pursuit of cycling involved Sundays. Weekends were good for additional study as exams approached. Life was busy, with prospects of a new school and weekend activities there.

Although uncertain about time constraints and managing potential future school pressures while continuing the DofE, I decided to press ahead with "me mates". I chose to continue with first aid and fitness tests. For expeditions, we moved to Snowdonia – wilder than around Moel Famau. Not hills, but mountains with tough terrain. It was also further to travel. For my pursuit, I continued cycling (the radius was increased to forty miles). On reflection, my growing interest in weight training would have been a better choice, since it didn't require weekends. Back then, I had no idea where my interest in weight training would lead – it would be such a surprise.

In August 1963, David and I spent three nights youth hostelling. Everything was booked in advance and the morning we received confirmation (Thursday 1st), we set off.

I left Grey Rock Street with David and at the bottom on West Derby Road I popped into Waterworths Fruit & Veg shop (where Mum was working) so she could give me something for lunch – which she kindly did. I was given 'pounds of oranges, apples and bananas, not forgetting some peanuts'. Then I tried wheeling my heavy bike with one hand across West Derby Road while carrying the fruit in my other hand – it wasn't easy, and crossing the road I managed to end up with the bike falling, and me dropping the fruit everywhere. Thankfully, the driver of a large lorry saw my struggle and drove around me and my fruit. After I retrieved it all, we left with plenty of lunch!

We cycled along the Welsh coast on a hot day through Rhyl and Colwyn Bay, along the A55 to Conway (Conwy), then a wonderful ride through the magnificent Sychnant Pass, before re-joining the A55. Just before Bangor, we turned off towards our Youth Hostel Bryn Hall (Llanllechid) and had to push our bikes up hills to reach it. It was evening but still hot, and we arrived "after much sweat and tears". We had covered seventy demanding miles with our full saddlebags – beyond the Gold cycle radius of forty miles. From the youth hostel as a base (where we did daily morning chores before going out), we rested from cycling and used buses and walking to visit places, including the Welsh railway station called:

Llanfairpwllgwyngyllgogerychwyrn-drobwyllllantysiliogogogoch

(or just Llanfair PG) en route to our visit to Anglesey's amazing South Stack lighthouse (near Holyhead), climbing hundreds of steps. The next day, we visited Caenarvon (Caernarfon) Castle for an interesting thirty-minute conducted tour, before returning home the following day.

My cousin Alf bought a new bike and together we did short trips, including overnight stays, to accustom him to distance cycling. Then in August 1965, we completed cycle camping over a few days in Wales. On the first night we camped in the country, a lady who was staying with her husband on the campsite brought us lovely cups of tea to warm us up. It was thoughtful and much appreciated. A day or so later, we stopped for lunch at a beach and spotted a man selling hotdogs from his van. We bought one each and they tasted great! So, we bought another round. Then we returned a third time. By then we were full, feeling much better, and fighting fit!

But back to 1963. For our Gold Award expedition, George Bunner gave us helpful evening lectures from around late September to December 1963 at Toxteth Tech's premises in Garston. After night school (Spanish classes), I caught the 82 bus to Garston. Then on 3rd November, along with George, my friend Robert Foyne, and other Tuesday class boys, I travelled for the first time in a Dormobile (listening to Mr Bunner's yodelling) to Snowdonia National Park to successfully climb Tryfan (in mist) near Lyn Ogwen. Our next climb/scramble (24th November) was up Crib Goch (a "knife edge" route up Snowdon) on a bitterly cold day, with high winds and pouring rain. It was a difficult day, but we enjoyed scree running. On Easter weekend, Thursday 26th March 1964, we spent five days until Easter Monday in Snowdonia, staying first overnight in a cottage by the A5 near Llangollen – it was our mock Gold expedition. Other times, we stayed in a cabin in Llanberis Pass. It had bunks – yippee!

After weekends of training, four of us (Reggie Gabbutt, Dave Black, Phil King and me) planned our sixty-mile camping expedition from 16-19th May 1964. Day one, starting at Capel Curig, was the longest, while we were still fresh. After a good night's rest in our tents, we rose early to make headway while the weather was good (hiking in rain wasn't enjoyable, although we had waterproofs – nothing designer). After a few days of camping and hiking at a regular pace, we finally reached our destination – Conway (Conwy) – without major mishaps. Our examiner (Mr D. Hoare) questioned us on the expedition. It was then written up in our personal books, and illustrated with small photos.

Eventually, we learnt that we'd triumphed over those challenges – yes!

Cycling incidents

For cycling, I had good friends that joined me, even though they weren't taking the DofE. David and Alan, mentioned previously, were on my Rhyl trip. Sometimes we were three but often we were just two. David was in my class at Sheil Road, lived near me, and liked cycling. We had many enjoyable days in Wales and elsewhere. On Sunday 28th July 1963, for the Gold Award, David and I cycled via Chester to Llangollen and the Horseshoe Pass on the A542 – on a beautiful hot day with amazing views when I pushed my bike up the pass – "A Day Well Worth Remembering". My face and legs were red with sunburn, and I was saddle-sore! It was a thirteen-hour trip and David's cyclometer recorded eighty-six miles.

Once, David stopped his bike at a zebra crossing to let pedestrians cross; unfortunately, I didn't stop in time. My front wheel collided with his back wheel, and I was catapulted over my handlebars, landing head-over-heels on the road in a heap. Somewhat embarrassed and apologetic, I stood up and brushed myself down. I think someone above was looking after me that day, as I had no injuries, despite no cycle helmet, and my bike was fine – David too was uninjured and his bike good. We carried on cycling home, thankful that all had ended well.

David's regular and reliable companionship helped me to achieve my DofE Awards. We also had "a lorra lafs" together, even beyond the DofE, when we were old enough to go to pubs (aged eighteen or over). A musical family, David's parents were friendly and welcoming whenever I visited them. His dad, also David, was a French-polisher. David would join the Royal Air Force (RAF) in the late 1960s, complete his initial training and become a musician. I had the privilege of attending his passing-out parade in Lincolnshire.

The family hired a taxi and we all squeezed in (driver, mum, dad, sister, me…) and made the long day-return trip.

Another school friend, Currie, sometimes accompanied me. One trip, on 4th August 1961, still stays in my memory, I called it "An Unlucky Day": cycling through the Wirral on the A41 near Little Sutton. We were riding and discussing which way to go and he was near the centre of the road when suddenly there was a screech of car brakes and a bang. A car suddenly came from behind and hit Currie. His bike was bent, but very fortunately he was unhurt, although thrown off and clearly shaken. The car driver was unhurt also, but his car was damaged. I was shaken but not harmed.

Ken and John Lawler were the grandsons of our neighbours, Mr and Mrs Winer. Ken and I became friends, and we cycled together. When Ken and I cycled on Sundays, this was fitted around his church attendance. If he hadn't attended the morning service at St Michael's, we would stop during our trip at an RC church. Ken attended the service while I hung around outside. With the service over, we continued cycling. We did this more than once, and it suited everyone, including his mum.

In the earliest days, I joined a school friend cycling with a large group of street friends, boys and girls, with a variety of bikes. It was interesting getting everyone together, and then keeping together, with nobody lost during the ride. It went well, but I don't think I repeated this again; the day was fun but rather slow, and the range of abilities and distances covered during a day restricted what I needed to achieve.

Another time, while cycling alone in Liverpool, I was attacked by two dogs which were neither on leads nor under anyone's control. They chased my cycle, barking ferociously. Now, there's precious little protection from dangerous dogs when you're on a pedal bike. I couldn't get enough speed up to leave them behind, and they weren't giving up the chase. 'What can I do?' I quickly thought. Stopping wasn't a safe option, as that could mean being bitten by both. There was only one option: kick! So, trying to balance my bike, keep on the road, not fall off, and not collide with any traffic or people, I kicked out. The kick caught one dog on the head, and it didn't like it! It yelped and quickly stopped barking and chasing. The second dog, thankfully, gave up the pursuit. It was an unnerving experience; afterwards, I gave that street a wide berth, choosing a safer route.

Finally, during my Silver Award, I had a nasty incident in Lime Street on 8th August 1962, which I called "Death – so Close". That morning, Ken and I went to Newtons cycle shop (where I originally purchased my bike) and I bought a saddle-bag carrier. After a delayed start, because of rain, we started our ride. To get to the Pier Head, we had to go through Lime Street. After Liverpool's trams stopped running (1957), unused tram lines remained for years. For me, the worst place was Lime Street. In the wide section in front of St George's Hall near the Lion statues (and opposite the railway station) were sets of tram lines.[112]

We moved into the centre of the road – I went first – and indicated we were turning right by holding out our right arms while looking behind at the busy traffic coming along e.g. cars, buses, lorries. Simultaneously, we watched the treacherous tram lines as a potential trap. The skill lay in swinging my front wheel across the tram line at a sharp angle. If the wheel angle was not wide enough, the front tyre was trapped in the tram tracks. Once trapped, I wasn't going to escape.

Well, despite many previous successful moves, my luck finally ran out. When my wheel was half across the tram line, the rubber tyre slipped on the wet tram line and fell into the gap. My front wheel was trapped, and the back wheel went its own way – Aaargh! I was quickly thrown up and backwards. The bike fell in a heap, and I was violently

---

[112] Then the magnificent St George's Hall had black external walls. Decades later during its restoration and cleaning white stonework was revealed - amazing! The black colour was from pollution.

thrown off – although my feet were in toe straps, this made no difference. I landed on the hard road surface. But the most sobering thing was looking to my right and seeing a large lorry wheel stop near me. I can still see it today! Fortunately, the driver quickly stopped, and I was saved. He checked that I was okay and amazingly I was – only a few scratches. But my bike's handlebars were slightly distorted. I met Ken outside the Empire Theatre, and we walked home together – ride cancelled – another visit needed to Newtons to fix the handlebars. I was very fortunate that I didn't hit my head. Once in Wales, we went across a cattle grid, praying for safety. Luckily, my wheels weren't caught, and I carried on safely downhill. But perhaps dismounting and walking over would have been better?

Hiking/mountaineering incidents

Some hiking incidents stand out. First, despite training in map-reading and using compasses, we sometimes got lost. Once we missed the route and had to cross fields, climbing carefully over narrow wire fences so as not to damage them, or ourselves. A farmer somehow saw us coming, and he wasn't pleased, so the conversation deteriorated to him saying clearly enough, 'I'll get my shotgun!' We moved off quickly, not wishing to provoke him that far!

On other occasions, we were told by landowners that we couldn't cross their land, so we needed alternative routes (not always easy, even with a good map: detours took time, and we risked coming across unwanted obstacles, such as cliffs). I think one of the issues was the relative newness of the DofE scheme. We had our individual identity cards, but weren't convinced that landowners understood it. They knew about the long-established Scouts and Youth Hostels, but not the DofE. So, we could be taken for just a troublesome rough group of lads. Of course, we reported this to Mr Morton for him to settle.

Once in Snowdonia, during a very hot spell, we stopped to rest at the side of a road. My feet were so hot and sweaty that I chose to stand in the nearby shallow stream with my boots and socks still on, just to cool them and my feet. Taking the boots/socks off to paddle would have taken too long. Fortunately, the boots didn't leak.

We were city lads in the countryside: dealing with animals wasn't our strong point. There weren't cows where we lived in Liverpool, although I had seen them in the Wirral from afar. So, hiking across fields with cows or bullocks present was new – we feared bulls especially. On our Silver expedition, we were in a field near a farm. It was raining, so we had large cycle capes (possibly bright yellow) draped over our shoulders and rucksacks. We looked like a camel train! We saw some bullocks coming along a hedge to our right as we were hiking to the fence and gate. Somebody lost his nerve, and the shout went up, 'Run! Run!' Reggie, a tall boy looking somewhat large with his cape, sprinted for the gate (as best as he could with a heavy rucksack). We followed. Surprising where the energy comes from, and how tired legs learn to move when confronted with danger! Well, the shout and the sight of our odd shapes running spooked at least one bullock. It stumbled and looked perplexed (if a bullock ever can look perplexed, but never mind). Our question was: 'Is it going to run with those behind and get to the gate first? And then what will happen with us trapped in the field?' The sight of a spooked bullock energised us further and we fled towards that gate, getting over it any way we could – no time to open it; just hurl yourself with your rucksack still on your back over the top bar. Fortunately, we were more terrified and faster than the bullocks (it was a close thing) and got over the gate before they reached it. The experience unnerved us, but we were safe, and continued our trek with throbbing hearts! No more bullocks!

While staying at the cabin with our team one weekend, I cut my left thumb. Later that day, our adult leaders saw it covered in a makeshift bandage; they decided it needed medical treatment. Luckily they had a car and drove me to the hospital in the town of Mold. I was put on a trolley under bright lights. My wound was washed, numbed and stitched. It healed fine, but I still have a scar.

In Snowdonia, we met low mist over the top of the mountain called Tryfan while we climbed, so visibility was poor. Whenever the mist cleared, we could see the A5 road below, looking tiny with its cars and the lake at the base. Few people wore climbing helmets then and setting a rock tumbling was a risk. I recall the loud cry, 'Below! Below!' Everyone then looked up quickly to move out of the path of the falling rocks. We crawled along the narrow ridge top of Tryfan; the beautiful scenery on either side below was in cloud. It was triumph to reach the top and to log the experience.

Another time, our team and instructor were lost on the Carneydds, in a thick mist. We lost our way on the path down and came to cliffs where a loosely-hanging rope showed how a previous group had extricated themselves. We planned another way: we were to throw our rucksacks down for a person to catch them. Sadly, the person missed mine and the rucksack bounced down the mountainside, accelerating all the way until with one giant jump it shot into the air and disappeared over the cliff edge! I tell you: that gave me an unsettling experience in my stomach and made me wonder: 'Would I see it again, with all my kit?' Then came the thought: 'That could've been me!' We continued and surprisingly found my rucksack, largely undamaged, on the way. Eventually, we got to our cabin rather tired and wet; but everyone was safe.

Further, while climbing the knife edge called Crib Goch (on the route up to Snowdon, although we didn't go that far), we recalled the story about the boys killed there: roped together, one had fallen and pulled the others down. Truly awful. Being on the top edge seeing both sides all the way down was an amazing sight, but unnerving! Prayer certainly came to my mind. However, we got down enjoying a scree run, and everyone was safe again.

Sometimes, unintended consequences followed from light-hearted comments. For example, on our Gold expedition, George Bunner told us to descend via the Devil's Kitchen;[113] but he took the easier route down the mountain. We queried this among ourselves before starting the difficult descent with rucksacks. But a little later, George returned, asking what we were doing – it was a joke which we'd misunderstood! We laughed, but almost cried.

Also, on the second night of our Gold expedition, when David and I were camping near the base of the Devil's Kitchen, we were woken by the force of the wind. Each of us grabbed an upright pole in the tent, shouting, 'Hold on!' as the gusts became wilder. We didn't want to lose our tent! To our relief, the gusts shortly subsided, and the tent stood firm.

A frightening incident occurred once after we returned from Loggerheads. On the ferry from Birkenhead to Liverpool, our team were playing a friendly game on deck. Someone threw sweets or chocolates up and we'd try and catch them. We were just having a laugh. Unfortunately, we knocked into a smartly dressed young man, with his friend(s), once or twice, and he became quite irate, threatening to pick us up and throw us over the side of the ferry if we didn't stop. He was deadly serious. We stopped the game but Reggie (who was tall and well-built) and others said, somewhat quietly: 'He won't be throwing me over the side!' We were miffed by the threat – especially as the Mersey looked cold, coffee-coloured (its normal colour) and rough that day.[114] Rather than start a fight, we walked away.

---

[113] The Devil's Kitchen is a rocky slope in the cliffs on the path between Llyn y Cwm and Llyn Idwal (where we camped that night).

[114] The Mersey was a terribly polluted river. But in May 1999 the *Independent* newspaper online ran the headline 'Salmon lured back to cleaned-up Mersey after 100-year absence'. Also, its ships/boats belched out polluting black smoke. See Matthew Sutcliffe and Kate Fox,

Reflections

Sadly, eventually, the Gold Award required too much time. In the period February-March 1965 I wrote a reflection, "Looking to the Future", on options for going cycling with companions but also on the pressure to do the best with my homework. If I could have taken the Gold Award later on, I could have continued by changing from cycling to weight training (not until 1969 was the age limit extended so young people aged fourteen to twenty-one were eligible). I'm sure that then I would have finished. But that's water under the bridge.

The DofE was a great opportunity that Sheil Road School encouraged us to seize. The work of Mr Toft, and the teachers, especially Ken Morton (who sometimes brought along his daughters Judith and Jill), and other instructors must be recognised and appreciated. It wouldn't have worked without their dedication or the school's provision of equipment.

I had learnt lessons for life: first aid; teamwork; Country Code; camping; hiking/mountaineering; map- and compass-reading; the joy of safe cycling; seeing new scenery/situations; writing up reports; leading and training others; and the sustained effort required to achieve and pass the physical standards.

Without realising it, these physical activities strengthened me physically and mentally. The hard exercise built a foundation for my developing interest in weight training. Mr Morton's emphasis on "stickability!" lives on with me.[115] Stashed in my loft for decades were my many DofE reports that I have now reread with joy.

Over many years, I corresponded with Mr Morton and

Who Saved the Mersey? Undated. Accessed 28 August 2022 at Who_Saved_the_Mersey.pdf (merseybasin.org.uk)

[115] For a fascinating study, see the pioneering psychologist Angela Duckworth, *Grit: Why passion and resilience are the keys to success* (London: Vermilion, 2017).

spoke to him on the telephone – even in old age, he spoke with such a strong voice, just like in his days as a teacher. He offered to get our son some items from Liverpool FC's shop. Sometimes, he sent me long letters and various items to read, and we exchanged Christmas cards for very many years. But then suddenly and sadly, after 1999 they stopped. We never heard anything, but were left to draw our own conclusions. The recent death of Prince Philip, on 9th April 2021, brought back so many memories for me.

(Also on front cover) Me, with Anne (in pram) and Gran Thompson in Grey Rock Street looking towards West Derby Road, c.1950/51.

Lilian Thompson (Mum) with her mum (Gran Thompson) in Barry Street, Liverpool. Late 1920s.

Lilian Thompson in her "Newsham" School uniform, 1935.

Stanley Dutch (Dad) on his first ship HMS *Glasgow*, joined 7th May 1938, aged nineteen.

Uncle Alf Thompson and Auntie Edie's wedding,
St Margaret's Church, 5th August 1939.

Uncle Alf and Auntie Edie's wedding.
Front from left: Gran and Grandad Thompson and
(Great) Uncle John Thompson.
Rear from left: Lilian Thompson bridesmaid, Uncle Alf and
Auntie Edie peeping through.

Uncle Alf in Rome, 28th June 1944 after liberation by the allies. His cap badge has the British Army regiment the Royal Ulster Rifles. Its Latin motto *Quis separabit* means "Who will separate us?" Taken from Romans 8:35 'Who will separate us from the love of Christ…?'

Great Uncle Walter William Henry Thomas – Gran Thompson's brother, c.1915. He was lost on the merchant ship the *Thracia* on 27th March 1917, aged 27.

Stan and Lilian Dutch's wedding, St Margaret's Church,
14th September 1946.
Front: Edna Thompson (little girl).
Centre, from left: "Pop" John Hoban, bridesmaid, Stan and Lilian,
bridesmaid (bridesmaids were Mum's work friends) and
Gran Thompson.
Back from left: Auntie Bel with Uncle Jim (?), unknown,
and Grandad Thompson.

Our young family - Mum, me, Anne and Dad, October 1951.

Sisters Pauline (left) and Edna Thompson at 30 Red Rock Street,
c.1949.

Grandad Alfred Thompson and me. Backyard, 57 Grey Rock Street,
c.1949/50.

Festival of Britain (May to September 1951) – Grey Rock Street party.
Me and Anne with the children and our neighbours.

Grey Rock Street showing the corner lane going into Boundary Lane.
No. 49 is the end house. Our house (No. 57) is on the far right, 12th
September 1967. Courtesy of Liverpool Records Office and Archives.

Me, Anne, and Christina outside 57 Grey Rock Street.

Cousin Alf (holding a dog) and my sister Christina sitting outside our friends' house in Grey Rock Street. The friend (on the left) is watching and her two children are standing by Alf, March 1960.

Front: Dad (right) sitting with darts team cup and shield trophies.
Back: Uncle Alf (far right). Dad and Uncle Alf drank at The Red Rock
pub so this is the likely location for their team, 1950s.

1950s workers - on the back row Uncle Alf (third from left) then Dad.

Coronation Day (2nd June 1953) for Queen Elizabeth II. Children and adults in Grey Rock Street. Sister Anne is sitting on the first row, far left. I am in the second row standing at the kerb, fourth child from the right, holding a flag.

Coronation Day (2nd June 1953).
Anne and me receiving our certificates before the celebration party.

At Radiant House, Bold Street, Liverpool, receiving my essay competition first prize, Monday 4th May 1959.

Christina (left) and Anne in the backyard at 57 Grey Rock Street, 1960.

Burbo Camp Meols family group by the marquee, c.1950/51.
Front from left: Stanley Dutch (Dad) with me, Lilian Dutch (Mum), Anne
Dutch (litte sister), Elizabeth Thompson (Gran), and
Alfred Thompson (Grandad).
Back from left: Auntie Edie Thompson, Edna, and
Uncle Alf Thompson.

Me, Anne and cousin Edna Thompson at Meols. Shore defences and
sea to the left. Right: Across the wall towards Burbo Camp, c.1951.

Burbo Camp Meols with someone's van. Dad, Anne, and me, 1954.
Dad said we would get a car one day – meanwhile, we took this photo!

Meols shoreline with Anne, Gran and me, c.1955. The top of the
Second World War pillbox can be seen in the distance on top of the
concrete defences.

Me with cousin Alf at Burbo Camp Meols sports day, standing on the races field surrounded by small caravans c.1959/60.

Mum and Dad outside our caravan in Meols, May 1961.

Me with David Kent at Rhyl (Wales) - an early cycle ride for the DofE Bronze Award 11th May 1961.

Uncle Jim and Auntie Bel at Burbo Camp Meols, September 1961. The caravan behind them belonged to our friends Ossie and Joyce O'Brien.

Quarry Bank High School, Liverpool, rugby team 1965-66. I am seated third from the right. Courtesy of Calderstones School, Liverpool.

Me weight training with a shoulder press at the University of Salford. Lifting around 120 lbs (55 kg), c.1967.

My weight-lifting medal for winning the Universities Athletic Union (UAU) Bantamweight class powerlifting championship in 1967 (above: inscribed side; below: UAU with unicorn).

Christmas in our new bungalow at Ashton-in-Makerfield.
Mum, me, Dad, and Christina. Anne is taking the photo, c.1967.

University of Salford – me conducting a physics experiment,
c.1968/69.

University of Salford Graduation for our BSc (Hons),
Friday 18th July 1969.

From left: Parents (Stan and Lil) then me. Next is Dave Casey with his
parents (Vera and John) and at the rear his maternal grandad (Sam
Haines).

University of Salford Graduation. Receiving my MSc, 22nd July 1971.

Susan's and my wedding at Bethel Temple Church Newport, Wales, 9th October 1976.

Family wedding group at Bethel Temple Church in Newport.

Front from left: Dad (Stanley), Audrey (Sue's mum), Linda Brett (Sue's friend), me and Susan, Wendy (Sue's sister), Frank (Sue's dad) and Auntie Bel.

Rear from left: Bridesmaids Christina and Debbie (cousin Edna's daughter).

Our second honeymoon, in California.
Visiting Edna, Rob and their children, 1977.

University of London Graduation. Royal Albert Hall, London.
My first theology degree, January 1984.

Teaching at Nairobi Pentecostal Bible College Kenya, Africa, 1988.

Three generations: Me, son Tim and Dad in Bristol c.1990/91.

Our family visiting Edna (left) in Griffin, Georgia, US in rear garden, c.1990/91.

Working as a tutor, presenting a paper on training at a conference in Guernsey.

Receiving my theology PhD at the University of Bristol, February 1999.

Teaching at a Christian leaders' conference in Burundi, Africa,
June 2002.

CHAPTER 8

Grammar School Years

August 1963: exam results

August 28th 1963 is remembered by many people for the stirring speech of the American Civil Rights leader Rev Martin Luther King Jr., who spoke for justice before 250,000 people in Washington. His "I have a dream" speech spoke to, and for, America's Black population.[116] For my family, mid-August was the critical time, when exam results were released. Oddly, I can't recall the days when I got them.

Success or failure? Well, I passed all seven ULCIs (four with distinction): chemistry; English language; English literature; geometrical and engineering drawing (GED); maths; physics; and woodwork. Triumph! And my O-Levels? Two passed: maths and physics-with-chemistry. But sadly, two failed: English language and GED. Resits required.

Overall, though, we were pleased, and I moved schools. Two friends also moved, one to a technical school and Hutch to Quarry Bank High School (for his A-Levels: maths, further maths, and physics). However, these transfers weren't arranged through a state system, but thanks to Mr Toft's interest, initiative, and individual contacts.

Once, he told me: 'You shouldn't be here. You're a grammar school boy.' But according to the state selection system, I was secondary modern material. Thankfully, Mr Toft could see beyond the system. As I didn't know about grammar schools, I relied on his wisdom. Fortunately, he contacted Mr W.E. Pobjoy, the headmaster at Quarry Bank

---

[116] See Clayborne Carson (ed.), *The Autobiography of Martin Luther King, Jr.* (London: Abacus, 2000), chapter 20 'March on Washington'. "Negroes" was a normal term then, used by King and others.

High School for Boys, and I was transferred. Its famous pupil, John Lennon of the Beatles, had started there in September 1952. He had initially played in the group the Quarrymen, encouraged by Mr Pobjoy, but transferred schools to Liverpool College of Art.[117] All pupils were aware of being at John Lennon's school.

First Year: 1963-64

For the Lower Sixth Form, I needed five O-Levels, but I only had two, so I was offered a place in the Fifth Form to repeat the year. 'Should I take it?' My parents and I decided – yes. After all, I was a summer-born baby and pupils in my classes were often much older; I was among the oldest in the class for a change. Afterwards, I hoped to study Advanced Levels – also known as A-Levels – in maths, physics, and chemistry. I started in September 1963.

Quarry Bank was miles away, in Allerton (south Liverpool) and the school day started at 8.30am (Sheil Road began at 9am). If I heard Ogden's factory buzzer at 7.55am, I needed to hurry. From Grey Rock, I walked along Whitefield Rd to Belmont Rd for a bus up Sheil Rd and Kensington before I caught another bus to Menlove Avenue. Finally, I walked up Harthill Rd to Quarry Bank, passing Calder High School – the girls' grammar school separated from Quarry Bank by a high sandstone wall. I had a free bus pass. Infrequently, I rode my bike. Sometimes I went via the Penny Lane/Allerton Road bus terminal roundabout (made famous in the Beatles' song *Penny Lane*, released 1967).

Menlove Ave is remembered as the place where John Lennon's mother was killed in a tragic car accident on 15th July 1958. And 251 Menlove Ave was where John lived from 1945-1963 with Aunt Mimi. Ron Jones notes that John's

---

[117] Chris Ingram, *The Rough Guide to the Beatles* (2nd ed. London: Rough Guides), 2006, p.261.

suburban home shows he didn't emerge from Liverpool's slums, and he was not working class.[118] In 2018, I visited Penny Lane and Menlove Ave with my wife Sue, on a fascinating Beatles' bus tour which jogged many memories.

Quarry Bank was a considerable contrast to Sheil Road. First, we wore school uniforms. Second, the spacious premises stood opposite Calderstones Park on tree-lined Harthill Rd. Third, it was well-equipped with: gym, swimming pool, tennis courts, cricket and rugby/football pitches near the school buildings. The gym had free weights for weight training, and this became important for me (there were no fixed machines, unlike in modern gyms).[119] A short walk away, off Mather Ave, there were more playing fields, with changing rooms. Moreover, we had an onsite kitchen for preparing good-quality food, and a dining hall. There was a library, many classrooms, workshops, labs, and the assembly hall. Amazingly, there was also a tuck shop. Teachers taught in distinguished-looking black graduation robes. And our physics master tended the school beehives!

Discipline was distinctly different – there was no corporal punishment (the young head had banned it in 1961, twenty-five years before Liverpool's general ban, in the mid-1980s). Quarry Bank boys were motivated without force and fear. Further, they were mainly middle class, quite different from the working-class lads I grew up with. One classmate, a softly-spoken Jewish boy, told me that he wanted to be a doctor, like his father. Such an inspiration. Another classmate's father was an English teacher in our school. A few boys drove cars.

A house system had been introduced by the first headmaster, R.F. Bailey. This system was expanded until

<hr>

[118] Ron Jones, *The Beatles' Liverpool* (Liverpool: Liverpool History Press, 2018), p.71.
[119] For a 1931 aerial view of the school in its rural surroundings see Colin Wilkinson, *The Streets of Liverpool Volume 2* (Liverpool: The Bluecoat Press, 2012), pp.154-155.

1967 had Mersey; Esmeduna; Wavertree and Sefton; Allerton and Childwall; and Aigburth and Woolton.[120] My friend Mick was in Mersey but I was in Sefton. After lessons ended at 3.05pm, pupils met in house groups to do homework or sports.

After I left Sheil Road, Mr Toft remained supportive. I remember having initial issues with maths and I would drop by unannounced at his office. My bus home passed the school, so I alighted a few stops early. He was pleased to see me and gave me his attention. He was good at maths and explained the solution(s). He always had an "open door". His generous heart, intelligent mind and hospitality were outstanding.

Anyway, our class had a ground-floor room, opposite the gym and tuck shop, with single wooden desks facing the blackboard. Most boys were preparing for summer O-Levels. However, a few of us, who'd transferred from secondary schools, were working to increase our O-Levels for the Lower Sixth – so we weren't preparing for precisely the same subjects.

Away from school, in October 1963 another exciting James Bond film was released (based on Ian Fleming's books), *From Russia with Love*, with Sean Connery as Bond, followed in October 1964 by *Goldfinger*, and *Thunderball* in 1966. We made sure we watched and enjoyed them in the cinemas. In the Cold War era, they were entertaining and enriching – Britain could more than hold her own against bad guys!

In contrast, on 15th September 1963, racial violence and injustice wrecked lives in the US; an explosion in Birmingham, Alabama, at its Sixteenth Street Baptist church killed four Black girls in Sunday School. The American Civil Rights movement was shocked, and so were we. Many

---

[120] Brian Davies, *The History of Calderstones School (1924-1999)*. Undated. Accessed 29 August 2022 at Calderstones School - History of Calderstones School

injustices existed, for example school and university/college segregation over colour in the US.

In November 1963, I resat English language and GED. But on the world stage, a disastrous event occurred that month when US President John F. Kennedy was shot and killed while visiting Dallas (Texas). He was a president whom many, including me, admired – especially when he brought us back from the brink of nuclear war over Russian missiles based in Cuba. Staff and students were shocked. At that time the satirical film on the Cold War: *Dr Strangelove; or, How I learned to Stop Worrying and Love the Bomb* was being made in London, with the actor Peter Sellers playing three roles. It was due to be released on 22nd November, which turned out to be the day of Kennedy's assassination, and was thus not released until late January 1964, with minor changes. I enjoyed seeing it, and it received many awards and honours.

I thought: 'What O-Levels should I take next summer?' I passed ULCI English literature and could possibly take it for O-Level. In fact, in my ULCI paper I'd studied Shakespeare's *Macbeth* and H.G. Wells' *The History of Mr Polly.* These were the same texts for O-Level. I had enjoyed reading them, so what should I do? My critical factor was English language. I needed to focus on passing this; English lit wasn't an acceptable substitute, although it was another O-Level. So, I just went for English language. In retrospect, taking English lit would have been sensible, but nobody tried hard to persuade me against my choice. I continued with English language but wondered how long this would take – summer 1964? I wasn't alone, as other boys similarly struggled. A small support class was arranged.

Another question was, 'What about learning a foreign language?' Quarry Bank boys had learnt Latin and French for years, so there wasn't any hope we could catch up. Teachers suggested Spanish evening classes in the city centre. A few of us tried them, but although the teacher was enthusiastic and friendly, it never worked. Sometimes after the Spanish classes, I went by bus to DofE classes. It was a very long day. In reality, there wasn't enough time, so we stopped and restricted our applications to the few 1960s universities that didn't require a language. Some able boys studied Russian in the Sixth Form. That option wasn't open to us.

Meanwhile, I had passed physics-with-chemistry and now I could take them as separate subjects. In maths, I attended class lessons, but there was no point in retaking this O-Level, as I had a good grade (sometimes boys retook exams to improve their grades for university applications). Soon we decided that I should study pure maths at O-Level as this was good preparation for the Sixth Form. Pure maths focused on calculus, trigonometry, and algebra. The school provided me with a textbook, *Elementary Analysis*, and I worked through it, mainly unaided. However, one boy, who had passed his A-Levels, was staying on in preparation for entering Oxford or Cambridge University and he was asked to assist me with trigonometry – one-to-one tuition! He was friendly and knew his stuff, so I learnt quickly. It was an unexpected and enjoyable opportunity. Some people might think me mad but, really, I found the subject fascinating, and worked hard.

We had Religious Education (RE) classes under state legislation and we "Christian" boys attended morning assemblies. Jewish boys were exempt. One teacher offered us the option of studying RE for O-Level in lunchtimes, looking at the New Testament. It sounded interesting and my church attendance had provided some understanding. Also, once a term our school had a service at Allerton Parish Church (All Hallows), Greenhill Rd. Although my singing wasn't good, I listened; especially when one minster said that he had a maths degree, but had decided to become a minister. Hmmm.

Anyway, for whatever reason, I didn't take RE. It was almost a massive mistake, as I needed those five O-Levels. Now I had three: maths; physics-with-chemistry; and GED.

And I was only taking four (English language, pure maths, physics, and chemistry). But maths and pure maths only counted as one subject and physics-with-chemistry didn't count if I had them as separate subjects. In effect, I was only going to have five, even if I passed all. My second failure at English language was surely a warning shot. We knew one older boy who was still trying to pass his five O-Levels for Sixth Form entrance. So, this was no theoretical issue. In retrospect, taking more subjects would have reduced the risk I was running.

Our physics master gave us regular short written tests, usually unannounced, to see how we were progressing. However, a pattern emerged. They were around half-term, so it became sensible to think ahead and revise just in case. Thankfully, such preparations paid off – it certainly kept us on our toes!

After Christmas, in early 1964, the exam results came out: passed GED, failed English! Happily, I didn't need to study GED further. But, 'Oh dear; my second English failure! What next?' I needed to progress.

In the outside world, in February 1964, the US boxer Cassius Clay knocked out Sonny Liston and became the world heavyweight champion. The fight was shown live on early morning TV. I didn't get up to watch, but my friend Mick and his dad did. His dad was out of the room making a cup of tea, and when he came in, it was all over – rather quickly!

Eventually, May/June 1964 arrived. I took my exams, including English (attempt three). In August I passed: pure maths, physics, and chemistry, but English language was another failure! What would happen? I had repeated a year but still only had four O-Levels. I thought: 'Was it a mistake to do the repeat year and strive for the Sixth Form? What next – must I leave?' Was not opting to take English lit and RE a case of putting all my eggs in one basket and dropping them? I waited…

Unexpectedly, and fortunately, Mr Pobjoy waived the

minimum number of O-Levels (five) and permitted me to enter the Lower Sixth. Unbelievable! I was so thankful. Presumably, other teachers agreed. Certainly, the maths teacher was pleased with my pure maths, saying, 'Well done!' Mr Pobjoy's specialism was languages, but he saw my potential in maths and science. After a struggle, I could now move forward.

However, many grammar school children didn't enter the Sixth Form, and took jobs. My cousin Edna left Holly Lodge to take up nursing and my sister Anne left her grammar school to be a dental assistant. But cousin Alf would study A-Levels. Marr notes that in 1964, at their height, England had 1,298 grammar schools and these educated 25.5 per cent of pupils.[121] I was privileged to be at Quarry Bank.

That summer, 1964, our family of five holidayed at Rhos-On-Sea in North Wales. Dad drove us and we had a flat near the coast for the week. There was the beach, a pool, and Forte's Ice Cream and Café, where we enjoyed meals and ice-cream sundaes (it's still there). Overlooking Rhos was Bryn Euryn, a limestone "mountain" 130 metres high. I enjoyed walking there, admiring the view. We had a lovely day out visiting the 37-acre Welsh Mountain Zoo in Colwyn Bay (opened in May 1963).

Lower Sixth: 1964-1965

So, in September 1964, aged seventeen, I started A-Levels. I already had the textbook *Advanced Level Physics* by M. Nelkon and P. Parker. Actually, it was my "Headmaster's Prize" from Mr Toft in July 1963 (I still have it). It was a step

---

[121] Andrew Marr, *Elizabethans: How Modern Britain Was Forged* (London: William Collins, 2020), p.105. Today, he remarks, the figure is around five per cent. And then many children had their lives damaged by the 11-plus. See further his chapter 13 'Schooling: The First Defeat of Socialism'.

of faith for him to give it then. It was very helpful, and friends bought copies too. Quarry Bank, of course, provided textbooks, but Nelkon and Parker was inspiring. Nevertheless, like other 1960s books, it was in black-and-white, with only two pages having photos. But its layout, explanations, examples, exercises and exercise answers endeared us. Curiously, the area I found very interesting, "atomic physics", was only covered briefly.

It was normal to study three A-Levels. I choose maths, physics, and chemistry. Early on, I considered swapping chemistry to further maths, but decided against it. Our O-Level chemistry teacher was excellent and friendly, so this probably contributed to my decision as he taught us physical and inorganic chemistry. Another teacher taught organic chemistry. However, in the organic chemistry lab, the water supply was intermittent. During one experiment, Mick spilt a chemical on his hand, so he quickly turned on the tap to wash it off, but found it was dry. The shock on his face was obvious! Fortunately, he grabbed a bottle of water off a boy and used that before any burns occurred – close shave!

We also took general studies and "Use of English". RE lessons continued, as did morning assembly, with prefects publicly reading Bible passages. The Beatles became famous worldwide. *Please, Please Me* (released February 1963) reached number one in the UK charts; *I Want to Hold Your Hand* (released November 1963) had sales worldwide, reaching ten million. There was Beatlemania, and an American tour in 1964, with an appearance on the Ed Sullivan TV show with millions of viewers. So, with John Lennon's connection to Quarry Bank, girls' letters arrived requesting penfriends. Mr Pobjoy read interesting, and hilarious, sections in assembly, and invited boys to write if interested!

Of course, I had to think yet again about English, and November 1964 retakes. So, further teaching followed, but this was terribly tiresome.

For A-Levels, we received weekly homework, which we

handed in for marking. Once, we had more chemistry homework than physics, and this bothered me, as I wanted more physics. I asked our physics teacher for more and he obliged, although it meant he had more marking. The extra question was worded "if you wish to try it". I don't think all boys did, but it gave me the necessary extra practice.

Maths was divided into pure and theoretical mechanics, with different teachers for each. Our pure maths teacher was a Quarry Bank "old boy" who, after finishing his degree, returned as a teacher. He also coached rugby. The mechanics teacher was older, and in our afternoon classes he would gently wake up anyone dozing off!

Back then, there weren't modular exams that counted towards final grades. Moreover, there weren't AS-Levels (Advanced Supplementary) to take after the first year. All the pressure rested on our summer exams after two years. We had to remember all two years' work – a tough ask! Of course, we had class exams.

During 1964, I started attending Christian Union (CU) meetings during lunchtimes. There were two meetings: the lower forms and higher forms. My friend Hutch wanted something extra to put on his university application forms (he was in the year ahead of me), and decided the CU looked good. He invited me and we heard interesting talks in the library. Once, we had a joint meeting of CUs with a missionary, in the large, tiered classroom and this was pretty full. Hutch got into university, so perhaps it helped him. I think it helped me. Besides meetings in the library, we had private study there. It was often crowded, and a master made sure there wasn't loud talking or bad behaviour. Sadly, sometimes we were caught talking and told to leave. Anyway, I took the November 1964 English exam (attempt four).

In December 1964, the Liverpool group Gerry and the Pacemakers released *Ferry Cross the Mersey* in the UK. It was written by Gerry Marsden[122], and did well in the charts, reaching number eight. Previously, in 1963, they had released *You'll Never Walk Alone* (sung at Liverpool's football matches). We saw an advert in the *Liverpool Echo* for extras for the 1965 film *Ferry Cross the Mersey*, but didn't audition as there were so many applicants it made it unlikely that we'd be chosen.

On 24th January 1965, we heard the sad news of the death of Winston Churchill, Britain's greatest wartime leader, who had encouraged the nation to fight on against the Nazis. His lying-in-state was seen by over 320,000 people, and his funeral televised.

Also, in early 1965, after assembly we stayed in the hall for Mr Pobjoy to read our exam results. Nerve-racking! Numbers one to six were passes, with one the highest. Failure grades were seven (just fail), eight, and nine (worse fail). Holding my breath – listening intently. 'Dutch, English language grade seven (or eight?). Fail!' Same regrettable result.

But for young men in America, things were much worse, when in March 1965 President Lyndon Johnston sent marines to Vietnam. So began a long, horrific war, which was shown on TV. Conscription followed, and we watched. Further, in February 1965, a voting rights march in Selma, Alabama resulted in 200 people being jailed, including Martin Luther King Jr., and many injured through police violence (see the 2014 film *Selma*).

Summer 1965 meant school exams. I did surprisingly well in physics, coming first, by a fraction. The boy who was second was miffed, and discussed the marking with the teacher, trying to get a slight increase, but the teacher stuck to his guns, and I remained top. This was a surprise and success for me. I cannot remember the positions I achieved in maths or chemistry. Nevertheless, for my studies I was awarded the Quarry Bank High School prize for Diligence

---

[122] Sadly, in early January 2021, it was reported that Gerry (the 'Merseybeat legend') had died from a short illness, aged seventy-eight.

Lower VI Science 1964-65, signed by Mr Pobjoy. It was a copy of *Nuclear Physics and the Fundamental Particles* (Harry H. Heckman and Paul W. Starring). I still have it.

I resat English language (attempt five) in summer 1965. My friend who was the same standard as me got tired of failing the grammar-syllabus paper, and swapped to a more scientific syllabus. Result? He passed! But I stuck with the grammar syllabus, and miserably failed for the fifth time! "Time to change – too many tough times and trials."

Rob Atkins, my cousin Edna's husband, was a chemist and salesman, who worked occasionally as a private tutor. While at Quarry Bank, he sometimes helped me with chemistry; his support was appreciated. When they moved from Liverpool to a new house in Formby, I visited and helped with child-minding and gardening.

In August 1965, we took a one-week family holiday in Wales, at Cemaes Bay, the most northern village on the coast of Anglesey. But Dad had been involved in a car crash on the way home from work. He was uninjured, but the car was no longer roadworthy. Fortunately, a friend kindly loaned him his automatic car, and we arrived in the dark, as my sister Christina recalls. The next morning, we woke to a bright blue sky across the coast. During this holiday, I met Philippa, whose parents had a holiday home opposite our rented flat. We became penfriends and met during school holidays, in either Liverpool or Manchester. She was a boarder in a private school, and certainly not working-class, but we got on well for years, writing regularly and meeting. In the long summers she was usually abroad.

Upper Sixth: 1965-1966

In September 1965, aged eighteen, I joined the Upper Sixth and was a prefect. I greatly enjoyed Quarry Bank, its ethos and environment. Pupils actually liked learning, rather than loafing around.

Months rolled by, with autumn and the thick, crispy leaves on the ground followed by winter; we looked forward to spring, with pink cherry blossom trees, and then summer.

During autumn, pupils applied to university. As stated before, most 1960s English universities required applicants to have an O-Level in a foreign language. Therefore, my choices were limited. I asked universities to post me prospectuses and considered: (1) three-year honours degree, BSc (Hons) in Pure Physics, (2) four-year degree in Applied Physics with one year in industry ("sandwich" course), and (3) joint-honours degree in Physics and Maths. I preferred a BSc (Hons) in Pure Physics.

The University of Liverpool was my home university (nowadays Liverpool has three universities), but the language restrictions meant I couldn't apply there, or to Manchester. Instead, I recall applying to: Lancaster University; Battersea (London – shortly to become the University of Surrey); Royal College of Advanced Technology at Salford (near Manchester); and Harris College (at Preston, north of Liverpool). Lancaster University offered me a place if I passed Use of English instead of O-Level English, but I don't recall being interviewed. The others gave me interviews.

To reach Battersea, I travelled by steam train from Liverpool and then by train in London. The return fare, Liverpool to London, was around £5 (a large sum then). The interview went well, including my answers to their physics questions. They clearly wanted me to study there, since I received a written offer with low grades, but the disadvantages made me reject it: Battersea's premises weren't good, and the travel costs were high. Somewhere more suitable was needed. I took the train to Harris College, which had smart premises, and the man who interviewed me was pleasant. However, the college didn't award a BSc (Hons) – just a route to be a Graduate Member of the Institute of Physics. This was a major disadvantage, as with a BSc (Hons) I could apply directly for membership. I turned that down.

The Royal College of Advanced Technology at Salford (to become the University of Salford in 1967) looked suitable: it offered a BSc (Hons) and wasn't far from home. Actually, when my parents left Liverpool in 1967 for a new bungalow near Wigan, this meant Salford was even closer, with reduced travelling costs. I had some wise advice from Rob Atkins. He explained the merits of studying closer to home: I could stay away (if desired) but get home easily (if needed). Rob's family lived in Bootle (north Liverpool) and as he studied at Manchester, he practised what he preached. I saw the merits of this and followed his suggestion. Salford was fine.

The college's large main building stood on the banks of the River Irwell, almost opposite the fire station, and was more modern in appearance and feel than Battersea. My interview with two academic staff went well. They asked me about radioactive decay, and what experiments we had done recently. I answered both clearly, and they looked pleased. When they made me an offer, I accepted. Now I needed to pass the A-Levels and, of course, English.

On Wednesday 17th November 1965, 9.30am-12pm, I resat English language, but swapped to the scientific syllabus (attempt six!). Before the English results came out in early 1966, I took the Use of English exam. Anyway, for the O-Level results we gathered (yet again) in the hall and pupils' results were announced. With bated breath, I waited at the back... 'Dutch: English language grade one. Pass!' I shouted out in astonishment. People looked at me – top grade after multiple failures? Staff and students were shocked. So, I passed with the top grade this "scientific" English language (paper B) syllabus! Now I had five O-Levels. Trials ended; triumph grasped. Now more time for A-Levels. But I still had to wait for the Use of English result: especially as Lancaster's offer depended on it. The shock was that when the results came out, I had failed! How can that be a sensible assessment system – mad – when I'd just passed English with the top grade? I never went to Lancaster.

On 17th March, my Lower Sixth form prize (mentioned above) *Nuclear Physics and the Fundamental Particles* was presented to me at our school Speech Day Distribution of Prizes held in the Philharmonic Hall.

Summer 1966 exams were held over some weeks. I kept to my revision programme. The night before my first exam, after I had studied intensely, my parents said: 'Come on! You have studied enough so let's go out for a drive.' Dad drove our second-hand Austin Cambridge car for a pleasant ride to relax my brain and it certainly worked. In May/June, England's evenings are long and light until around 10pm. It was relaxing – just what I needed.

Exams were stressful and tiring. Maths, physics, and chemistry usually had two three-hour written papers. Further, physics and chemistry had practical lab exams. The chemistry titrations were particularly lengthy, and called for precision measurements. Often, we took a three-hour paper in the morning, had lunch, and a three-hour paper afterwards. That meant revision time for the next exam was precious. I worked in the evenings. In addition, we took O-Level general studies. As an incentive to work hard, I opted to take special papers in physics and maths.

My A-Level revision focused on physics and maths to get good grades. Chemistry, although interesting, took second place. I found that in organic chemistry we were expected to remember the precise amount of chemicals needed in experiments. This seemed somewhat trivial, and would require rote-learning. However, I genuinely enjoyed physical and inorganic chemistry.

At the end of each exam day, my hands ached after writing for three to six hours. I sat the physics special paper on a very hot Friday: 10th June, 2-5pm. Our classroom windows were open, but it was still so hot. I had a pounding headache but no painkillers with me, and my right hand ached from holding the pen. Moreover, the sweat from my hand lessened my grip. So, the pen kept slipping, and I needed to wipe the sweat off so I could write faster. In the chemistry practical exam, we did precision weighing of chemicals in the little booths we sat inside (it reduced air flow, and made the process more accurate). I remember spilling chemicals – stress! All grades depended on those few exam weeks; we were expected to remember two years' worth of material, since we could be tested on any of it. Of course, there were back papers for practice, and usually some choice of questions; but it was still stressful – not enough time, no open books, no formulae, no calculators – perhaps a slide rule.

British education policy

Looking back, my academic success highlighted the issues of school selection policies. Mr Toft and Mr Pobjoy were essential in easing me across the divisions. They gave me opportunities that revolutionised my future. Marr identifies that by 1965 the failure of the state tripartite selection system was crystal-clear. Private or public schools creamed off about five per cent of children, leaving ninety-five per cent in the discredited state-education system – around one quarter in grammar schools and three quarters in secondary moderns (which were mediocre). Marr notes one 1965 author regarded "modern" as a euphemism for "less clever".[123]

Being a summer-born baby had hindered my progress in schooling. And growing up working-class, speaking Scouse rather than the Queen's English we heard on BBC TV, was another disadvantage. The road to recovery was uphill.

---

[123] Andrew Marr, *A History of Modern Britain* (London: Pan Books, 2008), pp.246-247. And Marr, *Elizabethans* (p.105) on the divisive education system, which failed millions of children and even the elite for life in modern Britain. Also see Brian Jackson and Dennis Marsden, *Education and the Working Class* (revised edition, Harmondsworth: Pelican, 1966).

Sports

At Quarry Bank, we played football, went swimming, and did PT in the gym. This made the classes more interesting, with ropes; the floor was polished wood, and we had proper changing rooms. Cross-country running was an option and I enjoyed this regularly in Calderstones Park. When we had inter-house competitions, I entered cross-country to gain a house point. However, I wasn't a natural long-distance runner, and usually counted my position from the end, for example fourth from last! Nevertheless, our housemaster was supportive, standing in the school grounds as we returned to the finishing line and cheering, 'Well done, Dutch!' The fact that I had entered, persevered, and finished counted for him. He was an encouragement.

I played rugby for the first time, and enjoyed it more than football. I made it into the school teams ("A" or "B" team), and played hooker. Our coloured shirts had black and yellow horizontal stripes. We had interschool matches on Saturday mornings but occasionally midweek after the school day. Physically, I was small (under five feet six inches) and weighed less than nine stone (less than 126 pounds). Most boys were taller and heavier than me, some much heavier. But I could sprint and was strong – and I even scored the odd try. Once, I went to a school session to become a blood donor. I was turned away as underweight. They thought I needed what little blood I had!

One year, I couldn't play rugby continuously because of an injury. This happened when I was staying with Edna and Rob. They had boys who were neighbours, and we were chatting in a friendly way outside their house. One boy said something, and I started to chase him, but he pulled their metal gate behind him and I ran into it, hurting my left knee. It didn't seem bad, so I played rugby afterwards. Regrettably, I got hit in that knee – painful. It took weeks to heal, and I stumbled around, although crutches weren't required. Even more than a year later, if I sat too long in one position, it ached.

I mentioned that I was strong. I attribute this to walking and cycling for hours during the Duke of Edinburgh's Award at Sheil Road, and weight training at Quarry Bank. One friend, Chang, who was Chinese and lived in Chinatown, as I recall, was powerfully-built, and good at lifting weights. There was no specialist equipment. The PE teacher was interested, but wasn't a weight-training coach.

I read books and learnt as we lifted. Also, I used "chest expanders" and added "strands" as I got stronger. Eventually, I purchased a barbell and weights as money permitted, and trained away from school. I bought "Body Sculpture" light green metal weights in various sizes up to 15 lbs (pounds then rather than kilograms). This allowed me to gradually increase the weights. There was little space in our house, but eventually Auntie Edie's front room in 30 Red Rock St became available (after her sister's family moved out, and then Edna and Rob moved to Formby). I could store and use the weights there. Eventually, I started reading the magazine by the British Amateur Weight Lifters' Association (BAWLA), to see what was happening in that world and what records were set, particularly for my weight class. Today, I still like lifting weights, including those I bought in the 1960s.

We had swimming sessions in the lovely school pool, and I took some lifesaving classes. The pool was deep enough to dive into. We had to rescue "drowning" boys and swim back to the bar with them. It was worth doing, although we weren't assessed for certificates. Often, we found rescues highly amusing, and started laughing, to the point where rescue became impossible! Abandoning the attempt, we frantically swam to the poolside, to save ourselves from spluttering and sinking.

Driving lessons

In the Lower Sixth, I learnt to drive, aged seventeen. My parents kindly paid for lessons with an instructor who had a small Austin A40 car. Dad had learnt to drive some time before me, but became frustrated at the way he thought the examiners kept failing him. In the end, he booked tests two at a time, so that if he failed one, he was already in the queue for the next date. He took about six goes to pass, but never gave up. Dad even bought his car while still a learner, to get more practice with friends who had already passed.

I learnt to drive using gears with a gear stick (then four forward gears and one reverse). Automatic cars were rare. I had to learn to operate three pedals: accelerator (or "gas") on the right, brake in the centre, and the clutch on the left to change gear. In the mid-1960s, when I learnt, proficiency in hand signals was required in addition to the car's indicators. This meant driving with the window open whatever the weather, so I could put my hand out. There were signals for right and left turns, and to indicate I was slowing down, or to let the driver behind overtake. Car radios weren't standard, or headrests, heated rear-windows or seatbelts. But roads were far less crowded.

I recall an early lesson driving around a park at night, where the street lighting was poor, and the headlights didn't give enough illumination. Fortunately, the instructor knew the road. Another time I got stuck ("frozen") at one busy junction from a side road to the main road, where it was difficult to see what was coming. Eventually, the instructor swapped seats with me and drove. Thankfully, he got us out safely. Completing successful hill starts took practice. I had to hold the car on the handbrake, have the gear lever in first gear, with the clutch depressed to the floor, and then slowly raise the clutch as I revved the engine. Then, as the engine noise changed and the car pulled forward, I released the handbrake and, hopefully, the car didn't roll back down the hill, but moved off slowly up and forwards in a controlled manner. At the same time, I had to use the rear mirror, indicate, and give the hand signal. Lots to learn. Emergency stops were fine.

After about fifteen one-hour lessons, I took my test in central Liverpool. I had a final one-hour practice with my instructor before the test started. There was no theory test then, just driving followed by Highway Code questions. I read a number plate at the specified distance (seventy-five feet), to show that my sight was good. Fortunately, I didn't do anything dreadfully wrong, or have an accident. Also, I used the correct hand signals and the electronic indicators. Nevertheless, the examiner wasn't satisfied – I failed!

I returned to school knowing the class wanted to know the outcome. Unfortunately, the Lower Sixth maths class had begun in the separate classroom block from the main building, and I had to enter late through the door at the front. The maths master, who was friendly and a good teacher, stood there and I had to give an explanation of why I was late. With all the boys watching, it went something like: 'Sorry sir, for being late. I was taking my driving test.' Master: 'Oh! How did you get on?' Looking somewhat downcast, 'Oh, I failed!' Response from the class: loud laughter! He was sympathetic, but I had to slink down, taking my seat amid loud laughter and smiling, amused faces looking at me. It was not really funny, and far too public. The teacher meant well, and the boys understood.

Eventually, after further lessons, I retook my test with the same examiner. That time, I did hand signals with the window open in the light rain. We recognised each other but fortunately, my performance was better, and I passed. Success!

Entertainment

There were many entertainment opportunities in Liverpool. Besides cinemas, we visited the stadium for wrestling, the museum, and the Walker Art Gallery. We could visit NEMS, the record shop run by Brian Epstein, who became the Beatles' manager. We went to the original Cavern Club, and others, including the Sink and the Mardi Gras, which I visited on Tuesday evenings, with live groups (Liverpool had hundreds!) and its licensed bar. Other clubs included the Iron Door, but I can't recall going in. The worst club we visited was off Dale or Water St. My, it was rough! When we returned to our table and seats after dancing, we found they were smashed up. Scuffles broke out, and we decided it was safer to leave sooner rather than later. Imagine our surprise when we reached the exit and saw bouncers wiping up a large pool of blood off a tabletop. We never returned.

One event I particularly recall was on 23rd September 1965, when David Kent and I went on the ferry to the New Brighton Tower Ballroom at the mouth of the Mersey. The famous US Walker Brothers were singing. In 1965, the ferries ran daily to New Brighton, which is no longer the case. Older people like me will remember that. Getting the ferry that evening to see the Walker Brothers is memorable for sitting on the top deck in the breeze (and it was dry) and watching the scenery on both sides of the river.

However, the organisers had an oversight. The evening performance finished after the last ferry had departed for Liverpool. So, we went not knowing how we would get home. Anyway, during the evening, the organisers appeared to have realised their mistake and made an announcement that the event would finish early! Which was good for getting home but disappointing when we had paid our money for the full performance – no rebates were given.

I guess the organisers woke up to the fact that leaving scores, or hundreds, of teenage fans stranded in New

Brighton would not go down well locally, with parents and the authorities. Seems odd that they didn't think about that in advance, considering many other performances including the Beatles playing (1961-63) had been held there previous years! Although, possibly the fact that 23rd September 1965 was a Thursday and not a weekend may be an excuse... Sadly, fire destroyed the Tower Ballroom building in 1969.

Then there were the pubs, once we reached eighteen. I had friends who liked drinking at weekends, and they had a strategy for more beer money. The dinner money given by their parents was not used to pay for the school lunches, but to buy cheap stale cakes or broken biscuits at local shops. The money saved became weekend beer money.

Quarry Bank had its popular annual school dance in the hall, with live music, but sometimes a local gang came and caused trouble. "The Red Rock" at 42 Red Rock was our local pub when I reached eighteen, and plenty of others were around. I had an African friend from Sheil Road school, who took a few of us in his car around pubs, having drinks and laughs. Interestingly, Gerard DeGroot's history mentions drug-taking and quotes: 'If you remember the Sixties … you weren't there.' I can't recall being offered drugs in schools, on the streets, or in clubs/pubs.[124]

On 30th July 1966, Britain watched the FIFA World Cup final at Wembley Stadium, London. England played Germany and won 4-2 in extra time. Queen Elizabeth presented the cup to captain Bobby Moore. However, it was not until 2021 that England reached another major tournament final – the postponed UEFA Euro 2020 – in the new Wembley. Over 96,000 watched at the stadium and 32.3 million on TV (I was one!). Unfortunately, England lost to Italy in a penalty shootout. But back to 1966...

---

[124] Gerard DeGroot, *The Sixties Unplugged: A Kaleidoscopic History of a Disorderly Decade* (London: Pan Books, 2008), p.1. Citing Robin Williams.

A-Level results!

In August 1966, my reward was a triple triumph. We were called in individually to Mr Pobjoy's office, where he and the school secretary sat at his desk with the results. 'Congratulations, Dutch, on passing your A-Levels!' My physics was an A (the top grade, no A* grades then), maths a B and chemistry a D. I also obtained the physics special paper and O-Level general studies. Now I had six O-Levels, three A-Levels, and special physics. After collecting my A-Level results, I met up with Hutch and we celebrated with friends and Hutch's girlfriend in a few pubs in Liverpool's centre. It was a great outcome for my parents and family, who had supported me sacrificially during my extra four years at school. They were proud. Quite a contrast with my first day at Whitefield Road School, and my attempted escape!

In July 1967, one year after I finished, Quarry Bank and Calder High closed and merged with Morrison Secondary Modern (on Rose Lane), becoming Quarry Bank Comprehensive School. Today, this is a specialist science school called Calderstones.

Quarry Bank School Speech Day:

February 1967

In 1967, I had my last contact with Quarry Bank. As an unexpected honour, I had been awarded a book prize for good results the previous summer: *Advanced Mathematics for Technical Students* (Part Two) by H.V. Lowry and H.A. Hayden, signed by Mr Pobjoy (Headmaster). It was presented to me by Mrs E. Rideout (School Governor) at the school's Final Speech Day ceremony on Thursday 23rd February 1967, held in Liverpool's prestigious Philharmonic Hall. The full programme included: remarks, report, orchestra, prize oration, prize presentation, choir (the opening chorus from Bach's St Matthew Passion), address, vote of thanks and finally the National Anthem. My name was listed under the GCE Advanced Level Prizes, the GCE Advanced Level Upper VI Mathematics (for obtaining passes) and boys gaining university entrance.

CHAPTER 9

University of Salford

Royal College of Advanced Technology

Now I had a place for a physics BSc (Hons) at Salford's Royal College of Advanced Technology (RCAT) on The Crescent near Manchester.[125] Salford was a city that had experienced the Industrial Revolution. It felt like Liverpool: bombed in the Second World War; old, terraced houses; smoky, and undergoing "slum clearance". Properties were being demolished, spreading dust everywhere.[126] Buses often stirred up dust behind them. I would close my eyes, but it still got into lungs, hair and clothes – tough. Salford and Manchester merged, like one built-up city. A weekend all-night bus service ran (charging double fare).

The RCAT became the University of Salford on 10th February 1967. HRH Prince Philip, the Duke of Edinburgh, was its first Chancellor. My first year was the RCAT's final year, but the university's first.

---

[125] For the RCAT/University of Salford in the 1960s, a photographic archive was available online in October 2021. But before 8th August 2022 this facility was removed from the University of Salford Institutional Repository.

[126] For a short silent student film of this demolition showing the University of Salford, see: Michael Goodger, *Demolition in Salford*, 1968 North West Film Archive, Manchester Metropolitan University, 2022 British Film Institute. Accessed 8 August 2022 at Watch BFI Player Watch Demolition in Salford online – BFI Player

First year: 1966-67

Accommodation

Before starting, I arranged accommodation; daily travelling wasn't an option. The college didn't have enough places in its halls of residence for all first-year students, so I looked for digs. I met a friendly older landlady, who had a semi-detached house for male students at 33 Hereford Road, Eccles, Lancashire – she lived in her daughter's adjacent house, but cooked us meals. Our house had a front garden in the quiet street close to the pub. It had three downstairs rooms: a kitchen, a front lounge, and a rear room, which doubled as a dining room and study. Although the accommodation and our landlady were fine, her large Alsatian dog was erratic; I was wary from the start. It, too, liked the kitchen! Outside was coal storage, but there was an inside toilet – and a bathroom but no shower. At home, I had my own small bedroom; but here there were two upstairs bedrooms with twin beds.

I accepted the weekly half-board accommodation and got used to sharing with Paul, Pete and Jim, all also first-year students. The bus from college stopped nearby, but sometimes I enjoyed long, quiet evening walks back (and it saved 7d bus fare). I can't recall how much I paid, but I have a friend who went to Dublin University in 1967 and paid £5 a week including B&B (bed and breakfast), evening meals, and three meals on Sunday. And he had his own room.

Before term started, Dad and Mum drove me around thirty miles from Liverpool to Eccles along the A580 (no M62 motorway then). I didn't have much stuff, which was helpful, since there wasn't much storage space in the bedroom that I shared with Paul. After I unloaded, they waved "ta-ra" (goodbye!), told me to 'keep safe,' and drove home. Besides clothes and toiletries, I had little else. No mobile phone, no computer, no radio, and no record player. It would be about one month before I next saw my parents. To contact them, I could write or turn up at home. Mum and Dad didn't have a telephone, and there wasn't one in our digs. Things improved when we moved from Liverpool in spring 1967, since our neighbours (Mr and Mrs Jones) had a phone, and eventually so did we, although it was a shared party line. The party line was a way of having access to a home telephone, rather than renting a completely separate line. We started off in Ashton, sharing a line with a neighbour across the street. But with a party line sometimes when we picked up our receiver to make a call, we would hear our neighbour, or his wife, talking to someone! There was no choice but to put down our receiver and return later, hoping their conversation was not too long. Such a line, of course, meant our privacy, and theirs, was potentially compromised. Difficult to imagine now, with mobile phones.

My sister Anne recalls going with Mum and Dad to collect me one time at Swinton (near Eccles) on the East Lancs Road. Apparently, I was stood at the roadside with my dirty washing wrapped in a sheet! Once, I hitched a ride home.

Starting studies

The college stood adjacent to where the River Irwell looped by the main road. Soap suds sometimes floated on the coffee-colour river, which reminded me of Liverpool's Mersey. In 1966, the RCAT was much smaller than the university is as I write in 2022 (in the academic year 2020/21 it had 23,955 students).[127] The main Maxwell Building was an imposing structure. On the ninth floor there was a large lecture room suitable for lectures and film shows. The sixth floor had the college's refectory, while the third floor had the

---

[127] HESA, 'Who's studying in HE: HE student enrolments by HE provider – Academic years 2014/15 to 2020/21?' 10 February 2022. Accessed 8 August 2022 at Who's studying in HE? | HESA

student union bar. The Department of Pure and Applied Physics may also have been on the third floor. The library was in the Maxwell Building. (Unfortunately, the refectory had very long queues at lunchtime, so we either returned later or went over the road to The Crescent Pub for an enjoyable drink and snack.)

Attached to the Maxwell Building via a walkway was the Maxwell Hall, where concerts, dances, debates and Christmas carol services took place. There was one large gym, and changing rooms with showers. Lockers for storing kit were in the Maxwell Building. Nearby stood the computer block, with its computer (yes, just one computer!). The tall chemistry block had two-man lifts that operated continuously: jumping in and out was tricky (they were known as paternosters). Beyond the grassed area and the Salford Museum and Art Gallery stood the old Salford Technical College ("Tech") in the Peel Building. Across The Crescent was the fire station; fire engines didn't have to go far when alarms sounded in the chemistry block. Some college buildings were outside the main campus, and for lectures we took the footpath besides the Irwell through Peel Park and across the footbridge. Eventually, the Tech vacated its old building, which became available to the university.

After arrival, we were given book lists and our timetable (lectures, lab experiments and private study). Wednesday afternoons were for sports. To broaden our education, we had elective short modules of non-assessed topics (such as psychology, exercise activities, and elocution). Our intake was around thirty students, while the BSc (Hons) Applied Physics, a four-year sandwich course, had far fewer.

The college didn't have a bookshop, so we shopped in Manchester. Most books were helpful, but sometimes we wished that we'd waited before purchasing ones we hardly used. Lecturers wanted us to buy many books – in the second year we were wiser! Visiting bookshops did, however, make us familiar with Manchester's streets.

Barclay's Bank was the first to introduce the credit card (the Barclaycard) to Britain, in June 1966, but I didn't have one. It wasn't until 27th June 1967 that the world's first Automated Teller Machine (ATM) was installed in Barclays Bank (London, not Salford). We queued at bank counters for cash withdrawals.

Where did my money come from? Fortunately, Liverpool Council's student grant system paid the course fees automatically to the college, and gave me a living allowance (which I didn't need to repay). We completed the forms for a means-tested grant. Dad was a bricklayer and his previous year's earnings meant a proportionate deduction came from the full living allowance, leaving me the remainder to live on. The deduction was the "parental contribution", which my parents paid by giving me free board at home during the holidays. The proportion of students that studied in higher education was much smaller back then (for comparison, the total number of students obtaining first degrees in the UK was 51,189 in 1970 and 350,800 in 2011) and the public purse could afford that system.[128]

First- and second-year modules/units were compulsory, and taught over the whole academic year (October-June), though we had some shorter classes. Lecturers took class registers. Besides physics, we attended maths classes. I bought the Teach Yourself Book *Calculus* by P. Abbott. Another book was *Advanced Mathematics for Technical Students* (Part Two) by H.V. Lowry and H.A. Hayden, the book I had received as my school prize from Quarry Bank for good A-Level results.

---

[128] Paul Bolton, *Education: Historical statistics*, House of Commons Library, Standard Note: SN/SG/4252, 27 November 2012, Table 8. Accessed 25 March 2023 at Education: Historical statistics – House of Commons Library (parliament.uk) For more recent figures see Paul Bolton, *Higher education student numbers*, House of Commons Library, Research Briefing, 21 February 2023. Accessed 25 March 2023 at CBP-7857.pdf (parliament.uk)

First-year physics modules included: Atomic and Nuclear Physics; Electricity and Magnetism; Properties of Materials, and experiments (such as on the properties of light). Most lecturers were men, but a woman taught Electricity and Magnetism. We also studied Acoustics, including listening to frequencies in a sound-proof chamber (a single anechoic chamber). Magnetism classes were delivered by the young-looking Professor Tebble, but with a drawback: he delivered the wrong modules accidentally to two classes, one being ours (swapped with a third-year class). My friend Dave Casey recalls, with ninety per cent confidence, that it happened while we were in our first year. Though amusing, it didn't inspire confidence.

All topics had to be memorised for the summer exams. Teaching was by chalk and talk. Proofs were developed line by line. There were no overhead projectors or electronic teaching aids in lecture rooms. Laptop computers were decades in the future. We copied notes from the blackboard and used textbooks. Photocopiers weren't readily available, so there were no printed handouts (except in one third-year class). One lecturer, J.G. Brown, had written the book for our second-year module *X-Rays and Their Applications*.[129] It was clear, with good diagrams, maths proofs, black-and-white plates, problems and answers. Moreover, he showed us the X-ray equipment for our lab experiments, e.g. in X-ray crystallography. The lecturers taught at a sensible pace. With around thirty students, we used small lecture rooms; sometimes, however, students fell asleep and needed stirring!

For lab experiments, we worked in pairs, which was good as we figured out what we were to do. It was drummed into us **not** to write the experiment results on loose-leaf papers, as these were easily lost. Rather, we recorded results in our lab books. The evenings before our next lab class, we would

---

[129] J.G. Brown, *X-Rays and Their Applications* (London: Iliffe Books, 1966).

usually finish writing up experiments, then discuss them with the lecturers before being allocated another. Often, this meant late evenings or early mornings. Consequently, when students arrived somewhat weary, a warm dark "optics" lab induced sleep. A friendly word from the lecturer asking, 'Are you okay? Is everything alright?' was sufficient to rouse us. And then, to the point: 'The lab is not the right place to sleep, is it?' 'No, sir!' And then back to the experiment, much more alert.

Nobody had electronic calculators; in the labs we used Facit mechanical calculators. These worked with a numeric keyboard and a rotating handle. Inside the grey box were mechanical cogs. We entered the numbers and turned the right-hand handle to do arithmetical operations. More complicated calculations required tables or slide rules.

Mum and Dad purchased a lovely slide rule for me, which was invaluable: a ten-inch-long Thornton cream-coloured plastic rule in a black plastic case with its instruction book. I still have it but, of course, decades ago, calculators replaced slide rules. I remember shopping for it, and it cost around £5 – a lot of money then. I was very grateful, and used it often.

Exams were not expected until the end of the academic year. However, staff decided to give us some earlier exams to monitor progress! So, we began to revise. The maths paper was on Friday 16th December 1966, with ten compulsory questions. I did fine. My exam question paper shows me ticking off questions without desperate comments. (Yes, I still have it.)

One area I focused on was atomic and nuclear physics. In particular, this had mathematical derivations that were needed to solve Schrödinger's wave equation. I mastered them, and they came up in the exam. However, the lecturer had changed the problem from what we covered in class. The particle's direction of travel was reversed. Fortunately, I noted this, and carefully worked out the solution. When the results were released, we found that many students hadn't noticed the reversed direction. Technically, they got zero marks! But so widespread was this error that the staff agreed to mark the question out of fifty per cent instead of 100 per cent, for students who made the error. Fortunately, I'd read the question carefully and answered it correctly, getting full marks! What a relief. Staff warned us previously not to expect full marks but as all my maths was correct, I did get 100 per cent. When we had our private conversations with a lecturer, I was fine on this, but my "properties of materials" needed more work – no time to rest on my laurels.

I enjoyed the pure maths. My A-Level course in pure maths and theoretical mechanics had prepared me admirably. This confirmed my previous decision not to take further maths as an A-Level but continue with chemistry, giving me a wider breadth in science. Our lecturer taught advanced calculus with considerable clarity.

On 21st October 1966, as I was starting at Salford, a national tragedy occurred at Aberfan (near Merthyr Tydfil), a Welsh mining village. The local coal mine (colliery) had left a 500-feet-high slag heap. It suddenly slipped down as an unstoppable avalanche upon the local primary school, wrecking it. The fatalities included 116 children and most of the teachers (twenty-eight). For us, it was a deeply disturbing disaster. My wife, Susan, who lived in Newport (South Wales) recalls being in the office at the Builders' Merchants in Screwpacket Lane when it happened.

Clubs and sports

The four of us in our digs (Paul, Pete, Jim and me) often did things together in the early days. The RCAT had a lunchtime Folk Club so we went along (remember it was the Sixties), and had a hearty sing (although I can't sing in tune), especially with the rousing choruses along with the instrumentalists. Sometimes we went to folk clubs in Manchester, or dances held by other colleges. We had our entertainment society, which arranged dances in the Maxwell

Hall with live music. Lunchtimes offered occasional musical events such as organ recitals. There was an annual Christmas carol service. Debates also occurred, and I recall briefly commenting on Christianity in my second or third year.

The college didn't have a pool, so we used the public baths. I continued weightlifting, and started judo on Wednesday afternoons. There wasn't a purpose-built dojo, so we put out mats from the gym's store and removed them at the end. The instructor was Japanese: young, friendly, and a black belt. He was good to train with. There was a mixture of grades and abilities – mainly men, but one or two women. I was ungraded – a white belt. Some students were graded at their home clubs. One man was a brown belt. I used a judo suit from my jujitsu days. We certainly had fun, and kept fit with exercises, throws and groundwork.

I met Alan Ryden and Larry Weaver taking judo. Alan was on my course; he had previously trained in judo. Larry was studying for a Joint Honours in maths and physics, and was powerfully-built. We three became good friends and after judo walked to the bus stop or all the way home; although they lived nearer to college. Unfortunately, we weren't given "gradings", so at the end of the academic year I remained a white belt, despite improvements. Nevertheless, I served as a committee member for the Judo Club. In weightlifting, I would wear a leather black belt. Actually, this was not through any grading system, but merely to support my back during lifting. Nevertheless, I trained hard, and made more progress than I originally expected.

Weightlifting club

When I arrived, there wasn't a Weightlifting Club, but like-minded students got together and started one. I was its first chairman and Eric Jackson its secretary. (As chairman, I represented the club on the Students Union sports committee.) Others became committee members. Eric was tall, well-built, good at weightlifting, organised and enthusiastic. Another student trained with us. He represented Britain at rowing, and used weights in his training. My housemate Jim often trained with us.

Initially, the college didn't have any weightlifting rooms, but we used the balcony area overlooking the gym. However, students kicking or throwing balls around in the gym made it hazardous: anyone hit while lifting weights could be injured. Facilities were basic. Apart from the weights, we had a bench for exercises (e.g. bench presses) and a rack to support the barbell/weights. Eventually, through the Students Union, we bought a basic squat rack and more weights (including an Olympic style bar). When the Tech moved its premises, rooms became available across the campus, and we obtained one for our new Olympic weights. The college PT instructors were interested in weightlifting, but they weren't coaches.

At school, I had become aware of the British Amateur Weight Lifters' Association (BAWLA). It had an active following with competitions (including junior ones), so I decided to begin competitive powerlifting. I chose powerlifting instead of Olympic lifting (with the three lifts: press; snatch; and clean and jerk) because powerlifting required less mastery of techniques with its three lifts, called "the Strength Set" (deep knees bend or squat, press on bench, and two hands dead lift). So, I focused on these. I was heavier than before (so I gave blood for the first time) but still in the lightest class, Bantamweight. Initially without coaches, I learnt what I could from books and experience. I still have *The Manual of Weight Training* edited by George Kirkley and John Goodbody.[130] I took protein and multivitamin tablet supplements but never met anyone using performance-enhancing drugs.

---

[130] George Kirkley and John Goodbody (eds.), *The Manual of Weight Training* (London: Stanley Paul, 1967).

One benefit when our family moved from Liverpool to Ashton around March 1967 was the Ashton Health Club in the centre of Ashton by the market steps. It was mainly used by bodybuilders interested in powerlifting competitions. I joined and trained there. Derek Gibbons, the owner, was a champion bodybuilder with a fifty-inch chest, who did strength acts in public competitions. I first saw him do one in the club. He took a six-inch nail, put some soft material around the head, and held it in his hand, then with one quick movement he drove it straight through a thick wooden shelf. Amazing! He also bent metal bars. He gave me advice, came to competitions, and encouraged me.[131] Once, I met champion weightlifter Precious McKenzie (only four foot nine inches, or 1.45m tall).

I competed in three types of events: (1) the annual Universities Athletic Union (UAU), (2) local BAWLA competitions, and (3) inter-university competitions. After the weigh-in and warm-up, we had three attempts at each lift. So, competitors had to plan lifts wisely. The first lift had to be heavy but achievable. If I failed it, I had to reattempt it in my second lift (effectively wasting an attempt). My second lift had to be around my best, and the third had to be my best or better. If I was going for a record attempt, the judges could allow another attempt. Of course, I knew from training and competitions what I hoped to achieve on the day. Sadly, sometimes competitors misjudged their ability.

On 11th February 1967, I travelled to Yorkshire (to Leeds or Sheffield) to compete in the British UAU championship. One student from Loughborough got his strategy wrong in my bantamweight class. He started too high, and failed his first lift. A referee asked if we could give him a chance by changing the lifting order, so he had a longer rest. 'That's fine with me,' I confirmed. This gave him the extra chance that

---

[131] Gaynor Clarke, 'Local bodybuilding legend mourned', 10 September 2021, *Wigan Today*. Accessed 8 August 2022 at Local bodybuilding legend mourned | Wigan Today

everyone was grateful for – especially him. In the end, it made no difference, unfortunately, as he was recorded with a "nil" score. So disappointing for him. It did not affect my achievement. I beat the other person (who was the same weight as me – eight stone nine pounds – 121 pounds) by twenty pounds total. I won the annual Universities Athletic Union medal inscribed "Weight-Lifting Strength 1967 Individual Winner 9 Stone Class". Actually, by then I was lifting in the bantamweight class (and other competitors were similarly in the BAWLA classes), but the medals that year weren't inscribed for the new system. The official printout records the pounds I lifted: deep knee bend (254¾); press on bench (164¾); two hands dead lift (340½); and total (760). Each was a record, so it finished: "All Junior British Bantamweight and 9 st[one]". I proudly retain my medal and printout. The University's Salford Union published in *Amus News* (Monday 26th February 1967, p.7) the article called: "Salford student breaks four British records", with a photo of me training.

The BAWLA also awarded certificates for reaching prescribed achievements witnessed in competitions. One certificate, dated 11th February 1967, issued by the North Western Counties Amateur Weightlifters' Association recorded my three lifts with a total of 760 pounds at my bodyweight of eight stone nine-and-a-half pounds. This gained me the award of "Strength Third Class Blue with Two Bars". Mum sewed the coloured awards onto my tracksuit top. At one junior competition, when the others in my weight class saw this award they replied: 'Then you've won already. We can't beat that level.' They were right – I did win. I became the junior North Western Counties Bantamweight Champion.

Once, Dad drove Mum, Christina and Auntie Bel to watch. I recall being told afterwards that it was unbearable seeing the effort and pain on my face during my lifts. In fact, it could have been Auntie Bel who said: 'Never again – I won't come along again.' It was understandable – I was pulling my guts out, and showed it! Nevertheless, I was so grateful that they had supported me. Whether the spectators cheered wildly or clapped politely, I can't recall!

Two BAWLA Award certificates that I have confirm my British Junior records. On 9th April 1967 at Wythenshawe, Manchester, three appointed officials recognised my records in the bantamweight class for: press on bench; two hands deadlift; and strength set total (790 lbs), thus achieving three British Junior records. My body weight was eight stone ten-and-a-half pounds (55.5kg). Then on 21st May 1967, at the Crosby Barbell Club, Crosby, Lancs., appointed officials confirmed my records for: press on bench (179 lbs); two hands deadlift (358½ lbs); and strength set total (795 lbs), thus breaking my earlier three British Junior records. I never quite made the deep knee bend record then. In one competition, I missed it by not taking a long enough break before attempting the final lift, and then going too low (below the required parallel thigh position) and so not having enough strength/energy to get back up. Anyway, my competitions appeared in the University of Salford students' magazine (*Amus News*). For example, on 5th May, *Amus News* p.7 headline read: 'North-West Counties champion!' This pointed out that my 'total was high enough to beat the next weight division up – featherweight'. I was interviewed once, and a photo showed me doing a training dead lift. The Students Athletics Union recognised my achievements. My records also appeared in *The Strength Athlete,* in April 1967.

One Saturday in 1967, I returned alone from an inter-collegiate weightlifting competition to Manchester railway station, to catch the last train home. It wasn't due for a while, so I went for a quick pub drink. As I returned to the platform, I saw to my horror the train pulling out. I'd missed it – having misread the timetable. Somehow, I contacted my parents and asked them to collect me on the edge of Eccles/Salford. With what little cash I had, I paid for a taxi and then walked the rest of the way to meet Dad driving his car and we got home. Such lovely parents.

Jumping ahead, I should mention that in 1968 I didn't compete in the British UAU championship. A few weeks later, at an inter-university team lifting competition, I met the UAU bantamweight champion for 1968 and beat him on the basis that we lifted the same total number of pounds. Because I weighed less than him, I was the individual winner. Sweet success.

Easter and environmental disaster

On 18th March, just a week before Easter Sunday, when we were on university holidays, a disaster occurred when the supertanker SS *Torrey Canyon* hit a reef off Cornwall's coast and spilt over 100,000 tons of crude oil; beaches were polluted in Cornwall, Guernsey and France. A massive clean-up followed. We watched the sad events unfold on TV. Fifty years later, in 2017, BBC reporters noted: 'Beaches were left knee-deep in sludge and thousands of sea birds were killed in what remains the UK's worst environmental accident.' Britain received compensation from the supertanker's American owners. The sunken ship still sits on the seabed.[132] That summer, we visited Newquay, Cornwall – fortunately its beaches were fine, but the environmental damage was disturbing.

New accommodation

My accommodation in Eccles was fine for a while. But the large Alsatian which shared the house became wild.

---

[132] Bethan Bell and Mario Cacciottolo with Chris Quevatre, 'Torrey Canyon oil spill: The day the sea turned black', BBC News 17 March 2017. Accessed 8 August 2022 at Torrey Canyon oil spill: The day the sea turned black – BBC News

Alarmed, I gave notice in early 1967 and moved before being badly bitten. Soon after, the dog went too. I had new digs with a devout Jewish family, at Hillwood Avenue, Middleton Road, (north) Manchester 8.

I was there Monday-Friday, going home at weekends. When they celebrated the Jewish Passover from Monday 24th April to Tuesday 2nd May, although not Jewish I was invited to participate at the family meal. It was an enjoyable and enlightening experience. Then on Monday 5th June, Israel's Six Day War broke out between Egyptian and Israeli forces in the Sinai region and other Arab nations. It was international news, and the family was very concerned; in response, their young son (about my age) volunteered to fight, but a prior medical condition prevented him from enlisting. We followed the media reports. Also on that Monday, I was busy revising for my first maths exam on the following day.

Leaving Liverpool

Back in Liverpool, my parents had been looking to buy their first house, and move from our rented terraced house, which would soon be demolished under "slum clearance". We moved to the market town of Ashton-in-Makerfield (near Wigan): about twenty miles by road from Liverpool. Dad, aged forty-eight, secured a mortgage on a new three-bedroom, semi-detached bungalow (which cost less than £3,000). We moved in March to an estate under construction. We said "Farewell" to Liverpool after I had lived there almost twenty years, and before me, my parents, grandparents and great-grandparents. Our bungalow had a long living room, three bedrooms, a bathroom/toilet and kitchen. At the front was a porch and small, open-plan garden, and a side drive to the back with a long garden. Finally, we had gardens and countryside views.

There was no garage, but Dad built one. Our family friends

Joyce and Ossie with son Harold bought the attached bungalow. We enjoyed meeting new neighbours. Surprisingly, the locals didn't speak Scouse, but used old English with "thee" and "thou", just as in the Bible! We were so happy in our new location – although we missed aspects of Liverpool, especially as we had left Auntie Edie and Alf in Red Rock and Auntie Bel in Harewood Street. But we visited. Eventually, Auntie Edie and Alf moved to a new high-rise flat near the East Lancs Road, and so did Auntie Bel (sadly, Uncle Jim had died in 1963, aged fifty-three), who regularly attended her Anglican church and drew strength from there. When she moved, she joined her nearest parish church.

Christina transferred to the local junior school (Evans County Council School) in March and after the summer went to Cansfield Secondary School, where she took her CSEs (Certificate in Secondary Education) and O-Levels before leaving in 1972. Anne had worked as a dental nurse in Liverpool's Dingle on a low wage of £5 per week (reduced further by deductions and bus fares). When we moved to Ashton, she again worked as a dental nurse, alongside her friend Sylvia Heath for a while. Then Sylvia left to become a nurse while Anne moved to Ashton-in-Makerfield public library as a librarian.[133] Sylvia worshipped, with her family, at Bryn Baptist Church.

Besides the garage, there were enough building projects to keep Dad busy: building low rear walls, eventually another living room (although Mum and Dad had accidents during this project – a broken nose and gash above an eye respectively). Dad built friends' garages, too. The gardens needed some work.

---

[133] For a photo of Ashton-in-Makerfield, Evans County Council School and public library in 1960 see the Francis Frith Collection. Accessed 8 August 2022 at Photo of Ashton In Makerfield, Evans County Council School And Public Library c.1960 (francisfrith.com)

Summer 1967: exams, work, holiday
and mission

In summer 1967, we sat maths and physics exams. My two maths exams were taken on Tuesday 6th June, on the top floor of the Peel Building (after Salford Technical College moved to new premises), which meant it was a long way down the stairs to the toilet. (In time, the Social Sciences and Humanities Library opened in this building.) Physics I and Physics II were on Tuesday 20th June and Friday 23rd June respectively (9.30am to 12.30pm). Each paper required us to answer five questions from eight. They usually stated: 'What is...' or 'Find, Describe, Show, Calculate, Distinguish, Deduce, Explain, or Apply'. There was a practical long lab exam over three hours. I had to wait until mid-summer for the results: maths (A) and physics (B). Some relief. No "resits".

With exams over, I returned home to Ashton. Dad got me a job at Wimpey's building site in Cantril Farm, on the edge of Liverpool. This was being built as a council estate – a suburb for Liverpool's "slum clearance" programme to house 15,000. Folk whose houses were demolished had relocation options. Cantril Farm was one (but it was a long way from Liverpool's centre). Over time, the council estate at Cantril Farm deteriorated and needed reviving. In 2016, the *Liverpool Echo* featured an article 'Was Cantril Farm really ever one of the worst estates in Europe?' with mixed views. Now it's called Stockbridge Village.[134]

---

[134] Tom Belger, 'Was Cantril Farm really ever one of the worst estates in Europe? ECHO readers share fond memories after Craig Charles returned to his childhood home', *Liverpool Echo* 11 September 2016. Accessed 8 August 2022 at Was Cantril Farm really ever one of the worst estates in Europe? - Liverpool Echo Also see: Kris McDonald, 'Stockbridge Village – A Community Regeneration Project', 30 November 2012. Accessed 8 August 2022 at Stockbridge Village - A Community Regeneration Project - YouTube

In my first two summers, I worked with the civil engineers on laying the footings and drains for the houses and maisonettes. I was paid as a labourer because I was over eighteen. In practice, I worked in the civil engineers' offices, drawing coloured diagrams of site drains (rainwater and sewers) that were around the concrete footings/foundations. I learnt the length of pipes. Then I recorded where drains were installed, including their positions and lengths. These drawings were signed off by the engineers and filed. Also, they were the source of bonus payments agreed by the engineers with the pipe-laying teams. I reported anything odd to the engineers, for action. Eventually, the pipes were concreted over.

Dumper trucks were used to move building materials. They had one driver's seat, and safety warning signs: 'Do not ride on the back of this vehicle. Doing so will produce instant dismissal.' I returned once to the office and asked where so-and-so was. 'Gone!' was the reply. 'What happened?' I enquired. 'Instantly dismissed for riding on the back of a dumper truck! Told to pick up his cards and leave!' 'Well, he'd been warned,' I thought. Management upheld the warnings – they weren't going to accept such disregard for safety that could cause serious accidents or death.

We clocked in and out on cards to record our working hours. We had three breaks: morning, lunchtime/dinner, and afternoons. Some men had large thirsts and, in the morning, they'd drink a pint of milk and eat a fried-egg sandwich (a "buttie" in Liverpudlian). One year, when I worked as a labourer, we were having our morning-break, enjoying our cuppa (of tea) in the big hut. The large foreman, who had a fist the size of a sledgehammer, came in rather annoyed that we were taking too long. He shouted and slammed his fist on a wooden top/table, which shook under its impact. Everyone jumped and rushed for the door, including me.

That year, I spent hours daily shovelling concrete over rainwater and sewage pipes. It was demanding, but at least

I was outside in the weather; a change from lectures and labs. And I was paid. The working week was Monday–Friday, but we'd work overtime Saturday 8am–1pm (paid at "time and a quarter" or "time and a half").

I travelled with Dad in his car with his mates along the "East Lancs", or he drove to a local pub's car park, where we waited for the company coach to collect us. In the evening, we were dropped off, collected Dad's car, and drove home. Sometimes, I fell asleep in the coach; I swayed but fortunately never fell into the aisle. Builders were used to the long, gruelling hours of manual labour. On occasions I remained on the coach into Wigan where I met friends, including Sylvia Heath, and had a good time swimming – I had just enough energy. For at least three summers there wasn't a strike, walkout, or work-to-rule. Dad was a union representative, so he would have discussions with engineers over any grievances.

An important event in June 1967 was the London-based preaching mission of the late Dr Billy Graham (the well-known American Baptist preacher).[135] He regularly came to preach in Britain, at the invitation of churches. There were "relay centres" set up countrywide, including the Empire Theatre on Liverpool's Lime Street, where the service was shown live on the big screen. At that stage, I wasn't a practising Christian, but my sister Anne was. She knew about the arrangements for tickets, and – much to her surprise – I asked her about the event. I had experienced a successful year at university studying science, but spiritually I was searching – so I decided to go along, even though by then we were living outside Liverpool. That was more than fifty-five years ago. Billy Graham had an international ministry and was born the same year as Dad (1918); he was just forty-eight when I first heard him. I went forward publicly

---

[135] 'List of Billy Graham's Crusades', Wikipedia, last edited 24 March 2022. Accessed 8 August 2022 at List of Billy Graham's crusades - Wikipedia

to "commit my life to Christ". In the counselling room, I met one counsellor who knew my sister, and at a distance I spotted Barry Crown from Sheil Road School and then at the University of Salford. We would meet up again in my second year.

That August, I had a memorable holiday in Cornwall with Auntie Edie, her sister Auntie Nettie, and my cousin Alf. We set off in a coach from Liverpool's bus station (in Skelhorne Street near Lime Street) one Friday evening at 7.30pm. It took a long, slow route. Seats didn't recline, and there weren't toilets. After about two hours it got dark, so there was little to see through the windows. After many hours, my left knee ached a little (from the earlier rugby injury). The coach collected passengers and had two main stops at Cheltenham and Bristol. It travelled all night, and we snatched sleep as best we could. I guess we stopped for breakfast, but can't recall. Anyway, by Saturday noon, we reached sunlit Newquay more than sixteen hours after departure.

The guest house was nice, and provided breakfast plus an evening meal. We got our own lunch. Alf and I had a room in the ground floor annex. Back then, we didn't have the luxury of en-suite rooms, so we shared the nearest bathroom with other guests. Newquay had many shops, and cafés or pubs for lunch; although Alf was too young to drink in a pub. It was summer 1967 (the "Summer of Love"), with Scott McKenzie's record *San Francisco (Flowers in Your Hair)*, which we enjoyed singing while playing slot machine games near the beach. We enjoyed the sun, sand and sea. On Sunday, we attended morning worship at the packed Methodist church by the beach. An excellent holiday, followed by a long trip home.

That summer was also memorable for the Beatles' release in July of *All You Need is Love* – and the death of their manager, Brian Epstein, from a drugs overdose in London on 27th August. He was buried in Liverpool's Jewish cemetery in Aintree.

During the summer, Anne and I had attended the local Methodist church and then Bryn Baptist Church. The Billy Graham Association helpfully sent me a Bible study course and asked the local vicar to visit me, which he did. Before returning to Salford in autumn 1967, I was baptised as an adult believer, on Sunday 24th September 1967, by the Baptist church elders. Mum and Dad had had me christened, but I never was confirmed at St Margaret's Church, Anfield. Now I wanted to be baptised by immersion, just as Jesus' followers were in the New Testament. My certificate is headed: 'One Lord, One Faith, One Baptism' (Ephesians 4:5). Family, friends and neighbours attended the service. Bryn Baptist was an active church and over the years I went with members in the church coach to the amazing Keswick Convention in the Lake District, caravanning or camping. Once, we went to Butlin's holiday camp in Filey, North Yorkshire, for a convention.

Second year: 1967-68

Accommodation

I returned to Salford as planned. First-year friends had agreed to find us accommodation; so, when I asked for the address, I mistakenly thought this was our place. But it was a temporary stay till our house became available. I slept on the living room floor with my coat as a blanket. Dave Casey recalls putting me up when he was sharing accommodation with four other physics students: Bernard Cahill, Malcolm Darvil, Paul Forman, and Clive Hughes (from Oldham). In particular, the five of us stayed up discussing/arguing scripture after I had become a Christian (or "been saved") over the summer. Good discussions.

However, soon we moved into a large student house at 194 Weaste Lane, Salford 5. Six students shared the house: Alan, Larry, Geoff, Mick (third-year physics), Chris and me. I had my own attic room at the front of the house. Three of my housemates ran motor vehicles, but I only had an underpowered 80cc Suzuki motorbike. Our house backed on to the rugby ground so, when a try was scored, we heard the crowd roar. Often, we ran upstairs to look. We could just see over the spectators' heads to the pitch, but only part of the stadium was in view – a stand to the right blocked other views.

As a new Christian, I attended the university's Christian Union (CU), and the local Eccles Evangelical Church, where I was welcomed and invited to meals. On Sunday 29th October, I walked there for the morning service, but found it closed. Somewhat puzzled, I realised that the clocks had gone back one hour at 3am to 2am (to give more light in the morning). Rather than walk back, or hang around, I went around to Dave's flat and gave them an early wake-up. On one subsequent visit, I found some of them sleeping in the lounge, and a strong smell of gas (then town gas not natural gas). Scary – it could have been fatal – there were no carbon monoxide detectors then. A large leak was found near the gas fire.

Restarting studies

Restarting in October, my first-year studies seemed distant. Physics modules included: Einstein's Special Theory of Relativity; Electromagnetic Theory and Light/Optics; Electronics; Heat and Thermodynamics; and Quantum Mechanics. Also, we studied the challenging module Mathematical Methods in Physics (including Fourier series, Bessel functions and Laplace transforms).

We had a Social Anthropology module for our general knowledge. Staff originally intended to include assessment marks in our final degree classification. Who thought that was acceptable? Anyway, after student representation, there was a U-turn. We just attended the classes which had some interesting aspects in the content.

Heat and Thermodynamics was taught by a likeable lecturer (Dr Bernard Yates, later Professor), and the textbook was helpful, so we were well prepared. Electronics included valves, transistors and field effect transistors.

Mr Bialek taught us physics, including modules on Einstein's Special Theory of Relativity (special relativity on the relationship of space and time) and Vectors (using the small book *Introduction to Vector Analysis* by G. Hague). Further, he addressed philosophy of science. We looked at the basis of science, its limitations and related issues, such as religion and death. He was a slim man of medium height, who sucked peppermints so much that the pleasant smell lingered. He thoughtfully said to us students, regarding death: 'If after death you wake up in another world then you can't say "I shouldn't be here – Newton's Laws do not allow it," since Newton's Laws only apply to this world/universe.' Very interesting observation. Also, he commented that the module was meant to help us in later life if we became disillusioned with science and its achievements/limitations. He was welcoming and thoughtful, willing to listen, and he encouraged me to think through issues, which I did. When asked to write essays on the module topics, I addressed, 'Is there life after death?' I met up with him a few times in his office to discuss science and faith issues. My interests in science and faith stemmed from my decision that summer to become a follower of Jesus.

Initially, I attended Eccles Evangelical Church. But by 5th November I was attending Bethshan Tabernacle, a Pentecostal church in Crowcroft Road, Longsight, Manchester (now Bethshan International Church), after an invitation from chemistry student Jack Hibbert in the CU. Then Dave Casey decided to attend. Jacky Davidge from Wales and in our CU also attended. We made friends there, including Geoff Hague, who drove Jacky, Dave and me to Blackpool's illuminations one autumn, in his Morris Minor. On the way, we were stopped in Eccles by a concerned policeman, who saw Jacky sitting in the backseat. He thoughtfully wanted to make sure she was safe before we were allowed to drive further. But when we arrived, we found the illumination season was over – we'd missed them. Also, Bob Jones took me to the Lake District across the passes on his 750cc Norton motorbike (much better than my 80cc bike!). It was a great day, but I felt stiff.

For Rag Week, Alan Ryden and Larry Weaver, among many other students, did an overnight walk from Lancaster Castle to the University of Manchester, leaving at 9pm and arriving around noon. Dave and I were the support team, using Dave's car. It was a very long walk, but they did it.

After the assassination of President John F. Kennedy in 1963, two further memorable assassinations occurred. On 4th April 1968, the civil rights leader Martin Luther King Jr. was sadly shot in Memphis Tennessee, aged thirty-nine. Then in June, US Senator Robert ("Bobby") F. Kennedy was shot in Los Angeles, aged forty-two. Meanwhile, the Vietnam war saw rising US casualties.

In the UK, the Central Electricity Generating Board (CEGB) continued building nuclear power stations. Moreover, Oldbury Power Station (north of Bristol) began construction in 1962, and started generating electricity in April 1968. It was a new nuclear design, with a concrete pressure vessel. Unbeknownst to me then, Oldbury would become important for my future employment. (It safely produced clean low-carbon electricity for over forty-four years, and shut down in February 2012.)

Part 1 exams: summer 1968

Our second year finished with the Part 1 examinations, which contributed towards our third-year marks. Mathematical Methods in Physics was one three-hour paper on Friday 17th May (9.30am to 12.30pm), with five questions to answer from nine. Physics had four three-hour papers on Monday 10th

June to Thursday 13th June (9.30am to 12.30pm). Each required us to answer five questions from eight.

After the exams, we relaxed by rowing in Heaton Park, Manchester, and playing pitch and putt. Also, in June, Dave, his girlfriend Naureen, Harry Perry (from church) and I went in Dave's car to Snowdonia's beautiful Llanberis Pass to camp overnight. From there we walked some distance along the Pyg Track up Snowdon. I wore my DofE anorak. It was a dry, clear day, so we could see a long way. Dave, a keen photographer, took photos (which I still have).

Also, that summer I was in a team who went to support a small church in Kendall (Lake District) for one week. Six of us from Bethshan (Bob Jones, Harry Perry, Jack Hibbert, Keith Frost, Brian and I) travelled together, lived on church premises, led services, and got to know people. We ate at the Chinese restaurant, enjoying its three-course lunches.

Again, during that summer, our family drove to Angle near Milford Haven in Pembrokeshire, Wales, for a caravan holiday on the coast. Anne couldn't come, so cousin Alf came. Christina recalls that we went out to celebrate my 21st birthday by having egg and chips. But afterwards we realised that it was the day before my birthday! I recall the coast path, and the magnificent night sky with the Milky Way: little light pollution there. It was a long drive, but worth it. Now I could vote. Not until January 1970 was the age lowered to eighteen.

Finally, the CU supported the "International Friendship Campaign" in London, welcoming overseas students. For about one week, I enjoyed meeting them and giving assistance as needed, including visiting one student in hospital. During this period, I stayed with John Nicholson (CU president) at his family's house. Then back to study.

Third year: 1968-69

Accommodation

For a while, I rented a flat with Barry Crown and Dave. As committed Christians, we had similar interests besides academic studies. Barry was studying civil engineering. The flat was a short walk from the halls of residence in Oaklands Road, Kersal, Salford. (I visited friends there, and on Saturdays countless students squeezed into the hall TV room to watch *Doctor Who* on a small black-and-white screen.)

On the top floor, we had a living room/kitchen with a gas cooker, bathroom/toilet, plus one small bedroom with three beds. Compact. There was a fire escape at the back, to a car park for Dave's car. (I no longer had my motorbike.) Another time, Dave and I had accommodation in a small ground floor flat in Mandley Park Avenue, Broughton. We crossed the park to catch our bus. Later, we moved out and students moved in, but sadly they were burgled, and a friend lost all his hi-fi equipment, which wasn't insured.

Subjects… and space

We started third-year studies in October 1968. Most students continued with the honours degree and chose four modules (from five options) but two students, who hadn't reached the required standard in Part 1, took ordinary degrees with fewer modules.

I chose: Electron Physics; Low Temperature Physics, Nuclear; and Solid State. Electron Physics was challenging but we had a helpful book *Electron Physics: The Physics of the Free Electron*.[136] Nuclear was divided into (a) models of

---

[136] O. Klemperer, *Electron Physics: The Physics of the Free Electron* (Revised; London: Butterworths, 1961).

the atom's nucleus and (b) nuclear reactors. It included sub-atomic particles. Solid State had the benefit of bound notes from our lecturer (Dr Mervyn Black). I enjoyed nuclear physics most. We had a short module on computer programming (or "coding") for the university's computer using ALGOL (from "**algo**rithmic **l**anguage"). My module choices were guided by my interest in taking an MSc (see below).

As a change from academic studies, I went with other Christian Union members (men and women) to weekend house parties. In November 1968, we stayed at Cloverley Hall Christian Conference Centre in Shropshire (Dave took photos). It was a time of teaching, prayer and fun. John Woodside from the Universities and Colleges Christian Fellowship led the meetings. Another time (perhaps winter of 1967/68 during our second year), we stayed in a youth hostel near Buxton, Derbyshire (in the Peak District). As we packed to leave on Sunday, it snowed and the coach driver got to our conference centre but couldn't get the coach back out. We were stranded, and it was reported in national newspapers! So, we stayed another night and returned to Salford on Monday.

Soon, the Christmas holidays arrived. As we were having our family Christmas at Ashton, on Christmas Eve 1968 *Apollo 8*, the US spacecraft, achieved its first manned mission to orbit the Moon. Viewers, including us, saw Earthrise and the far side of the Moon. The three astronauts, Bill Anders, Jim Lovell and Frank Borman, read from the Bible: 'In the beginning God created the heavens and earth…' (Genesis 1:1-10).

As 1969 moved on, I chose my compulsory research dissertation with my supervisor, Dr Allan Craig. We focused on mathematical modelling of the death of cells that had been hit at least once by ionising radiation. Under his direction, I used ALGOL to programme the computer via punched paper tape. With a blank tape in the machine, I used a keyboard to punch holes in it as instructions. When finished, I rolled up the punched tape, completed a form, and placed them in a cardboard box in the computer block's outer room. The next day, I'd return for the results. Unfortunately, if I made a simple error, such as typing a comma instead of a full stop, the computer wouldn't recognise my instructions and would reject the tape. Back to the drawing board. I changed the error, spliced in the corrected code, and returned it to the computer room. It was a slow process. Eventually, though, I did the necessary number of computer runs (with different conditions) to derive my results, printed on large paper sheets which moved along with sprocket holes on each side. Programming became an art in precision, otherwise the computer wouldn't converse with me. After analysis, the results were written up and my handwritten dissertation was submitted. It included neatly produced sections of code with results. I waited to see if I had passed.

After the final exams, Dave and I came back to my parents' house in Ashton, and we found one ton of sand by the back garden for Dad to build his garage. As the weather was good, we made a huge sandcastle. It was relaxing and fun.

Then one day we students were assembled and given an end-of-course form with a broad range of questions, some rather odd. One asked: 'What was the most influential book you read while at university?' My honest reply was, 'The Bible.'

When the results were provisionally released (and later confirmed), we had all passed. With such good news, I telephoned my former headmaster Mr Toft and asked, 'Is that Mr Toft?' 'Yes.' 'This is Robert Dutch and I've got my exam results – I passed my degree!' He was delighted: 'Congratulations!' It was fitting that he knew his hard work and encouragement had borne fruit. Triumph.

What next? A professor explained: 'If you are thinking about the USA for employment, then consider getting your PhD.' Some chose the PhD route, including my friend Dave, and John Bingham. Two classmates (Tony Cork and Jerry

Bell) chose a Diploma in Management Studies. I went for the twelve-months taught Master's degree: MSc in Physics (the "Radiological Health and Safety" course). As an aside, US jobs had risks: getting conscripted to fight in Vietnam.

My BSc (Hons) was conferred on Friday 18th July 1969 in the 3pm ceremony. Mum and Dad proudly attended, and we had a reception and photos, including a course group photo (with eighteen graduates present, although twenty-four students had passed). It was a defining moment of achievement after all the setbacks with O-Levels, but the success was worth the sustained struggles and hard work. It was a surprise that I could understand, and enjoy, maths and physics.

To celebrate, Mum and Dad arranged a party for me at our home with friends from Bryn Baptist Church and university friends Dave and Karl Unitt. Besides refreshments, we played at conferring "degrees" of various types on friends present.

Two days after the university ceremony, on Sunday 20th July, *Apollo 11*, the US space mission landed on the Moon. On Monday 21st, Armstrong and Aldrin became the first human beings to walk on the Moon (Collins remained in the capsule). It was televised. The US had beaten the Russians.

Summer 1969

Again, I think I worked at Cantril Farm as a labourer, but I was looking forward to a major trip to Spain with the Christian organisation called Operation Mobilisation. I was in a men's team and our leader was the late Peter Maiden. We took the ferry to Belgium for training classes, and I took my driving test to make sure I could safely drive their large Volkswagen camper vans. I passed "first-class" so I was "licensed to drive" in cities or countryside. We drove through France and along Spain's northern coast to Galicia. Once there, we stayed in churches, with Christian families, or camped (e.g. on the beach). Sometimes, I slept on the front seat of the camper van. Once, we stayed overnight in a hotel being renovated.

We worked with Protestant churches and helped in distributing Christian literature. And we had books and Bibles for sale by donations. Speaking some simple Spanish was important, and I did my share (from what I had learned at Liverpool's evening class).

We were generally well received. However, this was still Franco's Spain. The authorities were wary of anyone who wasn't Roman Catholic. As "Protestants" we came into this category, although we described ourselves, rightly, as Evangelical Christians. The police had eyes everywhere. (We were warned not to change uncovered on even empty beaches, for apparently the police surveyed with binoculars and we could be arrested.) When we distributed literature, we were twice mistaken for a particular sect, and arrested. After our arrests, we were interrogated using interpreters (if needed), and at least once the police telephoned the local priest, asking about our activities. Fortunately, in both cases we were soon released but warned what we could and couldn't do. (Apparently, it was common in previous years for teams to be held for one to two weeks.) On the first occasion we were arrested, one of our team even managed to leave the arresting police officer a Bible!

In August while in Spain, we learned that British troops had been sent to Northern Ireland (NI). Thus began a very long and dangerous commitment by the British government to defend NI against the IRA. After some weeks, we returned from a very enjoyable trip. Arrests and accidents, yes, but the Spanish Christians were thankful for our work and prayers.

MSc studies: 1969-1970

Accommodation

I returned to Salford in September/October. Dave began his PhD while CU friends Rodney Townsend and Gordon Moxton were taking chemistry PhDs. I discovered via a friendly university janitor that his son's terraced house was for sale in Spring Terrace, Lower Crumpsall. It had two bedrooms, a living room, kitchen and bathroom/toilet. Outside was a front yard and rear garden. Dave, Rodney and Gordon arranged a mortgage for the purchase price (£470). I rented. We probably moved in during autumn 1969. Once, we had an infestation of cockroaches, but rather than use the poison DDT,[137] I kept a cricket bat near the front door.

Another time while we were at university, it poured down and when we reached home, we found the ground floor flooded from a local river that we didn't even know existed. Fortunately, the water wasn't deep, and we were able to dry the carpets and clear up the mess quite quickly.

Starting studies

Our Radiological Health and Safety MSc attracted six students, including two from overseas. A Mexican student started, but family separation was too much – he went home for Christmas, and never returned. Our friend Manu was Indian. He was hardworking and supported himself with a weekend night-watchman job. On Monday mornings, he was really tired but, give him his due, he continued the

---

[137] DDT (dichlorodiphenyltrichloroethane) was developed as an insecticide in the 1940s and widely used. However, concerns arose over its health and environmental impacts. It was banned in the US in 1972 and in 1986 in the UK.

course. He shared his humour and culture with us, and took us to an Indian restaurant in Manchester, where he explained the dishes and we had a great meal. As he was a Hindu, we had interesting conversations about religion, god(s) and Jesus. One student lived at home and travelled in by bus. Jeff, Manu, Paul and I lived reasonably close to university. In fact, I could easily travel home at weekends, as the Wigan bus stopped opposite the university. A connecting bus then went to Ashton. Alternatively, I caught a train; I couldn't afford a car.

My studies were financed by the Science Research Council, which paid the course fees and a living allowance, which I didn't need to repay. It was around £500 for the twelve months: more than my undergraduate allowance.

Academic studies

Our small course meant we had most classes in a cosy first-floor classroom in the purpose-built "nuclear block" or "hot block". Its official name was the Cockcroft Building, and its construction was completed around 1966. Dr Craig, who supervised my degree dissertation, was our course tutor.

Besides lectures, lab experiments and discussions with Dr Craig, we had an older, friendly lecturer (the University Radiation Protection Officer). He was knowledgeable and taught us about physics, legislation, and radiation detectors. Visiting lecturers covered other topics. We visited Manchester's famous Christie's Hospital, which treated cancer patients using radiotherapy.

Labs were used in the nuclear block for experiments with radioactive sources. For biology, we had another lab. One experiment I clearly recall was about blood being damaged by radiation. We were going to look at normal blood under the microscope. 'But where is the blood?' we wondered. 'You need to take a sample of your own blood,' we were told. Well, I had become a blood donor at university, but I was never told to take my own blood! 'What is the procedure?' We were told: 'Jab a "sharp" into your thumb on the pad at the fingerprint.' Well, we had some painful goes. Others were successful, but not me, even after multiple attempts. After each painful failed attempt, I was less willing to really harpoon my thumb, and so less likely to draw blood. In the end, I approached the lecturer, who remarked: 'You've probably got an unusually thick layer of skin just there.' 'Great,' I thought. We eventually got a drop out, but only because he did it. So eventually I saw my blood under the microscope. I can't recall what I put in my lab book besides the struggle. Fortunately, further experiments were less physically demanding, although intellectually challenging.

When required, we entered the heart of the nuclear block through an access-controlled point where porters checked passes. Once inside, I wore my film badge to measure radiation, donned a white lab coat and overshoes, then crossed the barrier into the radiation-controlled area. On exiting, I carefully removed the protective clothing to prevent radioactive material spreading across the barrier, and monitored to check that I wasn't contaminated. I also used the hand-washing facilities.

Our radiochemistry module included lectures and experiments in the nuclear block, using radioactive tritium as a tracer to investigate chemical reactions. It was necessary to use additional safety equipment. I found that having studied A-Level chemistry helped.

One facility I used for my research was the massive radioactive cobalt-60 source, which emitted penetrating gamma rays. Because of the very high dose rates (enough to give us a fatal dose!), access was restricted to authorised persons. I was trained on the safety procedures and authorised as a user, so I could enter the area unsupervised. The source was in metal tubes that went below ground to provide shielding but then moved above ground to expose it. For obvious reasons, the whole facility was in the basement and set behind thick walls for shielding. A large special protective window set in the concrete wall allowed me to look inside the facility. Outside was the large panel with interlock mechanisms to ensure safe and secure access. Basically, it had interlock keys that I operated in a timed sequence (a wall-mounted clock was used). Also, I had to move a lever to complete the operation. A ringing bell gave an audible warning.

Before entering the internal facility through the shielded door and the labyrinth, I would collect the portable radiation monitor. I didn't assume that all the procedures had happened correctly. As a precaution, I checked with the instrument that the source wasn't still exposed. Extractor fans removed the atmospheric ozone created during irradiation. However, I could smell it a little. Exit procedures were followed to keep everyone safe. I completed a logbook with access/egress details.

Assessments

Practical experiments, though valuable for learning, didn't count towards our degree marks; assessment was by exams and a dissertation.

We had three three-hour written physics papers from Monday–Wednesday 19th–21st May 1970 (9.30am to 12.30pm). I missed my early bus for one exam and arrived just in time, somewhat stressed. All exams were closed book (meaning no notes/books). We had to answer four questions from seven.

After exams ended, we started our research until early October. Again, Dr Craig supervised me. Often, my research included Saturday mornings, then I caught the bus home before returning on Monday. During our research we discovered everyone had passed the exams. Holidays had to fit around the research. Peter was married that summer and I attended his lovely local wedding.

One problem impacted on our research through no fault of ours. The cell housing the radioactive source was being painted. No exposures could be done until the paint dried. Unfortunately, the paint didn't dry quickly; then someone realised the wrong paint had been used. The repainting meant unexpected delays when we couldn't do exposures. Eventually, we returned to our research, and I wrote up in time.

My dissertation was: *An Investigation into Some of the Effects of Cobalt-60 Gamma Irradiation on White Mustard Seeds (Sinapis Alba)*. It involved using the massive cobalt-60 source. Another student worked on irradiation of bacteria. (We never did research on animals.) My methodology involved irradiation of batches of mustard seeds under different conditions and taking controlled measurements, in a fixed environment, to determine the effects. Today, the International Atomic Energy Agency (IAEA) is involved with irradiation of seeds to produce crops 'that can resist disease and climate change' and give better yields.[138]

For writing up, we didn't have laptops, just old-fashioned typewriters, but I couldn't type. Fortunately, a young lady (Sandra Heath – Sylvia's sister) volunteered to help.

During my Master's the main university club I was associated with was the CU. At weekends, I attended church services, mainly at Bethshan. When in Ashton, I attended Bryn Baptist Church; a good community with a mix of young men and women and older people. Teaching and worship were good, and the people friendly.

Salford is dear in my memory, as it gave me an opportunity despite my lack of an O-Level in a foreign language. And my

---

[138] Laura Gil, 'Accelerating Growth: IAEA Launches Plant Mutation Breeding Network for Asia and the Pacific', IAEA, 16 August 2019. Accessed 8 August 2022 at <u>Accelerating Growth: IAEA Launches Plant Mutation Breeding Network for Asia and the Pacific | IAEA</u>

university education wasn't wasted. I recall standing alone on The Crescent at Salford as my studies drew to a close, thinking: 'I have enjoyed my studies. Now I want to go into the world to work and make a contribution.' I looked back at the illuminated Maxwell Building with its bright lights on the banks of the River Irwell as they glistened in the slow-flowing river. Soon I'd leave Salford, friends, family and the Sixties behind, but not forgotten, for my new role.

CHAPTER 10

Moving South: Working as a Scientist and Starting to Settle

Early on, I began looking at employment options. The two main contenders were a job through the university "milk-round" or one at university.

My friend Manu told me that the Central Electricity Generating Board (CEGB) representative was coming as part of the "milk-round" looking for new employees, and that I should arrange an interview. There I explained that I wanted to be involved as a scientist monitoring for radiation. The interviewer filled in the paperwork. Some while later, a letter arrived, inviting me to an interview at Oldbury-on-Severn Power Station. I'd never heard of it but found it was near Thornbury, north of Bristol. I travelled down after my exams, and had an interview.

I also had an interview with our physics professor, for the vacant university radiation technician position with part-time PhD study. The job also covered other areas, such as fire and flood. 'Do you think you can do it?' the professor asked. I replied, 'Yes.' I discussed my choice with friends and family. Should I take the job at Oldbury, or the technician position with a PhD opportunity? Other friends were studying for PhDs, and it would be comfortable to stay. But was this the best choice? Salary wasn't a major factor. I chose the CEGB and a move south, where I knew nobody. Why? More opportunities for professional development. But I wouldn't be studying for a PhD.

Now I needed a car, as Oldbury wasn't served by public transport. Fortunately, a man from Bryn Baptist found a four-door second-hand Austin Cambridge (1500cc engine) at a reasonable price. Dad loaned me the money and I bought it. Car insurance was arranged, and Dad showed me how to check water and oil levels etc. It had its MOT (Ministry of Transport) test certificate.

So, one Sunday evening in early October 1970, after last-minute changes to my research, I packed up, said farewell, and started south with a roadmap, but no mobile phone, satnav or accommodation booked. Everything was fine at home. Dad worked full-time and Mum part-time. She worked evenings as a silver service waitress and later waitressing in John England's catalogue office for the managers, near Wigan Park. Dad and Christina used to pick her up on Fridays after work – he loved doing that. Christina recalls that she worked there for years, and Dixi (our white toy poodle) used to wait for her to come home, staying by the living room window. As he couldn't quite see her, he'd jump up and down barking to get a glimpse and we remember his white ears went up and down as he jumped so excitedly. Anne was working in the library, and Christina was still at school.

Health Physics Assistant

In October 1970, I left the North for the South, to be a junior scientist on a nuclear power station.[139] Peaceful use of nuclear power interested me.

After three to four hours and a drive of around 150 miles on the M6/M5 and the A38, I arrived in the dark at the Swan Hotel in Thornbury's High Street, and booked a room. The next morning, I drove to Oldbury-on-Severn Power Station, which stood against the skyline as a massive building with a central block and cylindrical shapes at either end (one per reactor). It looked attractive with its white cylinders and vertical blue stripes. It's visible from the bridges over the River Severn.

---

[139] Paul Morley, *The North (and Almost Everything in it)* (London: Bloomsbury, 2014). See his chapter on Liverpool: Part Seven 'The rest of the world rubbing off'.

At the main gate, after security guards confirmed my identity, I parked in the car park, a short walk from the administration block with its ground-floor reception area, near our Health Physics (HP) Department's offices. The receptionist-cum-telephonist had her small office there. A wall plaque commemorated the site's official opening by the Labour MP Tony Benn, on 10th June 1969. Stairs and a lift led to the first floor to Reactor Physics' offices. However, I was a health physics assistant (HPA) in ground-floor offices, to the right of reception. Along the left corridor was an office, photographic darkroom, and two labs where health physics monitors (Basil and Tom) did day-shifts.

The Health Physicist (Hugh Tresise) had an office. Next door, our office had five desks in a block by the window, for me and my colleagues: John, Edwin, Duncan and Tony. Filing cabinets lined the walls. The Assistant Health Physicist (John Westmoreland) had the far window desk, next to a HPA (Edwin). One vacant desk at the window was for the new HPA (Duncan Ford), who would arrive soon from Berkeley Power Station. My desk was next to his. The fifth desk was used by the health physics foreman (Tony Kirkham) during morning and afternoon breaks, when a trolley service from the canteen served hot drinks and snacks. In our offices, I was the youngest; unlike me, the others were all married. However, they were friendly, experienced, and good to work with. Chatting over a cuppa helped me to get to know my colleagues. My breakfast was often a morning roll!

HP chargehands (later foremen), monitors and changeroom attendants worked shifts, including nights, since the site operated twenty-four hours a day, seven days a week. The Reactor Building included a foreman's office, lab, and a room where film badges, to measure radiation, were stored and issued.

Edwin did my induction training: introducing me to people, procedures and plant layout. He was leaving soon for another job. After completing the paperwork, I received my film badge, was told the procedure for wearing it to monitor my radiation exposure, and shown the mandatory monitoring procedures when exiting the Reactor Building.[140]

Near our office was the lecture room, used for first aid training and the National Blood Transfusion Service: donors came and recuperated afterwards with tea and a biscuit. On the opposite side of the nearby canteen/dining room was the medical room, run by a nurse. We had annual medical examinations there when the doctor visited. Next to this, a corridor led to the vast turbine hall, offices, workshops and stores. Garages contained a fire engine and Land Rovers.

On my first day, I left early to find digs; staying in a hotel for more than a day or two would be expensive. I was in the staff salary scheme, but I didn't get paid for a few weeks. I relied upon my savings (no credit cards then). Admin staff gave me a list of places to try for digs and soon I found a nice house by the A38 in Rudgeway, not far from work. Later, I moved to a bedsit in Bishopston, Bristol, after responding to an advert.

My early plant familiarisation included the reactors. One was shut down for routine maintenance, requiring us to access the pre-stressed concrete pressure vessel to examine the boilers. I entered with a team. In a university lecture, we had heard about inspections, and we had been amused. Now it was my turn, in my first couple of days!

We collected our film badges and donned personal protective equipment, then went to the pile cap access point, where we put on respirators before descending via ladders through the concrete pressure vessel into the boilers/reactor area. As the temporary lighting had been removed, we used torches in the pitch-black. An access control team watched our entry, surveys and exit, so we returned safely. We followed procedures for undressing, showering and

---

[140] Film badges used photographic film and filters to measure a person's radiation exposure.

monitoring, to ensure we weren't contaminated. My entry was a valuable experience of teamwork.

In our department, my role included: (a) responsibility for the issue/return, measurements and records of radiation dosemeters, (b) gamma spectrometry of samples, (c) radioactive sources for testing instruments, (d) measurement and disposal of low-level solid radioactive waste, (e) environmental monitoring, and (f) airborne monitoring for asbestos. Involvement also included periodic emergency exercises. I worked with HP monitors, as did Duncan, complying with regulations and procedures. Also, we worked with staff at Berkeley Nuclear Laboratories, Berkeley Power Station and Stone District Survey Laboratory, up the River Severn. Site inspectors enquired about our work. One worked for the CEGB and the second for the Nuclear Installations Inspectorate (NII) – now the Office for Nuclear Regulation.

So, at the start of my career, I was involved in environmental monitoring (called District Survey). For example, in the fields around the plant, we did gamma radiation surveys and tackishade measurements (these were like sticky lampshades on high poles, that collected dust in the atmosphere). To reach our sample points, we drove the four-wheeled Land Rover as far as we could and then walked the rest of the way; I had a test to qualify as a driver. While walking, we watched out for cows and bulls. We even did river surveys during low tide, and collected fish for our radiation tests.

Our department's professional staff, including me, worked normal days Monday-Friday, typically 9–5:30pm. The disadvantage of this was in the winter, when we travelled to work and back in the dark, but then so did millions of people. Some staff were on a standby rota. Outside normal hours, they could be contacted for advice or, in an emergency, they'd be first responders. As a junior scientist, I wasn't on this rota.

For two to three years, I was involved in a City and Guilds

course on radiation protection (Stage 1 and Stage 2) that was introduced by the Oldbury Health Physicist for training chargehands, monitors and changeroom attendants. Stage 1 ran twice over two years, and this provided enough "students" for a Stage 2 course. Some staff lectured; I supervised lab exercises. It was run in conjunction with Gloucester College.

In January 1973, we had a film badge which appeared to have a high radiation exposure. I investigated this and discovered what had happened. It wasn't a genuine dose but was caused by local heat from a high-powered lamp. The Health Physicist agreed that I could publish a report (*An Investigation into an Abnormal Film Badge Exposure*) with my findings, and this was circulated in September to health physics departments in the CEGB's nuclear power stations.

Here I restarted my first aid, which had lapsed after my Duke of Edinburgh's Award Scheme. I passed an on-site St John's Ambulance course. Oldbury, as a large industrial site, needed trained first aiders and I was pleased to be involved.

In 1971, New Year's Day was still not yet a public holiday. On 15th February, Britain changed over from its old currency (pounds, shillings and pence) to its decimal currency; life was easier for many, but critics voiced concerns over rising prices. The Vietnam war continued with terrible losses on both sides. It wasn't until 1975 that the last US troops left.

Just occasionally, insulation in the turbine hall would ignite, and the local fire brigade would arrive quickly to help our on-site fire-fighters. The problem here wasn't radiation, but the asbestos lagging which provided insulation. When this was disturbed/removed, asbestos fibres became airborne and could be inhaled. I monitored the airborne levels and people wore personal protective equipment. Asbestos can cause serious and fatal diseases.[141]

---

[141] Health and Safety Executive, 'Why is asbestos dangerous?' Undated. Accessed 29 August 2022 at Why is asbestos dangerous? (hse.gov.uk)

Living in Bristol

After my Rudgeway digs, I rented a first-floor bedsit in Bishopston (Tyne Road) at about £4 per week. There was another bedsit next to it and the houseowner Doug also lived there (and later his wife). Although it was a big house, we tenants only had access to our own bedrooms and the shared bathroom. We weren't allowed to use the downstairs sitting room, kitchen, garden, or telephone. Meals were not included; we had Baby Belling electric cookers in our rooms (but no fire extinguishers). Fortunately, during the week I was able to buy hot meals in the power station canteen.

Bristol to Oldbury was a return journey of about thirty miles. To save petrol, I joined a car club with other staff, including Norman in Reactor Physics, who had an MGB sports car. Sharing with colleagues, we learnt about their work and families. Nowadays, with climate change and the need to reduce carbon emissions, car clubs are encouraged once more. Fewer cars meant less congestion and lower emissions – we did our bit.

One year, I took two Evening Institutes courses: car maintenance and judo. A black belt taught us judo at a local school. I joined the British Judo Association, and still have my record book with a photo. On 21st November 1972, I was graded in Bristol's Victoria Rooms (Whiteladies Road). After two hard fights with bigger men, my forearms and body ached from holding on so tightly, but I got my yellow belt. My judo registration expired in October 1973, and I didn't have any more gradings. My attendance fizzled out. It wasn't like Wednesday afternoons at university: I had to go out in the dark after working a long day. It was decades before I trained again in martial arts.

Church in Bristol

I joined the City Temple Church in Jamaica Street; an Elim Pentecostal Church. The minister was the Rev Ron Jones. He was warm and welcoming, and preached very well. In one service, he briefly interviewed me about my job as a scientist, and the environment. Moreover, he was musical, and started a youth choir that I joined for a while. The fact that I can't sing was overlooked, and I tried not to put others off. I made friends in the youth group and learnt more about the Bible and Christian life. I became friendly with the assistant minister, Rev Stephen Hilliard, and we met for coffee, chats and meals. One summer, Stephen and I had a camping holiday in Cornwall.

A married couple, Frank and Maud Tharme, looked after me and others. I often visited for Sunday lunches; Frank was a church usher and car mechanic (he had also been in the Second World War and recalled crossing the Rhine into Germany). He helped when my cars needed repairs. In fact, he helped me buy my second-hand powerful Triumph Vitesse. After Sunday evening services, we went to the home of Maud's sister Vi and her husband Lee (nicknamed Slim), for egg and chips.

The church ran youth camps along the beautiful Gower coast in Wales, and these were enjoyable breaks physically and spiritually, with Ron Jones teaching in the small chapel. Dormitories were basic but no problem, given "me Liverpudlian background".

University of Salford degree ceremonies

After I started at Oldbury in October 1970, I would return home some weekends to work with Sandra on typing my MSc research. I would drive up on Friday nights, and then drive back to Oldbury on Sunday. Eventually, my dissertation went to Salford via family and friends for binding and submission. Later, when the university confirmed receipt and sent information on the ceremony, I paid for my gown and took time off work. At Salford, I met friends for the awards. But there was a massive mix up! We weren't getting our degrees. 'Why not?'

Dr Craig explained about the external examiner. Except for Manu, we had submitted our dissertations on time, but a student from the previous year had re-submitted a dissertation. Unfortunately, the exterior examiner gave it priority; ours weren't marked in time. We weren't getting our degrees, and there was "nowt" we could do. So, we sat and chatted, then went home. Not satisfactory. Manu had experienced problems and delays with submitting his dissertation. Another staff member told him that his dissertation was good, and he should submit it. I think that's what happened, and he got his degree eventually.

We returned in July 1971 for the awards ceremony – a notable occasion for my proud parents. After almost five years, I had my BSc (Hons), MSc, and my job as a scientist. My friend Dave was doing his physics PhD and another friend, John Bingham, was also undertaking physics research. Eventually, Dave got his PhD.

Visiting home

I usually travelled home to Ashton on Fridays after work. Initially, the M5 section around junction 8 (with the M50 towards South Wales) north to Birmingham and the M6 was only two lanes: effectively, a dual carriageway, unpleasant to drive along in the dark, and congested. When it rained, spray from lorries reduced visibility.

Dave and Anne Casey were married in 1971 at Bethshan by Pastor George Stormont, and I was the best man. Occasionally, I visited them at Ramsbottom (north of Manchester) for get-togethers with friends from Bethshan, and John Bingham, from our university course. In those days, I still had my long Sixties hair and John's was even longer!

Sometimes I stayed home Sunday evenings and travelled back Monday. Dad woke me at 4.30am and after breakfast I left at 5am for the three-to-four-hour drive. In the early mornings, the motorway traffic was noticeably light. In 1950, there were 2.4 million cars and vans on Britain's roads but by 1970 this was twelve million.[142] Anyway, effort was required to focus on a potentially boring drive, often in the dark and with no CD or cassette player. Preventing myself from falling asleep was essential – I still recall one close shave, but no accidents. Initially, the motorway ended north of Gloucester, and I took the ring road (A38) during the morning rush hour. Then country lanes brought me to Oldbury for another week. I felt tired by the end of the day.

Postgraduate Radiological Protection Course

While at Oldbury, I received training from the staff, such as on the regulations around sealed radioactive sources. In 1972, as part of training, I attended the Postgraduate Radiological Protection Course at Harwell, near Oxford (2nd-27th October). This informative international course, with thirty-three attendees, had lectures, practical/lab exercises and visits. I stayed on-site in the nice accommodation block, which provided breakfast and evening meals. It was a short walk to our lecture theatre. For lunch, we had sit-down meals and talked among ourselves (networked). While away, I received a rent reduction for my bedsit.

---

[142] Andrew Marr, *A History of Modern Britain* (London: Pan Books, 2008), p.176.

1973: Events and visiting the US

In 1973, some crucial events occurred. On 1st January, Britain joined the Common Market. But this wasn't without concerns, and in 1975 a Labour referendum was held on whether the country should continue its membership or not. There was an overwhelming "yes" to continue; I can't remember what I voted. The troubles in Northern Ireland continued such that in 1973 Britain had 27,000 troops stationed there to maintain peace in the face of IRA (Irish Republican Army) terrorism.

Back at what I still called home... After Edna and Rob lived in Formby, they had moved to Wivenhoe near Colchester (where we visited them) and then, while I was still at university, to the US. In October 1973, I visited them. My passport entry has "Oct 01 1973" and included a "Non-immigrant visa" valid "indefinitely for multiple applications for admission into the United States", issued in September 1973 by the US Embassy. I got this visa because Edna was my cousin. I had tried in my undergraduate years to visit them in New Jersey but the chartered flight arrangements for students fell through. Now they were in Los Angles (LA), I booked a flight from Manchester to London and a long-haul flight to LA. It was my first flight.

I was travel-sick, which surprised me – I hadn't been sick since being a child. Anyway, I arrived in LA on a cloudy day after about eleven hours. By then, I was no longer feeling dreadful, thankfully, and managed to meet up with them for three weeks. Their house was in Los Palos Verdes Peninsula (on the hill south of LA), with lovely views from their back garden to Catalina Island. Actually, they'd only recently moved from a nearby smaller bungalow to this larger two-storey home with a double garage (6912 Lofty Grove Drive). It was still being fitted with furniture.

While there, we caught up on family times and saw holiday destinations, including Disneyland and Universal Studios.

We visited the beaches and had plenty to eat, at places called McDonald's (unknown to us Brits in 1973) and similar venues, including drive-ins. Driving on the left in big American cars was interesting. Having seen the US on television, the experience was so different from what I expected. Plus, Edna and everyone else was so hospitable! I was to visit again.

Fortunately, the return flight was better than the outward, but there was a connection problem with delays so I couldn't get my flight from London to Manchester, where my parents were waiting for me. I had the ticket transferred to a train journey. But without a mobile phone it was difficult getting a message to them at Manchester airport. Nevertheless, everything worked out and we met up. I gave them their boxes of American duty-free cigarettes. Unfortunately, after three weeks, my car in Dad's garage wouldn't start and we had to get assistance. This caused one day's delay in returning to work.

New opportunity and power cuts

After a few years at Oldbury, I saw an advert for health physics assistants at Hinkley Point Power Station in Somerset. It had two power stations: Hinkley Point "A" (then producing electricity) and Hinkley Point "B" (being commissioned). Their Health Physics Department had responsibilities across both sites. I applied, had an interview, and was offered a position. My friend Peter Schwemlein from our Bristol church obtained another position in the same department and started in late 1973.

By then, Britain was experiencing power cuts. Before I left Oldbury, I was driving my car and passengers home one dark night. Streetlights were out on part of the A38. Thanks to my headlights, I saw the car ahead of me and the beam of its headlights showed two horses appearing as if from nowhere. One passenger saw them and shouted, 'Horses!'

Then, like a slow-motion film, the events unfolded before us. The car in front couldn't stop, and hit one horse side-on! The impact sent it into the air as the car continued forward. Then the horse bounced on its bonnet and landed on the roof. Unbelievable! It straddled the whole roof with its front legs on the left of the car and its rear legs over the right, staying there momentarily, but the image is permanent in my memory. It damaged the car, including its roof. Then that horse came off the car, landed on its hooves, and was moving around in the road between the pavement and the car, somewhat confused, as one would expect.

For what felt like a while, with my foot hovering over the brake, I watched. Someone shouted, 'Brake!', which I did, but I was still approaching the other car, which was slowing down. The horses might move onto the pavement, leaving a stretch of road for me to stop safely, but would they? A choice flashed into my mind: 'Go left and possibly hit the horses (and you know what damage one just did) or carry on and possibly collide with the car?' In the split second, I selected the second option. Slowing down but not stopping in time, I caught the rear of the car. Fortunately, our seat belts (which we always wore) worked, and we stopped. I put on the handbrake and switched off the engine. We were okay, and didn't need medical assistance.

We got out and went to assist the other driver (also wearing his seat belt). When I reached him, he was semi-conscious. The horse's impact had bent the roof down, and cut his head. I switched off the engine and put on the handbrake. Using my first aid training, I checked he was still breathing, and I could see he was not bleeding much, so I didn't rush to move him, instead waiting for the ambulance. One passenger (Peter Hosegood) directed traffic around the accident. The police arrived and took charge. Our cars were taken away by recovery vehicles. Someone collected us to get home; possibly Peter's wife. Eventually, my car was repaired, but I had no transport for a while, and relied on others. It didn't put me off driving, but it was scary.

A day or so later, I gave my statement at Thornbury police station, describing the incident with the horse landing across the roof and actually looking as though it was riding it. The police officer was so amused by the description that he apologised for laughing – he hadn't heard anything like it. When I asked: 'Where did the horses come from and what happened to them?' I learnt that someone had let them out of a farmer's field and left them. Wasn't the field secured properly, I wondered? Why would someone do something as stupid and not think of possible consequences?

What about the horses? The police tracked them down and found that a vet was stitching one up as it was suffering from a few cuts. The injured driver received medical treatment. Thankfully, all in my car were okay. My head had just touched the windscreen lightly, and I had another slight injury. We were so glad it wasn't worse. I wasn't prosecuted for the collision, but can't recall if they prosecuted the culprit(s) who released the horses.

So why wasn't there road lighting? There was industrial action and strikes against the government. In early 1972, the National Union of Mineworkers (NUM) asked for a pay settlement of forty-five per cent, and when this was turned down, they went on strike. Andrew Marr notes it was the first national strike since way back in the 1920s – the government was unprepared, with low coal stocks.[143] After that dispute was settled, in 1973 the miners made another massive pay claim, with the threat of a strike. But this was compounded by the October 1973 Yom Kippur War fought between Egypt and Israel. When the Arab world was humiliated, it responded by limiting oil supplies to the West, and increasing oil prices. The Tory government, led by Edward Heath, responded with "panic measures". Petrol rationing was planned, with coupons produced and issued.

---

[143] Marr, *History*, p.337.

To save fuel, the national speed limit of seventy miles per hour was reduced to fifty.[144] That was the context in which I found myself in the dark.

Farewell to Oldbury

As a junior scientist, I learnt much at Oldbury, and appreciated my time there. Before I left, I updated the procedures for my successor. However, as it was some while before he/she arrived, colleagues tried to make arrangements whereby I could return and assist them, which I was happy to do. But because of the urgent need to commission Hinkley Point B, this wasn't permitted – I was needed 100 per cent at Hinkley. As a farewell gift from colleagues, I received a *Road Atlas of Great Britain* – useful as there weren't satnavs. I still consult it. I was looking forward to my new role.

Hinkley Point: Health Physics Assistant

When I arrived at Hinkley in January 1974, I stayed in the temporary contractors' site next to the "A" Station. My friend Peter was already staying there. It had small, individual, basic rooms with shared toilet facilities. But paper-thin walls meant noise carried. Anyone coming back late and making a noise could disturb the whole block. This happened once. The next day, the culprits were told to find alternative accommodation; things were quieter then. There was an on-site canteen (with plenty of food), and a bar. Fortunately, the "B" site was just a short walk away.

I joined a large Health Physics Department led by the Health

---

[144] Marr, *History*, p.340. He notes that in January 1974 with the three-day working week there were many restrictions. It was 'the darkest day (literally)' in Britain.

Physicist, Phil Carter, and the Assistant Health Physicist, Trevor Stocks. Our offices were on the ground floor of the administration block. My appointment was in the health physics commissioning team at Hinkley Point B Power Station (HPB), which was great for the experience it offered. HPB was the new reactor design called an AGR (Advanced Gas-cooled Reactor) and construction started in 1967. We were involved in the radiation protection role. Hinkley Point A Power Station was already producing electricity for the National Grid; this was the older "Magnox" type of reactor (now being decommissioned). Our small team of professionals was led by the experienced and knowledgeable John Edwards. He was great to work with, and very supportive. I learnt much from John and I was able to make my important contribution to seeing HPB commissioned. The team included Chris Fincher and later Mike Oldfield. Sadly, in 2014 John died during retirement after a short illness, but was survived by his wife (Kath) and children.

At HPB, I learnt about people, plant and procedures. My responsibilities included commissioning instrumentation for measuring the radioactivity in the reactors' carbon dioxide coolant during normal operation and blowdowns. (A blowdown occurred when carbon dioxide was discharged from the pressure vessel in preparation for inspections.) Further, I commissioned the instrumentation for measuring gaseous radioactive discharges and reported the results to the regulators. For future vessel entries and inspections, we determined how this could be done safely in a challenging environment. We did this before the reactors were operated in earnest and when the plant was not contaminated by radioactive material. Our department also did on-site carbon dioxide surveys to protect people from exposure, and checked contractors using X-ray machines or radioactive sources. Bob Atkinson was the deputy station manager who led the commissioning teams, and I got to know him through attending site progress meetings, etc.

My friend Peter obtained a mortgage for a newish three-bedroom semi-detached house in Bridgwater – a quiet part, far from its smelly cellophane works. I rented, and we formed a car club with an engineer nearby who owned a Morgan sports car. However, Peter didn't have a house telephone – it was too expensive. Many people lived without one and used the GPO (General Post Office) coin-operated street phones.

Peter and I began attending a small Elim Pentecostal Church in Bridgwater off the main street. We were made welcome by the minister, Frank Livings, his wife Alice (a schoolteacher), and the general congregation. It was here that I first spoke on Sundays and at mid-week Bible Studies. Later, I became a lay preacher with the Methodist Church, visiting village churches and a main church in Bridgwater.

I was pleased with my job at HPB. I also got my repaired car back. Until then, Peter gave me lifts. After I got the car, I drove north for the weekend to see family.

1974: Great losses and gains

Tragically, on 1st June 1974, the Flixborough chemical plant in Lincolnshire exploded (the UK's largest industrial explosion) – leaving twenty-eight dead and thirty-six injured. I recall that some people (and media) expressed concerns over nuclear energy, safety and the environment, but Flixborough demonstrated graphically that other large complexes were hazardous.[145] Initially, the CEGB's coal-fired power stations discharged vast volumes of carbon dioxide and chemicals that produced acid rain in Scandinavia.

But for me, this was the year of personal loss. In 1973, Mum became ill. She suffered over many years with a

---

[145] BBC News, 'Flixborough chemical explosion: New memorial to 1974 blast', 1 June 2019. Accessed 29 August 2022 at Flixborough chemical explosion: New memorial to 1974 blast - BBC News

smoker's cough in the mornings. Apart from that, she always seemed healthy. Once or twice while I was at Sheil Road School, she was in hospital for tests, but nothing came of those. But in late 1973, she had gone into hospital for an operation on a blockage, and was released to "recover" at home before further investigations. She tried to be positive and so did we, encouraging her to take the prescribed medicines. At home, although she'd lost weight, she got around unaided, and when the weather was fine she went into the garden. Mum had a lovely place to live as we waited for test results.

A friend generously offered to take me home many weekends. I was working at Hinkley Point and living in Peter's house, which meant the journey home was longer than travelling from Bristol. Fortunately, I met Alf McCann at our Bridgwater church. He was a long-distance lorry driver and had relatives in Oldham, north of Manchester. He often drove me to see Mum. This saved me driving the long journey (about 200 miles each way) alone. Leaving after work on Friday evenings meant driving some of the way in the dark. Alf was good company and we shared petrol costs. He kindly dropped me off, then drove to Oldham, and collected me on Sunday for our return journey.

But the test results weren't good. Mum had terminal bowel cancer. Mum returned to hospital but hope for her recovery was no longer tenable. She was comfortable there but only had a short time left in this world. There was no hospice in those days that she could go to. So, we waited. Rev Ron Jones from the City Temple Bristol kindly visited her in hospital while travelling home from a conference.

However, Mum found a Christian faith that helped her in her final days. She was an Anglican and a member of St Margaret's, Anfield, where she and Dad were married.

Mum lived a good life and was committed to her family and friends, their needs, and helping us all whenever she could. She worked part-time, kept the house tidy and clean, fed us well, and took us on holidays. Nevertheless, in her illness she began to search more deeply for the meaning of life and spirituality and found truth in the Bible, as revealed in the four Gospels. She believed that Jesus was the Messiah (Christ) who came to give us forgiveness of sins and eternal life. Through his death, resurrection and ascension, she could know that life. This new realisation greatly helped her with the assurance of God's love. She attended church when she could.

One Sunday, I was going to lunch at the minister's house with his wife. But something arrived that day: a telegram was delivered to me at Peter's house. Telegrams conveyed urgent and usually bad news. I didn't need to open it to know. It was from Dad. Mum had died on 30th June in St Helen's Hospital. She had her birthday earlier that month, when she was just fifty-three. Such a tragic loss so young! I went to the public telephone box and spoke with Dad.

I gave my apologies to the minister, who invited someone else to lunch in my place, and I drove the 200 miles home. Work granted me compassionate leave and I took some holiday entitlement to stay for a week. On a wet day, Mum's funeral took place at Bryn Baptist Church, and after the service she was buried in the graveyard at St Thomas' Anglican Church on Warrington Road, Ashton-in-Makerfield.

Mum lost her life to cancer aged fifty-three and her brother, Uncle Alf, had died from lung cancer aged forty-six. Both children died much younger than their parents (my maternal grandparents). In 1952, Grandad died of a heart and lung condition aged sixty-four; while in 1956, Gran had died from cancer aged sixty-three. I understand the fear of cancer.

Anne and Christina were living at home at the time. Anne was a librarian at Ashton's public library and Christina had transferred in 1972 from Cansfield School to Wigan Tech to study her A-Levels in biology, English literature, and sociology. They would support Dad. But it was tough for everyone, even though we knew that the cancer was terminal. Mum and Dad's friends Ossie and Joyce still lived next door, and supported us.

In September 1974, life improved when I met a nice young lady called Susan at Paignton in Torbay, on Devon's south coast. I had arranged a holiday at Paignton with my friend Rev Stephen Hilliard (former assistant minister in the City Temple, Bristol), who had moved south as the minister for two churches at Wimborne and Poole, near Bournemouth but we had kept in touch. Fortunately, his mother lived near Paignton, where an annual Christian conference was held for a week at Pontin's Holiday Camp. This provided accommodation, dining halls, venues for meetings and refreshments. Stephen and I stayed with his mother and visited the camp daily. During the same week, we met Frank and Maud from the City Temple. They introduced me to Susan from Newport (South Wales), who was at the conference with her mum Audrey and her friend Hettie. We hit it off and kept in touch. I visited her regularly over weekends in Newport as the M5/M4 motorways linked with Bridgwater via the (old) Severn Bridge.

Sue's mum Audrey had a spare room in her house, so I stayed at weekends. However, Sue worked in Hughes, Forrest and Evans (builders' merchants) Monday to Saturday mornings each week, so that gave us just Saturday afternoons to spend time together. Sunday was church attendance at Bethel Temple morning, afternoon and evenings: Sue taught at Sunday School in the afternoons. After the evening service, I'd drive back to Bridgwater. Weekends were pretty full!

However, in September, I started part-time studies. Our site managers supported staff development and advertised a postgraduate Diploma in Management Studies. I applied and was accepted on the three-year, part-time course at Bridgwater Technical College (extra-mural centre) through Bristol Polytechnic (now the University of the West of England) and validated by the Council for National

Academic Awards. We had one afternoon attendance each week during termtime, and stayed in the evenings until 8.30pm. The CEGB paid my fees and gave me time off to study in the afternoons, and to attend the annual one-week residential course. (The first year this was held in a hotel near the seafront at Weston-Super-Mare, Somerset.)

In December I went home for Christmas and I'm pretty sure that was when I caught the flu and was in bed ill – a nasty experience and I was exhausted. Also, it was our first Christmas without Mum and the four of us missed her sorely.

1975: Work and holidays

– Swanage and Yugoslavia

January 1975 marked a year since I had started at Hinkley. The very important commissioning work was proceeding on-site.

Our team was investigating "vessel entry". This was for man-access to the reactor pressure vessel after the reactor had been operating, and the inside was physically hot and contaminated with radioactive material. Led by John Edwards, we were researching the best personal protective equipment to use under those future arduous circumstances. We went down vertical steel ladders giving access to the vessel. This was shortly after I had flu, but I had returned to work and felt okay. However, although I felt well going down the ladders, my legs became wobbly, and I had to leave the vessel as a precaution. Recovery from flu takes a while.

Another area I was involved in was checking plant interlocks on doors and alarms to prevent inadvertent personnel exposures when irradiated fuel went through facilities.

I continued my management studies. I found the course material and lectures fascinating, finished all assignments, and took exams in June 1975 (such as "financial analysis and control" and "statistics"). In August 1975, I found I'd passed. Although eligible to enter the second year, I deferred one year, restarting in September 1976.

I think I took two holidays in 1975 – fortunately, the CEGB had a generous holiday allowance. First, Susan and I went on holiday with Dad and Christina to Swanage, on the coast near Bournemouth. It was, admittedly, a long way for Dad to drive, but they did it. We stayed in a hotel, or B&B, not far from the beach, and had a week with good, sunny weather. Our nearest beach section was the busiest part, but when we walked towards Bournemouth, we found a quieter part. It had a suitable sandy section a short distance from the water's edge, so we could swim or paddle. In the evening, we walked along the front.

Further, Peter and I planned to visit Yugoslavia for three weeks. Susan wasn't able to come, as she only had an annual holiday allowance of two weeks. But she did visit me for day trips at Peter's home.

Peter took his small Hillman Imp car, packed with the tent and other equipment, leaving just the two empty front seats. At Dover, we caught a ferry to Belgium, and camped the next night. We travelled into Germany, where we met Peter's friends and family. Peter spoke some German. His friends were wealthy, had a large house, and lived a good life. But we talked about their ongoing fear that the Russians would invade West Germany and they would lose everything. It was the Cold War, and it was dreadfully real for them. We saw Peter's relatives and stayed at a pleasant campsite by a lake. It was noisy and the insects problematic.

Then we drove from Germany to north Yugoslavia, where we camped in different locations along the coast. Putting up the tent in the heat of the afternoon was a challenge! Relaxing, sight-seeing and swimming to small islands off the coast in the warm water were all so enjoyable. But we always took a small inflatable with us, in case of cramp or worse. Once, we woke up in the night with stomach-ache, and sprinted to the toilets. Thankfully, this wasn't an ongoing problem. Staying in the tent in the morning wasn't possible – it was too hot.

Eventually, we left Yugoslavia for Italy (stopping for pizza and ice cream in a small restaurant) and Switzerland (or Austria?). We camped up in the mountains at a lovely site, but it was a contrast to hot Yugoslavia. We had our sleeping bags and inflatable Lilo beds on the ground sheet, but it was so cold overnight – even in August. Furthermore, Peter's Lilo was leaking, so through the night I heard him blowing it up. During the night, I put on additional clothes and by morning I had my anorak on but still it was too chilly. Imagine our surprise when we used the toilets in the morning, to find they were warm: we wished we'd slept there instead.

Peter drove on and the following night we pulled off the side of the road to sleep. We didn't camp. Instead, we slept soundly in the front seats. We reached Germany, stayed with Peter's relatives, then caught the ferry to Dover and headed back to Bridgwater.

During this time, we hadn't been in contact with anyone in England. However, before I left on holiday, Susan had put some letters in my luggage for me to open throughout our holiday. That was a nice thought! So, I read these with interest (we still have them). I didn't keep a diary of the holiday, which I regret now. But I did get some good photos. Sadly, in the 1990s Yugoslavia descended into civil war. In 2021, I read a more accurate account of the conflict than that shared previously by the Western media.[146]

In 1975, my sister Anne married John Elton at Bryn Baptist Church, and they set up their own home. Sue came to their wedding with me. Christina stayed with Dad in Ashton.

In summer 1975, Peter and I made a large sign: "Free

---

[146] John R. Schindler, *Unholy Terror: Bosnia, Al-Qa'ida, and the Rise of Global Jihad* (St. Paul, MN: Zenith Press, 2007). When writing, he was Professor of Strategy, US Naval War College.

Georgi Vins! Religious Freedom in the USSR", and joined a Christian march in London on a hot day, to demonstrate for religious freedom. Vins was a Baptist pastor and leader who was persecuted and imprisoned for his faith. In 1975, he was sentenced to five years' imprisonment and five years' exile.[147]

For a while, I had saved to buy a house. Then in 1975 – the year our professional staff had around a thirty per cent pay rise – I got my first mortgage for a link-detached house at 20 Puriton Park, Puriton, near the M5 motorway junction 23 for Bridgwater. I exchanged on 4th November 1975 for £11,000. This rise was fantastic. I knew the nation had a serious issue with inflation but fortunately our employment terms and conditions meant we were given corresponding pay rises.

For professional development, I attended company courses and occasional conferences. In late 1975, I attended the four-week "Introduction to Nuclear Power" course at the Nuclear Power Training Centre adjacent to Oldbury Power Station. Around fifteen professional staff attended. Hotel accommodation was provided at Stone in Gloucestershire on the A38 and a coach ferried us daily. We had lectures, practical activities and visits. It was assessed, so it was important to learn the material. Fortunately, I'd studied nuclear physics in my BSc (Hons). I passed.

A one-week course immediately followed this in December 1975 at the CEGB's Management Centre in Buxton, Derbyshire. It included two trade union officials from our department and me. Its focus was on management-union issues, not nuclear power. So, after seeing Susan over the weekend, I nervously drove there by myself in the fog one Sunday evening. Although I started on the M5, the conditions were too hazardous because of speeding motorists overtaking me in the fog so, I left it for the slower but safer A38.

---

[147] Felix Corley, 'Obituary: Pastor Georgi Vins', *The Independent* 17 January 1998. Accessed 29 August 2022 at Obituary: Pastor Georgi Vins | The Independent | The Independent

1975: Moving to Puriton

Puriton Park was a small new estate, with a selection of brick-built three- and four-bedroom houses with open-plan front gardens. Some Hinkley staff lived there already, including John and Sue Weston. John was also a HPA in our department and his wife Sue was a scientist in reactor physics.

My house, 20 Puriton Park, was a linked detached; the garage was linked to the neighbour's garage. It had a porch before the main door into the hall. The ground floor had a cloakroom, lounge/dining room, kitchen, and toilet. The lounge/dining room walls were yellow, and the carpet was red (it reminded Sue's sister Wendy of "custard and jelly"). A basic kitchen had Formica worktops, a sink and some units, but no built-in white goods. The hall stairs went to the landing (with an airing cupboard), three bedrooms (two with built-in wardrobes) and a bathroom/toilet (no shower). From the back windows over my small garden, I could watch the farmer and his cows trekking to the milk shed twice a day. The large front lawn had an adjacent tarmac drive to the garage, with views over a quiet street. The garage space was great for doing some car maintenance!

There was a gas central heating unit for warm air heating. With no white goods, I needed a cooker, and quick. A colleague gave me a free refrigerator. Dad gave me a matching smart mahogany table and chairs from his home – although I don't recall how he got them to Puriton from far-off Ashton. I bought wall units, etc. Initially, I slept on a mattress on the floor. The previous occupants left a pram, which I gave away to Mrs Thame in Bristol, for her daughter. There wasn't a telephone, so if someone from work needed me, they rang a colleague along our street, who walked down with the message. Then I'd use the public telephone box to call back.

Puriton had a few shops, a church, and a garage for car

maintenance and the annual MOT test for vehicle safety. It was on a bus route to Bridgwater, which helped. Along a road was the Royal Ordinance Factory (where government munitions were manufactured for the armed services), which I could see from my house. Fortunately, there weren't any health and safety issues or explosions while I lived nearby.

At night, I saw vehicle headlights on the M5 motorway as it wound its way north to south. However, while I lived in Bristol, the bridge section between junctions 18 and 19 across the River Avon was under construction. So, vehicles used the A38 road for a while. Summers were bad as holidaymakers drove to Cornwall. The A38 at North Petherton was often a bottleneck on Saturdays.

When Dad and Christina visited me, Dad, as a bricklayer, inspected the brickwork on my house. One summer we drove to Newquay (Cornwall) for a short hotel break. It wasn't unusual for single men to buy houses/bungalows. Peter had a house, and our car-club friend owned a bungalow. As I had only met Susan a year earlier, I didn't ask for her view on the property.

1976: Hinkley, home and happiness!

Our team continued its commissioning work as the time drew nearer for generation. Sometimes we worked outside office hours, and I recall returning late and staying at John Edwards' home overnight when Kath looked after us – evening meal plus bed and breakfast. Another time on a Sunday morning after commissioning all night, I returned to my house in Puriton, lay on the bed, and fell asleep while the local church bells rang for morning worship.

Thankfully, HPB began generating clean, low-carbon electricity on 5th February 1976, when I was present and proud of our site's achievements. It was the first AGR in the UK to generate electricity. Since then, it safely produced low-carbon electricity for forty-six years, which is over fifteen years beyond its initial expected life. But in August 2022, it was finally closed down, having reached the end of its life as the UK's most productive nuclear plant.[148]

That winter of 1975/1976, we had local weather conditions with some massive snow falls, but staff managed to keep Hinkley Point A Power Station generating electricity. In summer 1976, Britain had a very long heatwave (reaching record temperatures), with droughts and water restrictions followed by floods. We sweltered in our offices while foremen came in wearing shorts. After work, I went with a friend to Bridgwater's Lido on Broadway – an outdoor swimming pool (demolished in the 1980s). It was packed, there was hardly enough room to move or swim, and it had smelly changing rooms; but it was just what we needed!

Importantly, after a couple of years "courting", in May 1976, I popped the question and Sue and I became engaged. We chose a nice diamond ring. Sue's mum, family and friends made the arrangements, and we were married in Newport on 9th October 1976 at her church (Bethel Temple, Stow Hill) by the minister Rev Eric Dando. Friends and relatives came to our happy day and to the reception in a hotel on the edge of Newport (now the Holiday Inn opposite the Celtic Manor).[149]

We had four bridesmaids: Linda (Sue's best friend), Christina (my sister), Debbie (cousin Edna's daughter, who came from LA with her family), and Wendy (Sue's sister). Mum sadly had died so she never met Sue. The family photo on the church steps shows Susan and me; the bridesmaids; Sue's mum and dad (Audrey and Frank) with my dad and Auntie Bel. Another shows my sisters (Anne with her husband John; Christina with a boyfriend); Dad (Stan);

---

[148] Dave Harvey, 'Hinkley B: UK's most productive nuclear power plant closes', BBC News 1 August 2022. Accessed 29 August 2022 at Hinkley B: UK's most productive nuclear power plant closes - BBC News

[149] In 2018 Bethel Community Church was gutted by fire started in an adjacent nightclub. Rebuilding started in 2020.

Auntie Bel; Auntie Edie; Cousin Edna with her children (Andrew, Debbie and Steve) and finally Mr Atkins, Edna's father-in-law. Tragically, her mother-in-law (Mrs Atkins), whom we knew, had been killed in a car crash.

Our first night, we stayed in Puriton. When we looked out the next morning, we saw a clothes line with white washable hanging nappies across the front of the house with other items! We guessed it was friends from Hinkley that came silently in the night – but nobody owned up. Our ten-day honeymoon followed quickly after, as we flew from Cardiff Airport to Majorca. We had a smart hotel with a balcony overlooking the Mediterranean Sea. It was quiet and usually sunny in the morning, overcast in the afternoon. Bad weather one evening meant the hotel lost its electricity, and trying to find our room in the dark was challenging. The outside swimming pool was perishing. After a short time, I had to dash into the hotel shower to warm up! It was a good honeymoon with a pleasant hotel and food, day trips, walks along the beach in the sunshine, a trip along the coast on a hired tandem, scary only when we came back too quickly down the local hill (no helmets).

When we arrived home, Sue settled in and bought us some nice new furniture: a long dressing table, double bed, and a wonderful light-brown leather three-piece suite for our lounge. It began to look like home! There wasn't much painting to do. We started to learn about gardening. Sue met the neighbours and the church folk. In fact, she formed a little group of church ladies led by Miss Blackmore with Mrs McCann, and learnt how to make small teddy bears with moveable joints. Also, she helped out with a children's church group. Moreover, she was more musical than me, and when I preached on the Methodist circuit, she accompanied me. She gave advice on hymns and sang in tune – I still can't, even though I grew up in Liverpool during the Swinging Sixties. Plus, she'd tell stories to children. We complemented each other.

Eventually, Sue started contract office work. It was somewhat different from her previous full-time job in Newport, but she gladly got on with it. At first, we had two cars: her Hillman Imp, and my Triumph Vitesse. But we reckoned one was enough. Peter bought mine, and we kept Sue's economical one. I travelled in a car club, and there were local buses.

One year (1976/77?), Auntie Edie visited. She had moved out of Liverpool under the city's slum clearance programme in the late 1960s. Rather than move to the new dwellings at Cantril Farm (where I had worked with Dad during university holidays), she chose a high-rise flat in Croxteth on the edge of the East Lancashire Road with her son Alf, who recalls: 'she was fed up of looking out of the kitchen window at walls', so chose the high rise. We visited Auntie Edie there, and I must say she had magnificent views from her Altbridge Park flat (ninth floor).

Auntie Edie had many happy US holidays visiting her daughter Edna, Rob, and their children. I enjoyed her showing me the photos when she returned from America. Sadly though, Auntie Edie developed problems and went blind through pressure build-up in her eyes (glaucoma). It was an inherited disease, but it seems she didn't know enough about her past to have this potential problem identified in time. Subsequently, I remember Edna and her children being routinely checked to ensure that they did not develop the same devastating condition.

We invited Auntie Edie to visit, possibly some weeks after the wedding. She was brave enough to make the trip alone on public transport, and we greatly admired her for it. She travelled the long distance from Liverpool on the coach into Bridgwater. But somehow her coach arrived before we did and when we arrived, we saw Auntie Edie sitting patiently by herself waiting in the quiet coach station. 'I knew you would turn up, so there was no need to worry!' What an amazing attitude.

It was her birthday (born 16th November 1916) when she visited. We had a small fold-up table in the kitchen – just enough space – so we sat around it for the meal. Then we had a small cake with a single candle on it. We lit it, sang "Happy Birthday" and, holding the cake a little distance away, we asked her to blow it out, knowing she couldn't see precisely where it was. Well, she blew hard, but simultaneously her head shot forward over the burning candle. Fortunately, we quickly separated her and the candle before she was burnt. The flame had singed the hair in her nostrils! A moment later, we were laughing loudly. Edie had a good sense of humour. After her holiday, she got home safely. Sue's family and friends also visited, and one year her dad bought us our first TV.

After a few years at HPB, I moved under job rotation to widen my experience, and became the HPA for the on-site laboratory that served the "A" and "B" sites. We measured site air samples, issued dosemeters, measured airborne asbestos, and had responsibility for portable health physics instruments, including calibrations. Here we bought a programmable calculator, which I programmed. Further, we had some dose records kept by a link online (novel back then) and again I did some programming – what I had done at university gave me the necessary confidence.

I had deferred my Diploma in Management Studies, but decided to restart on Stage Two in September 1976 for two more years under the previous arrangements. These were valuable years. I attended the annual week away, but now at the nice new management centre at Bristol Polytechnic (where I used my first aid when a student had epileptic fits). One year, I was to travel from Puriton to Bristol, and it snowed hard overnight so that I couldn't drive off our estate. Sue's dad (Frank) offered to drive from Newport in South Wales and collect us. Unfortunately, his car broke down and he was rescued by the AA, who then collected us, and we headed to Bristol with his car on the low-loader. He got home and I got to my residential week!

Our department was providing radiological protection for the whole site. Professional staff with sufficient experience of the nuclear plant, procedures and safety rules were interviewed at the company headquarters, Nuclear Health & Safety Department, before becoming Accredited Health Physicists. I successfully passed the London-based interview, and was appointed as an Accredited Health Physicist in writing on 25th April 1977 by the station manager, P.T. McInerney. This enabled me to give formal written advice in Health Physics Certificates. Moreover, during my time at Hinkley I became a member of the Institute of Physics and the Society for Radiological Protection.

1977: Second honeymoon

For our honeymoon, we had hoped to visit California, but things didn't work out, so we had a superb "second honeymoon" in summer 1977, visiting Edna and her family (Rob, Andrew, Debbie and Steve) in LA. Coincidentally, it was the Queen's Silver Jubilee, commemorating twenty-five years since her accession to the throne.

We had fun at home, food at restaurants, and joy at beaches. Our visits included: Disneyland, Los Angeles Farmers Market, Knots Berry Farm, Marineland, Palm Springs, TV studios, Universal Studios, and an LA court in session (a murder case). Then Sue and I hired a car and drove north along the Pacific Coast Highway to San Francisco, where we visited the piers, Alcatraz prison, and travelled across the Golden Gate Bridge to Muir Woods (for the giant redwoods). On our return, we came inland through Bakersfield, seeing the Kern County Museum with its outdoor historic exhibits. Magnificent! After our return flight, Sue's dad collected us at Heathrow, and I drove us home to Bridgwater.

1978: Family visits, Dad retires, and I learn New Testament Greek

My cousin Edna often visited England with her children. In summer 1978, Andrew and Stephen stayed with us for a few days. They played war games with my small Airfix Battle of Waterloo soldiers (which I had collected and painted from my time in Bristol). We had a battle ground and farm buildings and sometimes they'd play into the night. During that trip, they played hide-and-seek in our home, but we couldn't find them. Eventually, they were located on the shelf in the airing cupboard behind bedding. It was a good place, but we wondered why the shelf hadn't collapsed.

That summer, when I finished my Diploma in Management Studies, Sue and I drove with Andrew and Steve to the University of Bath for a viva on my dissertation to see if I would be awarded a distinction. It went well and I got it – certificate dated 12th July.

In 1978, aged sixty, Dad retired through ill health, with back problems from being a bricklayer. He'd had medication from his GP, but it turned out the problem was a slipped disc, so he wore a lower back support. Unfortunately, he had no private pension; although he had worked for Wimpey's over many years, he wasn't staff. So, he lived on a disability pension. Fortunately, Christina still lived with him in Ashton.

I became interested in New Testament Greek. Why? Well, the part of the Bible called the New Testament (which includes the Gospels about Jesus) was written in Greek. In preparing my talks, I sometimes saw references to Greek. Also, I met people who quoted "what the Greek says", but I would wonder if they were right.

My interest in Greek was unusual, considering I didn't learn languages at school or university. Nevertheless, I found that London Bible College (now London School of Theology) ran a distance-learning course using J.W.

Wenham's *The Elements of New Testament Greek*. I enrolled and found the lessons and tutor helpful. The book was understandable, with a good "Introduction: English grammar". Lesson notes were received, and I sent work to my tutor. He returned it marked with model answers. My first lesson was received by him on 3rd July 1978.

Hinkley back to Oldbury

In 1978, I saw an interesting vacancy for a tutor at the Nuclear Power Training Centre next to Oldbury Power Station, where I had worked previously. I applied and was offered the promotion! In my last weeks at Hinkley, I updated documentation. Sue and I travelled to the Bristol/Thornbury area and looked at houses. We decided on one in Bristol and by 19th January 1979 had a surveyor's report. Our Puriton house was put on the market for £22,500 (freehold) while I travelled daily. I left Hinkley in January 1979, much wiser than when I arrived, to start a new position. And I continued learning Greek: by 21st May 1979 I would complete Test XV.

CHAPTER 11

Scientist, Tutor, Engineer, Theologian

"Winter of discontent" 1978-79

While at Hinkley, and when I moved to Oldbury in early 1979, the country experienced the UK's "winter of discontent", because of significant industrial disputes and serious strikes under the Labour government led by Prime Minister Jim Callaghan. There was social chaos and heartless actions: schools were shut, and ports blocked. The rubbish rotted and bodies were unburied. Things were bad in Liverpool, with more than 300 bodies awaiting burial.[150] People watched the news and experienced it: discontent damaged the nation. Historian Dominic Sandbrook calls 1974-1979 *The Battle for Britain*.[151]

After the government was defeated in March, an election followed. Also that month, the Irish National Liberation Army assassinated the Tory MP Airey Neave, using a car bomb at the House of Commons car park.[152]

In May, a major change occurred when Conservative Margaret Thatcher became Prime Minister – Britain's first woman PM. She revolutionised the country. In August, an IRA bomb killed Earl Mountbatten on his boat in Ireland.

---

[150] Andrew Marr, *A History of Modern Britain* (London: Pan Books, 2008), pp.373-375.

[151] Dominic Sandbrook, *Seasons in the Sun: The Battle for Britain, 1974-1979* (London: Penguin Books, 2013). This is Sandbrook's fourth volume in his history of post-war Britain when: 'Far more than, say, the late 1950s or the 1960s, this was an intensely politicized period' (p.xxi).

[152] Stephen Kelly, 'The life and death of British spy turned politician Airey Neave', updated 28 March 2019. Accessed 5 October 2022 at <u>The life and death of British spy turned politician Airey Neave (rte.ie)</u>

And we were still in the Cold War. These were the conditions in the year we moved.

Nuclear Power Training Centre (NPTC)

Travel and moving

I started as a tutor at the NPTC on Monday 5th February 1979, travelling daily (Monday-Friday) in our little Hillman Imp (a 1000cc rear engine car). The training centre occupied the same nuclear licensed site as Oldbury Power Station. Fortunately, it was motorway (M5) until junction 16 at Almondsbury (north of Bristol), then the A38 north to Thornbury and along country roads to Oldbury. One Friday afternoon, during our weekly staff meeting led by the principal Peter Myerscough, it started to snow. I left early for home, but snow on the engine meant the car wouldn't start. As I opened the engine to dry it, more snow blew in. Fortunately, somebody had a can of WD40 and using this spray, quickly dispersed the snow. I reached home without being stranded.

I made this journey, forty-six miles each way, until we moved on 8th May. We were trying to sell our house and move to a semi-detached in west Bristol, but our buyers had repeated troubles in their chains, and dropped out. Eventually, someone completed. The procedure took so long that my company gave us a "bridging loan", for which we were so grateful (they paid the interest payments on our Bristol house while we paid the mortgage at Puriton). Although living in Bristol, we still maintained our Puriton house until we exchanged contracts and completed in mid-September. When we sold it, its purchase price had jumped from £11,000 (July 1975) to £21,500; but house prices had risen in Bristol too.

The CEGB was generous with the bridging loan, but they also paid for travelling expenses (at 6.5p/mile); estate agent and solicitor fees for house sale and purchase; surveyor/valuation expenses for the Halifax Building Society; house removal expenses; and a settling-in grant.

Facilities and courses:

working as a tutor

The NPTC had opened in February 1973 and provided training for professional staff at the CEGB's nuclear power stations. I had even attended a four-week "Introduction to Nuclear Power" course there while I was working at Hinkley Point Power Station. Its facilities included: three lecture rooms (holding twenty students each), a project laboratory, a simulator hall, library, seminar room, and offices.

Initially, operations engineers completed the "Introduction" course, followed by plant familiarisation and either a "Magnox Operations" course or an "AGR Technology" course' (each four weeks), depending on whether they were working on Magnox reactor power stations or Advanced Gas-cooled Reactor (AGR) power stations. We also ran a "Nuclear Safety" course and various other courses. In 1979, the training centre staff included: the principal (Peter); three senior tutors; six tutors (including me); two reactor simulator engineers, and three administrative staff. Visiting speakers complemented us and an Advisory Committee oversaw the courses and made recommendations. Over the years, NPTC expanded its facilities, courses and staff to meet the training needs. Staff joined us on secondments.

As tutors, we arranged courses, booked speakers, and managed the courses when they were running. We produced handouts, lectured, assessed students, and developed new courses. When I arrived, I developed a "Radiological Safety" course to provide training for operations engineers who had responsibilities for writing and issuing safety "permits", including the radiological conditions to be observed. After this central training, the staff returned to their power stations and site-specific training on issuing safety documents.

My main role was in the Operations Team, led by Stuart Birnie, to commission the AGR reactor simulator for Hartlepool and Heysham 1 Power Stations (then under construction). These sites had the same plant and central control rooms, so one simulator served both. Once commissioned, we used it for staff training courses on reactor operations. Also, I worked in a team on the Hinkley Point B simulator and taught, for example: atomic/nuclear physics, health physics (radiation protection) and later fire protection. Over the years, I mentored new staff. We weren't a research institution, but a training centre where teaching was highly valued. However, the CEGB did have research facilities, such as Berkeley Nuclear Laboratories (later renamed Berkeley Centre) on the River Severn between Bristol and Gloucester.

As a Liverpudlian (northerner), one of the advantages of working on the reactor simulator or running courses was the link to Heysham (on the west coast near Morecambe) and Hartlepool (on the east coast by Stockton-on-Tees), both of which I visited. Returning from Heysham once, I was grateful I could pop in to see Dad, who was recovering from a heart attack. Visiting regularly was difficult now we lived down south. Further, I lectured on courses for staff at Trawsfynydd in Snowdonia National Park.

Tutors participated in professional development through staff training. For example, in March 1984 I was attached to the operations shift team at Hinkley Point B Power Station for six weeks, and in March 1991 I completed a one-week "PWR (Pressurised Water Reactor) Overview" course on the new Sizewell B Power Station. I also participated in site secondments, working with staff in the Health Physics Department at Oldbury Power Station.

As mentioned, a benefit of being in the operations section and commissioning reactor simulators was the opportunity to visit sites for meetings and training courses. I entered the concrete pressure vessel at Hartlepool, and saw the reactors/boilers being constructed. Another time, we visited Heysham 2 Power Station and I entered the reactor core in an early stage of construction. After my experience commissioning the simulator and training staff, I applied for Chartered Engineer status as a member of the Institution of Nuclear Engineers (now the Nuclear Institute). Following my application detailing my qualifications, I had an interview and was successful – scientist, tutor and engineer. I was so pleased.

In addition to my tutor's role, I completed first aid training at Oldbury Power Station and became an "Occupational First Aider". For this, we received additional training beyond the usual legal requirement for first aiders. We were authorised to use the first aid rooms and administer "gas and air". The site's resident nurse worked days Monday-Friday; but as the site operated around the clock, including weekends, and was some distance from Bristol hospitals, it was essential to have out-of-hours Occupational First Aiders. Once I administered "gas and air" to a tutor with a severe migraine. He was eventually hospitalised for a few days.

Sometimes during lunch hours, I went swimming with other tutors at Thornbury's pool, to improve my fitness. I received an award for achieving 1500m.

After years in the operations section, we were reorganised, and I joined a section led by Colin Chapman, as a health physics tutor with responsibilities for courses and teaching radiation protection, atomic/nuclear physics, reactor physics, etc.

Oldbury Training Centre (as it was eventually called) was a respected centre, and it was a privilege to work there. Before I started as a tutor, I complemented my physics degrees with a Diploma in Management Studies. This gave me considerable knowledge and experience achieved over the years. Moreover, I had studied distance-learning courses called "Modern Power Station Practice", taking modules in nuclear power and chemistry. Oldbury gave me the opportunity to train very many staff and contribute to safe operations at our nuclear stations. We were primarily training professional staff holding Higher National Certificates, Higher National Diplomas, or degrees. Sometimes, managers attended courses. Also, we ran short introductory courses for administration staff and courses in Glasgow for the South of Scotland Electricity Board staff. To save travel time, we flew from Bristol to Glasgow and stayed in hotels while running the courses. Occasionally, I helped organise and run on-site courses on radiation protection.

Family life

We moved into our semi-detached Bristol home on Tuesday 8th May 1979. Now Sue and I had enough space to grow our family without needing to move again. It had front and rear gardens, with a drive down the side of the house to a garage. A small porch led to the main door and the hall, with a toilet under the stairs. We had two reception rooms with original double-doors to make it into one large room. There was a breakfast room leading into a kitchen. Upstairs, we had three bedrooms and a bathroom/toilet, and on the next floor a loft conversion. In the hall was a telephone. At Puriton, we didn't have a phone for ages, until Sue's dad paid for us to have one.

We didn't have much furniture, but brought what we had. The suite fitted nicely into our rear room. The wall units I had bought went into the front room, but we had to buy more furniture. The lovely mahogany table and chairs that Dad had given me in the early days were in time given to friends Karen and Roger in Bridgwater. Sue's dad (Frank) and mum (Audrey) gave us for a wedding present a round solid wood table with chairs; and the little table at which we celebrated Edie's birthday went into the breakfast room. On the busy moving day, our new next-door neighbour Mrs Shaw brought us cups of tea. While we were in Bridgwater, Dad had bought us a small hardy fuchsia, which we planted next to our patio. More than forty years later, having survived harsh winters, it's a magnificent large red-and-purple plant – a reminder of Dad.

In Puriton, our house was relatively new, so we didn't do decorating or repairs, but our 1920s Bristol house needed attention – our surveyor gave us a long list of work. Dad pointed the front and side outside small walls. Downstairs rooms needed woodworm treatment. Guttering required replacing. The garage downspout needed a soakaway to be dug in the garden, which I did. The kitchen looked okay, but on inspection it was a patchwork job of pieces, and the units had no backs. The flat roof on the kitchen had a gash in it. So, Sue's dad once again stepped in, and funded a new roof and kitchen. Over time, we replaced the carpets and decorated. Little did we know that we would live there for more than forty years.

Somehow, we got to know the neighbours, probably through Sue, as I was working full-time. We made friends at church and they visited, as did family members. Dave Casey and his wife Anne also stayed, and we visited a cheese-making farm in Somerset.

When Sue and I first moved to Bristol, we attended the Mount of Olives Assemblies of God church on Blackboy Hill. The minister was Rev Warwick Shenton, whom we knew because he had been the assistant minister at Susan's church in Newport. Our daughter Laura was dedicated by Warwick in early 1980. Now we were three, and for us as proud first-time parents, life got even busier, especially with Laura's demands for sleeping and feeding! We were kindly invited by church friends (David and Lyn Gee with Paul and Rhoda Marshall and their children) to a September holiday with them at a caravan park near Bude on the Atlantic coast. We enjoyed our static caravan and relaxing with them. I recall swimming in the sea while Sue sat on a deckchair cuddling little Laura.

Studying Theology

Preliminary Examination in Divinity

1979-80

While working as a tutor, I finished my Greek distance-learning course with London Bible College (started 1978). What next? Back then, theology colleges prepared their students for the demanding University of London Bachelor of Divinity (BD) exams.

After Sue and I discussed options, I enrolled as an external student for four papers in the University of London's Preliminary Examination, covering New Testament Greek (two papers), General Introduction to the Study of the Old Testament, and History of the Early Church to A.D. 325. Again, London Bible College provided tuition. Taking the papers was a bold step for me. But with Sue's support and prayer, I started it around work, family life and church. Often, I studied before breakfast, read in the lunchtime at work, and used audio cassettes for learning Greek vocabulary.

I bought a *Greek New Testament* to study Mark's Gospel, and in summer 1980 I took four three-hour exam papers at Bristol Baptist College. The exams didn't allow use of Greek-English dictionaries. The papers required me to translate Greek texts into modern English or give comments, but one paper also had English sentences to translate into Greek.

For the Old Testament, I knew the stories. Fortunately, London University offered Saturday teaching, so I attended that with Rev Coggins. Early church history was challenging. Okay, in science I had learnt the history of scientific thought and discoveries, but it didn't help. The material was interesting but putting it together to answer questions was tough and required perseverance along with time management.

Then in the summer, a letter arrived. I opened it in trepidation: had all my studying been successful? Amazingly – yes! I passed, with my best grades in Greek – triumph. 'Not bad for someone who took multiple attempts at English O-Level,' I thought. Time to register for the main degree. It felt like I'd stepped into another world. Meanwhile, I continued enjoying being a husband, father, scientist, and tutor.

Relatives, holidays and live TV

Back in Liverpool, Auntie Bel and Auntie Edie were living in high-rise flats near the East Lancashire Road. Uncle Jim had died, so Bel moved by herself to 191 Randle Heights Liverpool 11. When Sue and I visited, we helped Auntie Edie (living in 95 Altbridge Park, Croxteth) by decorating, as she was suffering with glaucoma. My cousin Alf had initially lived with his mum. In 1980, we took Laura to see them. For Auntie Bel, this care had travelled down the generations: from rearing Dad, to me, to Laura; and we were glad Bel could cuddle her.

On 22nd November 1980, Alf married Amanda Daniel. We went to their wedding in the evening, where Edna and her children were present. But Auntie Edie was too ill to attend. That Christmas, Sue, baby Laura and I squeezed into our little car and visited Dad and Christina at Ashton. We visited Edie in hospital; it would be our final time of seeing her. On Christmas Day, while at Dad's, we had a phone call to say that sadly dear Auntie Edie had died, aged sixty-four. It appeared she had hung on until Alf married. We had a service in the cemetery's chapel and Edie was buried in the family grave with her husband Alf and our maternal grandparents. Edna's daughter Debbie attended the funeral, since Edna was in the US.

In summer 1981, we holidayed at Newquay, Cornwall, in a Bed & Breakfast. Laura was still small, and we had the top room of the B&B. When the seagulls woke Laura up early, how would we make warm milk for her? I don't recall what we did but somehow, we coped. Also, there was no attached bathroom/toilet; so, when I was ill after eating a mint ice-cream cone, I had to run down two flights of stairs to be sick in the toilet – and only just made it! Laura enjoyed digging the yellow beach sand and when we came home, she tried digging up our yellow carpet – without success.

While Sue was pregnant in 1982 with Jessica, our second daughter, our home was chosen for a live BBC TV Christian programme, *This is the Day.* By the Saturday before the Sunday broadcast, our home was transformed. Surplus furniture went upstairs and the double-doors between our reception rooms were opened. The back room had TV cameras with the cameraman Crawford (our church friend). The front room had seating and a chair for Warwick, who spoke. There was a table with bread and a candle (which I had to light live on TV). The street was full of vans, and a security crew watched our home, since the breakfast room window remained open for the power cables. On the Saturday in the nice weather, people used the garden and recorded prayers and Bible readings. We had multiple practices. Then on Sunday morning we were live across the nation. Our little girl Laura stayed with friends, as having a toddler in a live broadcast was too unpredictable. Warwick gave a good talk, and we enjoyed the service. The audience didn't know that one of the production staff was hiding behind our settee, able to secretly prompt us. Sue and I were also interviewed by the BBC Points West presenter Graham Purches, for the local news.

How did they choose us? Well, Warwick initially provided a list of church members' homes. It just happened that we were visited first, and the producer liked ours straightaway.

I asked if he wanted to see other homes, he replied, 'No, this is fine!'

Falklands War: April to June 1982

By 1982, Prime Minister Thatcher's popularity had diminished, but then came a change within months: surprisingly, she became our heroine.

An Argentinian dictatorship organised the invasion of the British Falkland Islands in the south Atlantic. However, Mrs Thatcher was determined to regain the islands. In May 1982, a decision was made by the war cabinet to land forces. The UK sent the fleet (over 100 ships) and 25,000 men. Many went to see the fleet sail on 5th April from Portsmouth – I recall a foreman at Oldbury going.[153] We watched the news with concern, seeing fighting, death and destruction with ships sunk. Colonel H. Jones was killed while attacking an Argentinian gun position. Although Britain recaptured the islands, the cost was high. I was pro-British but many, like me, were saddened by the controversial sinking of the *General Belgrano* by a British submarine. Over 300 sailors were lost. I could identify with both sides, given Dad's Second World War navy service.

Theology studies: 1980-1983

I continued my distance-learning degree in autumn 1980. Also, I attended Trinity College Bristol, for classes on John's Gospel and sixteenth-century Church History, which were given to their Anglican students in preparation for ordination. These were tough times for our family, fitting in serious

---

[153] See the YouTube channel Shatner Method: Dan Rather, 'British Armada Set Sail for War in the Falklands', CBS Evening News 5 April, 1982. Accessed 29 August 2022 at British Armada Set Sail for War in the Falklands - CBS Evening News - April 5, 1982 - YouTube

studies with family life and full-time employment. But I learnt a lot. I studied in the week and on some Saturday mornings. Fortunately, I could use our loft conversion as a study.

For the final degree, I prepared for nine three-hour exams. Students could sit up to four one year in advance (I took three at Oxford). My topics were: Christian Doctrine and Philosophy of Religion (one paper each). Four Biblical Studies papers: Old Testament General Paper with Selected Texts in English and/or Hebrew; New Testament General Paper – Historical Background, Introduction and Theology; Translation, Criticism and Exegesis of John and Romans; The Theology of Selected Portions of the New Testament in Greek, with Translations Therefrom. Plus, three Church History papers: Religious and Ecclesiastical Movements, 1789-1948; The Church to A.D. 451; The Church in the West in the Sixteenth Century.

I took my remaining six exams in London staying with my friend Peter Schwemlein. No aids were permitted – everything had to be remembered. It was a trying time for the family, with me away and under pressure. When the results came out – triumph – I passed. My BD (Hons) certificate was awarded on 1st August 1983. Sue, her dad and I went by train to the Royal Albert Hall for the long awards ceremony. A woman sitting next to me explained that some students in her college had failed their BD exams – yes, they were demanding.

Auntie Bel

Early in 1984, we lost another dear family member – Auntie Bel. Years before, in Harewood Street, she had been rushed to hospital for an emergency operation on her stomach, and thankfully recovered. Now it looked different. By arrangement with Dad, I took the train from Bristol to Liverpool's Lime Street station, where he collected me and drove to the hospital where she had been for some time.

Auntie Bel and I talked and prayed together, and she was cheerful as always; but that was the final time we met. She died on 27th January 1984, aged seventy-five. Her death was caused by cardiac failure, renal failure, and chronic obstructive airways disease. Bel had donated her body to medical research, so there wasn't a funeral, but instead a memorial service at her local Anglican church. We expected her body to be returned in due course to the family for burial, but that never happened, and we don't know why. Uncle Jim had already died, and she didn't have any children besides our "adopted" dad. Her father, John Thomas Hoban, had helped bring up Dad.

Miners' strike 1984-85

After the Falklands War, I recall the 1984-85 miners' strike controlled by Arthur Scargill (leader of the National Union of Mineworkers); it was intended to stop mines being closed, bring down the government, and conduct a class war. The media publicised the considerable destruction, violence and intimidation. At coal pits and coal-fired power stations, scores of police formed barriers. Although ours was a nuclear plant, the mineworkers established a token picket of protesters at the site boundary for months, with some even staying in a small caravan. But one morning we were met by very many more members returning along the site access road after picketing our site. They didn't try to prevent us going to work but we found that the training centre was packed with police officers having breakfast. They had been bussed in to control the mineworkers' picket.

Back in 1972/73 Edward Heath's Conservative government was brought down by the miners, but the Tories weren't going to be beaten again. They had planned ahead, piling up stocks of coal, retraining the police on picket line tactics, and providing them with riot gear. By April 1984, four in every five miners were on strike. The Nottinghamshire miners played an important role in support of the operating power stations. Ten months on from the start, droves of miners returned to work in January 1985, and more in February. Scargill had failed, and sadly so many people had suffered. Importantly, our staff in the nuclear power stations had helped keep the nation's lights on. Nuclear was providing clean, low-carbon electricity.

Meanwhile, the Provisional IRA continued its bombings – on 12th October 1984, the Conservative Party Conference in the Grand Hotel, Brighton was bombed, killing five people and injuring thirty. The attempted assassination of PM Margaret Thatcher failed. We watched the TV reports in shock.

First theology teaching in Africa

Shortly after attending the Mount of Olives Pentecostal church in 1979, Sue and I had met Peter and Jenny Kay. Peter was ordained and had a theology degree, while Jenny had a chemistry degree. Later, they decided to go with their two children, Abigail and Joshua, to live and teach at Nairobi Pentecostal Bible College in Kenya. When they were home on furlough, they often stayed with us (I was managing their finances). They invited me to visit them.

So, in 1988, the year after completing my London University postgraduate Diploma in Education (studying history and philosophy), I visited them in Nairobi and taught at the college and a local church. For example, in April I taught "New Testament Survey" at college. On a Wednesday evening on 4th May, I spoke in Dandora Church on "Why study the Bible?", which was translated. The congregation was responsive. It was great to see the Kays again, and some splendours of Africa with its lovely people: the Nairobi National Park, the Rift Valley, and even Langata Giraffe Centre. The Kays were enjoying their time teaching, supporting the college, and preaching in churches.

After two weeks, I flew home and caught a coach from

London to Bristol. Sue, who was pregnant with our son Timothy, collected me at the bus station, with our two girls in the car. Her mum had been helping while I was away. Our Timothy was born later in the summer. We were five.

North Sea oil & gas:

Piper Alpha tragedy 6th July 1988

Just after my return from Africa, on 6th July 1988, there was a terrible tragedy on the Piper Alpha oil platform, at their North Sea oil field off Scotland. Explosions were followed by terrible fires.[154] This became public, and one colleague admitted that he had a relative on Piper Alpha. He wanted to drive some distance to his family to try and find out about him – was he still alive? I became involved, as the occupational first aider. My colleague was clearly too distressed to drive himself safely, so I recommended that another colleague should drive him. This was accepted and he reached his destination safely, although still in shock. Of the 226 people on board, tragically, 167 men died – my colleague's brother was one of them.

Visiting Edna and holidays

I mentioned in chapter 10 that I visited my cousin Edna and her family in Los Angeles in October 1973; and again, in June 1977; a year after Sue and I were married, we went for our second honeymoon. We visited her in the US so many times thereafter that I can give just a sample of these trips.

---

[154] Fiona Macleod and Stephen Richardson, 'Piper Alpha: The Disaster in Detail', *The Chemical Engineer* 6 July 2018. Accessed 29 August 2022 at <u>Piper Alpha: The Disaster in Detail - Features - The Chemical Engineer</u>

Somewhile after our second honeymoon visit, Rob and Edna sadly divorced. First, she moved with their children to Denver, Colorado, then to Kentucky, and finally to Griffin, Georgia. With our girls – Laura (then seven) and Jessica (then five) – we caught up with her and second husband, Earl Fisher, in October 1987. Their large house was set in a couple of acres, surrounded by beautiful pine trees, with a large garden swimming pool. After a lovely time, we gave Edna a break by driving to Orlando's theme parks, Florida, and then Clearwater on the coast. We stayed in motels. Then, when we returned home, we discovered that "the Great Storm of 1987" (overnight on 15th-16th October) had caused destruction in the UK. Thankfully, our house was undamaged.

We visited Edna and Earl again with our toddler Tim, leaving for London on Friday 12th May 1989, flying direct to Orlando. We hired a car and stayed in the Comfort Inn; we remember the lovely breakfasts and the kind waitress who helped feed Tim in his highchair at 6.30am! The next day we started seeing the tourist attractions: Gatorland Zoo; Cypress Gardens; Water Mania in Kissimmee (Florida's biggest wave pool); Kennedy Space Centre; MGM Studios; swimming in the hotel pool and visiting the mall; Disney World (my favourite ride was the Pirates of the Caribbean). On Saturday 20th May, we drove to Daytona beach and rented a motel room on the coast. Here, we built sandcastles, jumped the waves 'and Timothy ate the sand and he chased the waves.'[155] Sunday was spent at a park, attending a Baptist church, and eating at Denny's restaurant before a storm. After our sunny adventures in Florida, we visited Edna in Georgia. Some years later, when Edna and Earl owned a condominium at the beach resort of Destin in Florida, we stayed there.

---

[155] The list of places is from Laura and Jessica's diaries. Quote from Jessica.

Over the years, we visited the Atlanta Cyclorama, which told the Civil War story of 22nd July 1864 Battle of Atlanta, when Major General William T. Sherman's army destroyed Atlanta. Also, in the museum we saw the original large *Texas,* one of the steam locomotives in the war's military raid, in April 1862, called the Great Locomotive Chase, or Andrews' raid; as a youngster, I had enjoyed Walt Disney's film version *The Great Locomotive Chase.*

Privatisation, studies and redundancy

In 1987, the Queen's Speech to Parliament said the national-owned CEGB would be privatised, under the Thatcher government when Cecil Parkinson was Energy Secretary. This was resisted with good reasons, and the Chairman Lord Marshall resigned in 1989. But the inevitable happened. The Magnox power stations were reaching their end of life; so, they would stay with the government, but the AGR stations would be sold. Of course, it caused considerable concern among colleagues. But 1989 thankfully brought the fall of the Berlin Wall and the end of the Cold War.

In September 1990, I was pleased to receive my Long-Term Service Award (£110) from Nuclear Electric, for twenty years' service (and I chose theology reference books). After completing my Diploma in Education, I returned to Trinity College for two years of Old Testament Hebrew. I had a good arrangement with my employers: when I did overtime, I took it off as time in lieu (rather than being paid). This allowed me to attend Hebrew classes, such as in October 1992 with Rev Dr Philip Jenson.

But things in the industry continued changing, and under the new regime the company offered staff voluntary severance. All our training centre staff received written terms, and were interviewed. Although I liked my job, I volunteered to leave and begin more studies, for which the company kindly paid my fees. They also gave me typing training (necessary for writing future essays). Nevertheless, moving from being a well-paid scientist in a secure post to a postgraduate student had challenges, including saying farewell to colleagues. Over the years, I had enjoyed working with tutors including Lorna, Sue and Sally, and Brian Sellick on secondment from Sizewell A Power Station. Also, I missed teaching staff.

Biblical Studies 1993-1994

From Friday 18th June to Saturday 26th June 1993, I returned to Nairobi Pentecostal Bible College to teach, before I left my employment as a tutor.

I started my full-time MA degree in October 1993, at Bristol University's Department of Theology and Religious Studies. Sue accompanied me as I enrolled. Most modules that I attended were at Trinity College; I did a few modules at the university, and my dissertation was supervised by Dr Diane Treacy-Cole, lecturer in New Testament and Early Christianity. Classes included advanced Greek and Hebrew. It felt odd becoming a full-time mature student and losing the satisfaction, security and status of a well-paid job (but leaving meant another person would have a job). We still had the mortgage to pay, and five mouths to feed! Nevertheless, I bought a computer and learnt to use it for writing essays. But Sue was much faster at typing than me, so I started off handwriting essays and thankfully she typed them up. We worked together on any changes. Eventually, I got faster, but Sue was invaluable.

In early 1994, we moved from the Mount of Olives Pentecostal church to our local Cairns Road Baptist Church. We knew the minister Rev Tony Matthews and his wife Jan, because their daughter and our Jess and Tim attended the same primary school in Henleaze. The church was great for children; they played football in the upstairs hall after the

Sunday morning service! The youth met in a local home and enjoyed soft drinks and snacks with a friendly group. Over time, Sue became a Sunday School teacher, as she had been at the Mount of Olives, and for very many years enjoyed the preparation and teaching.

When Easter 1994 came, I had a break from studies as our whole family drove to the Christian festival "Spring Harvest" in Skegness. It was a long drive, but worth it. We stayed in self-catering accommodation while Sue's sister Wendy had a place including full board. After a couple of days, Sue and I were called out of the morning meeting. It turned out that during a controlled game, a child had sat on Tim's arm, and they suspected it was broken. We spent that day getting his arm checked and plastered, and rechecked the next day. We had to leave Laura and Jess with Wendy who, thankfully, arranged for them to be fed with her for meals. After six weeks, Dad and I took Tim to Southmead Hospital, Bristol, to have his plaster removed. Thankfully, it had healed well.

While working on my dissertation, in July I became a distance-learning tutor with St John's College, Nottingham (until January 1999), covering New Testament, Old Testament, and Greek. We squeezed in our summer holidays in a caravan in Combe Martin near Ilfracombe, kindly loaned to us by Tony and Jan, and had a lovely time. In October, I successfully completed my MA – awarded on 16th January 1995.

From October 1993 until March 1996, I worked as an associate tutor for Oldbury Training Centre. In 1994-95, some taught modules were being converted by companies into computer-based training. My role was to evaluate their modules and write reports for Oldbury staff. This gave me useful home-based employment and income.

Dear Dad

Sadly, and suddenly, things changed drastically in late 1994. In retirement, Dad regularly visited us in Bristol, driving the 170 miles each way by himself. As he got older, he became less confident driving so, eventually, he travelled by bus or coach. He helped with our children and did jobs in the house and garden: installed secondary glazing in the breakfast room; fixed new hinges on a window; built a small garden wall; erected a garden shed, etc. When he came, he was happy and enjoyed our company (despite the noise!); he often stayed a week or so.

Often, we took holidays together with Dad at Haldon Court, a Christian hotel at Exmouth, Devon, and one year in Lydstep Haven caravan park (near Tenby). There we rescued starfish on the beach, and along the coast path we spotted an adder (Britain's only poisonous snake). In August 1990, we went with my sister Anne, her husband John, and their children, Matthew and Victoria, to Crantock near Newquay, Cornwall, and stayed in two large caravans. We walked down to the beach and back uphill, which was a struggle for Dad with his heart. One night, our caravan and others on the site were robbed while we slept. It was an unnerving experience. The police were informed, and happily, Sue's purse was found in a field. A £5 note was still in it. We enjoyed a good holiday nevertheless, but when I returned to work, I became unwell (including dropping off to sleep). I felt quite ill and visited my GP, who diagnosed sepsis (then called septicaemia) – which can be fatal – and put me on antibiotics. Thankfully, I recovered.

Dad had a stroke and was recovering in hospital in St Helens, so Jess and I took the train and visited him for the day. Christina collected us at the station. Dad took some while to recover and regain his speech, but he persevered when he visited us, and we encouraged him. He found walking to church a challenge.

Dad's final visit to us included a sunny day, so he joined Tim (then six) and me for a little game of cricket in the garden. After his stay, he returned home. Then I heard terrible news from Anne, who phoned: 'Dad has died from a heart attack.' It was 13th September 1994, and I was stunned – it was completely unexpected. Anne told us that Dad had just visited her, and had been waiting at the bus stop to go home. Then Anne realised he had left something behind, so she followed him. After she arrived, Dad collapsed. A passing ambulance stopped, and they did their best, but he couldn't be revived. He was seventy-six. On 19th September, we had the funeral at Bryn Independent Methodist Church, because when Dad visited Anne and John near Manchester, he attended their Methodist church. He was buried with Mum at St Thomas' Church, Ashton. Such a sad loss to us all, of a wonderful father.

Latin, classical civilisation
and doctoral studies

After working as an associate tutor for Oldbury, in September 1995 I started studies at Filton College, north of Bristol, taking Latin O-Level and Classical Civilisation A-Level. Why? Well, I thought it necessary to broaden and deepen my knowledge of the Graeco-Roman world in which Christianity first began. The classes were engagingly taught by Sally Knights and Gill Greef. As both part-time courses were attended by mainly adult learners, I wasn't out of place.

Earlier, I had applied to study at Bristol University for my PhD, including a scholarship, but was informed that I hadn't been awarded it. 'What should I do next?' I wondered. With a family and a mortgage, could I take on unsupported PhD studies? After a while of thinking and praying, we decided I should start. Surprisingly, while I was out, Sue had a telephone call from university staff saying that a scholarship had suddenly become available – was I interested? It was great news; my answer, 'Yes, please!'

So, in October 1995, I started research studies with Dr Diane Treacy-Cole. It was interdisciplinary research in classics and theology, with a focus on education, following on from my MA dissertation.[156] Initially, I registered for a Master's research degree, and later wrote an upgrade report and had a (tough) interview with my advisor and the Classics' teaching fellow Onno M. van Nijf. I passed and he was helpful in terms of the direction of my research.

During these studies, I continued at Filton College, with Latin and classical civilisation, and passed in summer 1996. I continued with A-Level Latin from 1996-97 – and again passed. Also, for my PhD I attended classes in the university's Department of Classics and Ancient History.[157]

Filton College arranged classical studies tours, so, encouraged by Dr Treacy-Cole, in March 1997 I went to Greece; we visited various sites and ancient Corinth, which fitted in remarkably with my research. Eventually, I submitted my dissertation. On 20th November 1998, in my PhD oral exam (viva), the examiners commended me on my range of sources, and I only had minor changes to make. I attended the university awards ceremony and my degree was conferred on 16th December 1998. Remarkably, in 1970 I had chosen to work as a scientist in the nuclear industry and not taken a part-time science PhD. Almost thirty years later, I received my interdisciplinary theology PhD! Then in October 1999 on another classical tour, we visited Turkey – ancient Asia Minor – and saw many sites, including ancient Troy and Ephesus.

---

[156] Tragically, she died unexpectedly in July 2006. See Ursula King, 'Dr Diane Treacy-Cole', 5 September 2006. Accessed 29 August 2022 at 2006: Diane Treacy-Cole | News and features | University of Bristol

[157] In 1996 I attended 'Leisure in Ancient Rome' (Dr Catherine Edwards); in 1997 'Rome in the East: culture and imperialism' (Dr Onno van Nijf).

I attended my first British New Testament Conference at Trinity College, Bristol, where I presented my paper *The Elite in First Corinthians and Ancient Education Models* at Seminar 7: The Social World of the New Testament, led by Professor Philip Esler. I enjoyed attending annual conferences of NT scholars and doctoral students, e.g. at the universities of Cambridge (2002), Birmingham (2003), Edinburgh (2004), Liverpool Hope (2005), and Exeter (2007). At Edinburgh, I signed up with Peter Oakes (University of Manchester) to become a book reviewer for the annual *Journal for the Study of the New Testament Booklist* and submitted my first review that year – I'm still a reviewer. Also, over summer 2004, I revised my PhD, which was published as: *The Educated Elite in 1 Corinthians: Education and Community Conflict in Graeco-Roman Context* (2005). Here, I argued for the important role the Greek gymnasium, an elite educational institution, played in understanding 1 Corinthians.

Dutch Consultancy Limited:

science and theology

In late 1998, with my PhD finished, I was considering options when I had an unexpected phone call from Dave Barraclough of Astec Services Ltd about scientific consultancy work – was I interested? It was based near Cardiff at Forest Farm, Whitchurch, working within a team for Nycomed Amersham plc. After an interview, I started initially full-time in January 1999 until September 1999. I was the training consultant in the Health Physics Department on course design, development and delivery, writing handouts and assessments. Other members of this contractors' team addressed instrumentation, waste, safety cases, etc. The focus was to update systems/procedures in preparation for a relicensing exercise with the Nuclear Installations Inspectorate. Starting in January meant driving in the dark and recognising that if I stayed in the slow lane on the M4 motorway, this often sent me off the motorway.

Encouraged by Dave Barraclough, I started my own company called Dutch Consultancy Ltd – I was the director and Sue the secretary. Over many years, I worked with Astec Services Ltd. After Nycomed Amersham, I quickly moved to BNFL Magnox Generation Berkeley Centre as a safety case consultant, author and trainer, working with various staff, including Colin Wilkins, Keith Hoyle and Wilf Hudd. To support my consultancy work, I later completed courses at the City of Bristol College, including integrated business technology, health and safety, and National Vocational Qualifications (NVQs) Level 3 (1999-2000) and Level 4 (2000) in Training & Development. Further, I completed an Open University (OU) Master's degree in education (2004). Later, the OU wrote to me about research for a doctorate, but I decided against it.

More, mainly US, holidays

Each time we visited Georgia, we saw Florida. Once, we stayed at Panama City Beach, on the Florida Panhandle with its emerald sea, driving through Alabama on the way. This reminded me of the 1960s civil rights demonstrations. On another visit, we attended with Edna a large Sunday service at a church experiencing a revival in Pensacola, where the balcony shook under the worshippers!

After some years of visiting Edna as a family, we decided that with the children growing up, I would take them separately. Laura and I went one week after the infamous terrorist attacks on the Twin Towers in New York on 11th September 2001 (9/11). We wondered about cancelling but decided to go, as we couldn't get our money back. The flight was packed with people desperately returning to the US after being turned back in mid-air on 9/11. Atlanta airport was very quiet. One trip was visiting the Martin Luther King Jr. memorial in Atlanta, seeing the church where he preached, and his dad before him, and taking the tour of his boyhood house. I had watched the civil rights marches on TV, but being there with Laura was memorable.

Afterwards, Laura worked on the Greek island of Kos in Kefalos, as a children's worker with MasterSun. In 2002, Sue and her friend Bryony visited Laura one week and later I visited with Sue's sister Wendy, when we learned to sail small boats. We enjoyed seeing ancient sites. The staff baked me a large birthday cake – I love cake!

One year, while visiting Edna, she told us she had something wrong with her, which was thought to be a cyst. We hoped it was, but sadly it turned out to be cancer and she only had a short time remaining. By then she'd moved with Earl from Griffin to Fayetteville, Georgia, to a lovely new home on a smaller plot with no swimming pool to maintain. Sadly, she died, on 29th May 2003 in Fayetteville, aged sixty-two. My sisters Anne and Christina went to her memorial service, but regretfully I couldn't attend, as I was on contract to teach at the University of Gloucestershire.

In July 2004, after Tim had finished his school GCSEs (General Certificate of Secondary Education – part of the National Curriculum exams taken at sixteen), I took him to the Greek island of Samos (off the west coast of Turkey) for a two-week holiday, where we stayed in a lovely seaside hotel. It was a Christian holiday centre and Tim enjoyed attending the youth activities, making friends, eating, etc. I enjoyed eating, relaxing, reading and visiting sites – we took the ferry for an amazing tour of ancient Ephesus.

As mentioned, in the summer of 2004, I updated my PhD for the publishers before Laura and I left on 20th October to 2nd November, to visit Earl in the US. We flew with Delta from Gatwick to Atlanta. Then went to his condominium in lovely Destin, Florida, on the Emerald Coast, and enjoyed the Gulf of Mexico, food, etc. Earl's friend Betty went with us. On Sunday, we worshipped at the First Baptist Church of Destin. The service was pleasant, but unfortunately over-ran, meaning we didn't have time to speak with any folk afterwards, and we were late meeting Earl.

We had our last family-of-five holiday abroad in June-July 2006, at the Bali Rethimnon resort in Crete, staying at the Bali Star hotel, arranged through MasterSun. It's on the coast, with mountains, lovely views, and a swimming pool. By then, Laura was working in the UK as a nursery nurse, Jess as a hospital nurse, and Tim had finished his A-Levels. It was our thirtieth wedding anniversary. Laura, Jess, Tim and I planned a Jeep tour of the island, which included the amazing family-run "German War Museum", with an elderly man who had witnessed German parachutists capturing Crete in the Second World War. However, Jess was ill and missed the trip. Regretfully, the Jeep driver wasn't in a hurry to return, and Tim was stressed as we nearly missed the World Cup match. I had an injured knee, so I couldn't tour the ancient site at Knossos. Sue enjoyed the sun, rest and company.

But back to the US. Tim and I visited Earl and Betty (then married) for our last time in September 2008. Earl took us target-shooting in the woods using his rifle and pistol. We weren't bad shots. We drove to Destin, of course; the whole trip took eight to nine hours. Tim was brave and did parasailing while we stayed in the boat. I went jet skiing with him – it was scary, but we survived! In Georgia, we visited the thirty-three-acre Atlanta History Center, seeing how the wealthy and their slaves lived before the Civil War. Further, we saw its magnificent American Civil War exhibition. Today it's a resource, for example, on the civil rights movement.[158] Also, we saw Atlanta's spectacular Georgia Aquarium.

---

[158] Atlanta History Center, 'Civil Rights Toolkit – The Children's March: Stories from the Birmingham Children's Crusade', 2020. Accessed 29 August 2022 at Civil Rights Toolkit | Atlanta History Center

Martial arts

Amazingly, more than thirty years after obtaining my yellow belt in judo, in my late fifties I decided to take up karate. A church friend had found a good club to train at and obtain his belts, so he suggested, 'Give it a go.' Our son Tim was in his teens, so in July 2004 we both started weekly classes. I was grateful that Sensei Ricki took me on at my age. By 24th November 2004, we had passed our yellow belt gradings. From then on, we trained regularly for years and practised at home. Sue also joined us, and we passed our coloured belts and earned black belts. Triumphs! It kept us fit.

University teaching, Kenya and Burundi

In early 2000, while working at Berkeley Centre as a training consultant, I had a phone call from Dr Gavin D'Costa at Bristol University, explaining that my advisor was going on sabbatical and asking: 'Would you like to teach modules in Biblical Studies?' The contract was from August 2000 to July 2001. I taught three modules: (1) The Corinthian Correspondence (Level 3), (2) Women in Primitive Christianity (Level 3) and (3) Health and Medicine in the Bible (Level 2). I enjoyed meeting students and teaching. But in summer 2001, we part-time lecturers were told our contracts wouldn't be renewed – the university was short of money. All my student handouts couldn't be reused! Nevertheless, in April that year, over Easter, Laura and I had an excellent group visit to ancient sites; once more I was in Turkey seeing Perge, Aspendos, Olympus, Phaselis, Termessos, Side, Sagalassos, Hierapolis and Nysa.

I taught Saturday day-schools at the universities of Bath (2002) and Bristol (2003/4 on women in the New Testament). And from February to June 2003, I taught two modules at the University of Gloucestershire (in Cheltenham): (1) Studying the Gospels and (2) Luke and the Teaching of Jesus. Simultaneously, I worked at Berkeley Centre.

Over this period, I visited Kenya again and taught in Burundi in 2002 and 2006. So how did these opportunities come about?

Previously, I mentioned my visits to Kenya while Peter and Jenny Kay were living there. However, they returned to Bristol for some years and Peter became the minister at Ivy Church in St Werburghs, Bristol. During this time, he visited Kenya and Burundi (near Rwanda) to provide periodic training seminars for pastors and church leaders in the many FECABu churches.[159] I first visited Burundi in June 2002 with Peter, and three ladies from Ivy Church, during our trip from 10th-27th June. We travelled via Nairobi and stayed at Nairobi Pentecostal Bible College for a few nights, meeting students. I spoke at two churches and in a morning assembly for staff and students at Pan African Christian College (sponsored by Canadian Assemblies of God). We had time to see Nairobi National Park, but most animals were hiding!

It was a short flight to Burundi, but because the civil war made travel outside the capital city Bujumbura very dangerous, we were restricted to the city, and used the church headquarters. We all stayed nearby in the secure guesthouse called La Par with mosquito nets, guards and a guard dog. Peter and I taught in the church's large, enclosed courtyard, with temporary awnings shading us and the visiting pastors and church leaders against the hot sun. The floor was bare earth. Worship, of course, included singing and dancing. I taught a series on the Apostle Paul's letter to the church at Philippi (Philippians). We also taught in

---

[159] FECABu is Fraternité Evangélique du Christ en Afrique au Burundi. Their work is administered through the Christian charity Creative Solutions. See 'Burundi'. Undated. Accessed 29 August 2022 at Creative Solutions - Burundi (creative-solutions.org.uk). It notes: 'Burundi is a small mountainous country, the size of Wales, in central Africa, just south of Rwanda.'

churches through interpreters, working from English to Kirundi. The hospitality of the Christians was amazing, and they kept us safe, providing escorts for the walk between La Par and the church HQ.

Surprisingly, in between my Burundi trips, I found that Larry Weaver (my friend at Salford University) who worked in Canada was returning to Wales with his family. On 12th November 2005, he was inducted as the pastor at Duckpool Road Baptist Church (Newport), and I was the invited speaker. Alan Ryden, also from our Salford days, attended the service. One year later, just before returning to Burundi, I preached at his church's Sunday evening service.

In November 2006, I returned to Africa to meet Peter and Jenny in Nairobi, en route to Burundi. Unfortunately, on the flight from London, the crown on my tooth fell out during a meal! Fortunately, I didn't swallow it, but kept it safe. On arrival that Friday, Peter took me to his dentist, where they did a great job of fixing it. The next day, we were to fly together to Burundi for teaching at seminars and in churches.

Jenny was too exhausted to fly, so just Peter and I went on 4th November. We taught a five-day seminar called "Freedom in Christ" at the church HQ in Bujumbura. I had never taught it before, and Peter had only taught it previously alongside Jenny, drawing upon her preparatory work and experience. It addressed the horrors experienced in the civil war. There was a section called "the healing of the wounds workshop", which Jenny had developed to help "the pastors confront and bring to Christ the terrible consequences of the war: multiple bereavements, terror, violence, betrayal, exile, loss and the helplessness of extreme poverty... God helped us wonderfully!"[160] We remained healthy for the whole seminar, and the interpreters' voices held. People shared testimonies on how they were helped to overcome the terrible things

---

[160] Personal communication with Peter and Jenny of 'Report of Burundi Seminars: November 2006'.

they'd seen and suffered.

As it was now safe to travel outside Bujumbura, the next week we taught at a seminar in a country church eighty miles away, near the Tanzanian border. I taught a series on Paul's letter to the church at Corinth, called "Leadership and Lifestyles in 1 Corinthians: Ancient and Modern Contexts". The pastors/leaders and Peter were excited by my teaching. Peter taught on 2 Timothy; the letter Paul wrote to Timothy about remaining faithful. One day, we had torrential rain with dark skies, and everybody had to gather around the teaching desk with its one emergency rechargeable light by which to read our notes. They greatly benefitted from the teaching, as their testimonies showed. Cairns Road Baptist and Ivy Church Bristol sponsored the two seminars. I gave my time freely and paid for my own flights. We flew back from Burundi on Saturday 18th November: Peter remained in Nairobi, and I returned to England.

Peter and I admired the Christians we met in Burundi, for their faithful witness to Christ and gratitude in the midst of poverty and persecution. Their joy and willingness to forgive the wrongs they had suffered encouraged us. The pastors/leaders were eager to learn, and engaged, and the church was strengthened. When I returned, I told Sue about my trip, including my visit to the dentist.

Sue also studied theology, through a distance-learning course run by St John's Extension Studies, Nottingham. She started by taking the module "Leading Children" (completed June 2003) to support her long-term commitment to regularly teach children in Sunday School. She found this so interesting and informative that she enrolled on the "Certificate in Christian Studies" and completed assignments for: Old Testament; New Testament; Evangelism; English Church History; The Holy Spirit; and World Mission. Her certificate was awarded in 2012, after ten years because of problems with her eyes. She persevered.

Trinity College (Bristol):
tutor and examiner

I had studied at Trinity College while taking my degrees. Later, an opportunity arose to teach intermediate level Greek, after the lecturer left for a post in the US. Then in September 2007 I began teaching a class on "Basic New Testament Greek" and "Introduction to Biblical Languages". Students taking the "Introduction to Biblical Languages" completed eight sessions with me before transferring to Hebrew sessions. Other students continued on my basic course two days per week from September to May. Fortunately, Dr John Bimson, who previously taught this module, gave guidance. I enjoyed teaching NT Greek over many years and helped struggling students learn. Eventually, this class was changed to a ten-credit module "Beginners' New Testament Greek", taught one hour per week over the academic year. Bristol Baptist College students taking Greek also joined my classes.

Besides teaching Greek, I sometimes contributed to colleagues' modules. For example, I supported Rev Dr David Wenham teaching introductions on his modules "Paul's Early Letters" and "Advanced NT Studies", when I set the letter called 1 Corinthians in its social and cultural context. I particularly enjoyed working with David, who is an accomplished author and teacher. His father, J.W. Wenham, wrote the first Greek book I used: *The Elements of New Testament Greek*. In 2020, I had the pleasure of providing feedback on a draft copy of David's book *Jesus in Context: Making Sense of the Historical Figure*. In 1968-69, David lived at St Aidan's College, Birkenhead, across the Mersey from Liverpool, doing some teaching while researching his second-year PhD at Manchester University.

Further, I was an examiner for Trinity's students wishing to progress from Master's research degrees to PhD registrations in New Testament. This entailed reading students' upgrade reports, agreeing questions with a colleague, and together interviewing individual students. We reported back to Bristol University. I held honorary academic status as a "Teacher in the School of Humanities".

Family times

Sue and I enjoyed happy times with our children, relatives and friends throughout these busy years. I always appreciated our garden, as my Liverpool house didn't have one. Of course, we had the holidays mentioned previously, particularly enjoying visiting Edna in the US. While at home, besides activities in the week, our children spent Saturday mornings learning ice-skating, playing tennis and football. We spent hours supporting them in tennis competitions and Tim in school football matches. Sundays included church meetings and young people's classes, followed by football in the church hall. Sometimes, we had university students around for lunch after church. When they were older, our children often went away with friends on various Christian activity weeks, making new friends and enjoying new adventures.

Relatives and friends visited us, or we would go away for Christmas, for example, to see Sue's sister Wendy and her family (with Nick and Amy similar in age to our children) in Hampshire. When Nick and Amy were younger, they went with Wendy and her husband Findlay to Mali, Africa, for a few years, visiting us when they came home. Often, Peter and Jenny Kay, with Ab and Josh, stayed with us while on leave from teaching in Kenya. Over the years, our three children all visited Africa, going to Mali, South Africa and Zambia.

Children love animals, so we looked after the school hamster and our own pets, notably guinea pigs and our old tortoise (given to us by our minister Warwick when his family moved to a smaller house/garden). Children and adults loved seeing our tortoise, but had to be careful when they fed him, as he could accidentally bite them, although he hadn't any teeth!

With our children, we made many church friends and knew families through "home groups", children's/youth groups, and Sunday School. This included Christmas parties provided by our friends David and Hazel Bussey (Uncle David and Auntie Hazel) and times with Ruth Morgan (Auntie Ruth). She taught evacuee children in the Second World War, and later trained as a teacher. Ruth lived to be ninety-nine.

Over the years, I found that my qualifications and experiences helped when it came to encouraging children with their homework and exam preparation. One advantage of my consultancy work was that I could decline contracts if necessary. In particular, I didn't want to spend long periods working away from home, leaving Sue with the children. I recall friends telling me of well-paid consultancy work around the country, but I decided that wasn't good for us – we had enough to live on. When I was growing up, Dad had spent time working away (especially weeks at a time in Ireland); but he needed to do it just to keep a roof over our heads and food on the table.

Over thirty years, as could be expected, we sadly lost dear family members, including Sue's mum (2000) and her dad (2006). Nevertheless, it has certainly been interesting combining science and faith.

CHAPTER 12

Reaching Retirement

and Reflections

Dutch Consultancy Ltd

As mentioned in chapter 11, in January 1999 we started Dutch Consultancy Ltd, with Sue as the secretary and me as director. It was well worth running it for scientific consultancy and theology teaching. My main focus was on scientific work, but I also taught theology, and assessed students for universities and Trinity College, Bristol.

In my consultancy work, I continued my contact with Oldbury Power Station, preparing the company's peer-reviewed *A Consolidated Safety Case for Continued Operation of the Radioactive Waste Management Facilities* (2004). I also prepared a *Periodic Safety Review Stage Submission* for Wylfa Power Station in Anglesey. It was under construction when our family had a holiday nearby in Cemaes Bay, when I was a schoolboy. I didn't know then that I would contribute to an important safety report.

Eventually, though, we decided to wind down our consultancy in summer 2006. Our reason for this was having fewer regular contracts while expenditure was still required (e.g. paying accountants). Also, there was the effort of completing government forms, with threats of fines if not done in time – it felt like the government gave little support, but it certainly wanted our taxes. Closing down took time, but afterwards the lack of pressure was worth it. When more scientific work was offered to me, as an Astec Services employee, I accepted; and this worked. My teaching at Trinity College continued under similar arrangements. But then I saw an advert for a part-time course administrator at Bristol Baptist College and applied. After an interview, I was offered the post, although in my early sixties.

Bristol Baptist College:

course administrator and tutor

In January 2009, I joined Bristol Baptist College as course administrator, for twenty hours per week (initially two days and two half-days). The college was founded in 1679.[161] It was a thirty-minute walk from home. In the 2012 Olympics, the torch bearer ran past the college as I was walking to work, giving me a great view. It was also the Queen's Diamond Jubilee year (1952-2012).

The principal was Rev Dr Stephen Finamore, and the vice principal was Rev Dr Ernest Lucas. Surprisingly, the librarian Shirley Shire and I recognised each other – Shirley was also in the Salford University Christian Union at the same time as me.

I worked for the college manager Fran Brealey, but with Rev Ken Stewart (Director of Pastoral and Mission Studies) I ran our Prepare for Service (PFS) course. It was a part-time access-level course, run over three years, for people who wished to become lay pastors or preachers, or Saturday students who were interested in learning. Each year, we offered four different modules over eight Saturdays. My experience of part-time study gave me the confidence to support these students, and help them achieve their objectives. Ken taught one module and we booked other experienced speakers for the remaining modules (they also marked student assignments). I also had

---

[161] See Ruth Gouldbourne and Anthony R. Cross, *The Story of Bristol Baptist College: Three Hundred Years of Ministerial Formation* (Eugene, Oregon: Pickwick Publications, 2022).

admin responsibilities for our students taking University of Bristol certificates, diplomas or degrees, to ensure that they chose and completed the credits in mandatory and elective modules, including placements. This was done in partnership with Trinity College admin staff.

At the time of my appointment, I was already teaching Greek at Trinity College to Trinity's students (future curates/vicars), but my classes included Baptist College students. What makes me smile is the situation of me teaching New Testament Greek, although as a teenager I had great difficulty passing O-Level English language, and no qualifications in a modern or ancient language. I continued enjoying teaching college Greek until retirement. My early school struggles and triumph through studying theology made me sensitive to fraught students.

I liked working with Baptist (and Trinity) college staff and students. Part-time regular work suited me, as it left time for opportunities as a book reviewer, being an examiner for research students, involvement in scientific and engineering professional memberships, plus writing a book proposal. Moreover, I completed a part-time MA (2009-2011).

While working at college, I approached Christian publishers, with a proposal on nuclear energy viewed from a positive Christian perspective, based on my experience as a scientist/engineer in the nuclear industry and my theology qualifications. Although publishers showed interest, they didn't think that it would sell enough copies, so this was postponed until after my retirement on 31st August 2014.

Rev Ken Stewart, who also had a first degree in science, was supportive. Also, the US publishers Wipf & Stock were suggested by a friend, Yongbom Lee, and Ernest Lucas, who holds two PhDs, one in science and one in theology. In September 2015, I submitted a proposal and signed a contract in January 2016. *Let There Be Light! Nuclear*

Energy: A Christian Case came out in 2017, aimed specifically at the non-specialist on the merits of nuclear energy.[162]

Professional societies, Christians in Science and The Faraday Institute

I retain my membership of professional societies. I became a member of the Society for Radiological Protection in 1978 while at Hinkley Point. Then, in March 2008, I was registered as a Chartered Radiation Protection Professional. Especially enjoyable was attending the society's 50th Anniversary Conference (May 2013) at the Harrogate International Centre. Sue and I travelled there by train, stayed at the hotel, and enjoyed its breakfasts; while I learnt at lectures, she enjoyed Harrogate's tea and coffee!

Also, I remain a chartered engineer through continuing professional development. This has included local lectures, e.g. at the University of Bristol South West Nuclear Hub and during Covid-19 restrictions in 2020-2022 via educational webinars.

Moreover, I am a member of Christians in Science. This network of members connects issues of science and faith. Its first aim is: 'To develop and promote biblical Christian views on the nature and scope of science and its interaction with the Christian faith, bringing a biblical Christian perspective on scientific issues into the public arena.'[163] The

---

[162] Robert S. Dutch, *Let There Be Light! Nuclear Energy: A Christian Case* (Eugene, Oregon: Wipf & Stock, 2017). For a review see, 'Is there a Christian case for Nuclear Energy? by Rev Dr John Weaver', JRI Blog, 9 August 2017. Accessed 30 August 2022 at Is there a Christian case for Nuclear Energy? by Rev Dr John Weaver – The John Ray Initiative (jri.org.uk)

[163] Christians in Science, 'Why Christians in Science?' 2022. Accessed 30 August 2022 at About CiS - Christians in Science

Bristol Local Group has talks by scientists and theologians. For example, in 2018-19 it ran the series "Our Fragile Planet – a Christian Perspective". Professor Andrew Halestrap (University of Bristol), then Chair of Christians in Science, encouraged me in writing my book.

Christians in Science has links with The Faraday Institute for Science and Religion, which mourned the sad loss of Reverend Canon Doctor John Polkinghorne KBE FRS in March 2021, aged ninety. It notes his 'huge contributions to the science-religion field'.[164] I enjoyed learning from his talks, publications, and a personal discussion. Other scientists who are Christians have also contributed to this debate, including: Denis Alexander, Rodney Holder, John Houghton, John C. Lennox, Ernest Lucas and Alister McGrath.[165] McGrath's book *Enriching our Vision of Reality: Theology and the natural sciences in dialogue* (2016) reminds me of the philosophy of science classes taught by Mr Bialek at Salford University during my physics degree (chapter 9). The Faraday Institute has a paper on *Religion and the Rise of Science*.[166]

I attend the Bristol Classical Association meetings in Bristol (and their webinars). My interest here is from my PhD linking classics and theology, focusing on social history. My

---

[164] The Faraday Institute for Science and Religion, 'In Memoriam John C. Polkinghorne (1930-2021)', March 2021 Newsletter No. 176. Formerly Professor of Mathematical Physics at Cambridge University before studying for the Anglican priesthood. Later President of Queens' College, Cambridge and knighted. His Faraday Papers No. 1 and 4 are online. Accessed 30 August 2022 at Faraday Papers | Faraday (cam.ac.uk)

[165] Sir John Houghton's scientific work, publications and presentations explain his concerns over climate change and its consequences. See John Houghton with Gill Tavner, *In the Eye of the Storm: The Autobiography of Sir John Houghton* (Oxford: Lion, 2013).

[166] On the positive relationship of science and religion see Peter Harrison, *Religion and the Rise of Science*, Faraday Paper 21, March 2021. Accessed 31 August 2022 at Faraday-Paper-21-Harrison-web.pdf (cam.ac.uk)

visits have included: Ancient Corinth, Athens, Epidaurus, Marathon, Mycenae and Olympia. In Turkey, I've seen Ephesus and Troy.

The South West Coast Path

Despite the pressures of working, Sue and I had time for family holidays. My last US trip was in 2008 so afterwards we had holidays in the UK. One exception was Normandy, in 2016.

Sue, Tim and I have appreciated walking on the South West Coast Path. Often in the past, our walks were based around where we were on holiday. For example, one August, while staying at Haldon Court in Exmouth, Tim and I walked the Coast Path along the stunning Jurassic coast to Sidmouth and arrived there during the music festival. Two days later, we started the section Sidmouth to Seaton, which is 10.3 miles. However, I found it was far too hot, and despite the magnificent views the demanding gradient (severe then strenuous) meant, we only reached Beer – in time to get the land train, rather frustrated, to Seaton.[167] Then we took the bus to Sidmouth for our connection to Exmouth. Rather a tricky return trip, just getting us back, rather hungry, for our evening meal!

During other holidays at Haldon Court, Sue and I have walked from Exmouth to Dawlish and Teignmouth. We once took a ferry across the River Exe, and then enjoyed walking along the coast and returned on the bus and ferry. Along this particular section, the path runs by the beach next to Isambard Kingdom Brunel's GWR train line, providing

---

[167] That day we saw off Branscombe the remains of the MSC *Napoli* disaster in January 2007. See Tianna Corbin, 'Looking back at the MSC *Napoli* shipwreck disaster 13 years on', DevonLive, updated 14 February 2020. Accessed 31 August 2022 at Looking back at the MSC Napoli shipwreck disaster 13 years on - Devon Live Spilt oil caused damage.

stimulating views accompanied by the sounds of the clattering engines and coaches' wheels along the tracks. On other occasions, we stayed at Teignmouth, Paignton, Brixham, Sidmouth, and Lyme Regis (climbing Golden Cap the highest point on the south coast in glorious weather with breath-taking views!). We are particularly fond of Weymouth in Dorset.

Tim and I first visited Weymouth from 25th-28th March 2011. We walked from our Bed & Breakfast (The Brunswick) in Brunswick Terrace on the first morning along the seafront into Weymouth, then via the Rodwell Trail to Ferrybridge and up to Portland Bill on the Coast Path. Very enjoyable. From the Clock Tower to Portland Bill is eleven miles.[168] We then discovered that at that time of year there weren't any buses back to Weymouth, so we quickly walked to the local town, Southwell, while eating our late lunch! We manged to get there and catch the last bus around 4.30pm.

On 13th September 2012, Sue and I caught the bus from Weymouth to Wool train station and walked to Lulworth Cove then along the coastal path to Durdle Door before reaching Osmington, where we caught the bus back to Weymouth. It was a brilliant walk, with warm weather and blue skies. Then in September 2013, we walked from West Bay to Burton Bradstock, and the following day from there to Abbotsbury. Another time, we did Abbotsbury to Ferrybridge (Weymouth). It took us from noon to 7.30pm to walk the 11.3 miles because heavy rains had made the paths muddy, but it was worth it.[169] We've been back regularly over the years as the Weymouth area provides good walking opportunities, beaches, plus history with the Nothe Fort, Armed Forces Day, The Castletown D-Day

---

[168] South West Coast Path, 'Distance Calculator'. Accessed 31 August 2022 at Distance calculator - South West Coast Path

[169] South West Coast Path, 'Walk – Abbotsbury to Ferrybridge (Weymouth)'. Accessed 31 August 2022 at Abbotsbury to Ferrybridge (Weymouth) - Walk - South West Coast Path

Centre (opened 2017), Portland Castle, Maiden Castle, Dorchester and the Tank Museum at Bovington. We often stayed at B&Bs in picturesque Brunswick Terrace, or in caravans at nearby Bowleaze Cove. Second-hand book sales on the promenade were useful.

Visiting Normandy's beaches

As mentioned, on 26th June 2016, we started a family holiday to visit the D-Day landing beaches and the Battle of Normandy. I was with Sue and Tim, plus our daughter Jessica, her husband Simon and our grandsons Harry (aged three) and Stan (a baby). This particularly interested me, as Dad was based in Portland and served on HMS *Grey Fox* on D-Day, 6th June 1944, supporting the American landings at Omaha Beach.[170]

We booked overnight cabins on the Portsmouth/Ouistreham ferry, just after the UK voted to leave the European Union. We had a marvellous, if sobering, time visiting the cafés, sites, museums and beaches (including Point Du Hoc), plus Bayeux. We saw the museum at Pegasus Bridge, where the first liberators, the British 6th Airborne Division arrived on gliders to capture bridges on the night of 5th/6th June. We visited Sainte-Mère-Église and saw where an American paratrooper had landed and got lodged on the church clock tower (now shown with a dummy). At Arromanches, we saw the remains of the innovative Mulberry harbours, which had supplied the allied armies. We also saw, with great sadness, the large, beautifully kept, Normandy American Cemetery and Memorial.

---

[170] The centre brings back memories of Dad's service on HMS *Attack*. Nearby are two Mulberry Harbour sections and the disused Jolly Sailor Pub where I imagine Dad drinking. See 'D-Day Centre'. Accessed 31 August 2022 at Castletown D-Day Centre – Castletown Regeneration Project

As a child growing up in Liverpool, the Second World War was close to me, and to other children and adults. Uncle Alf served in the army, while Dad was in the Royal Navy. My father-in-law Frank served with the Royal Air Force in India. Liverpool had endured the Blitz. As a child and teenager, I read war stories in comics and books and watched war films; and as an adult I have continued my interest, including reading about Bletchley Park and visiting it in 2017. In 2019, I researched and wrote a family record of Dad's time in the Royal Navy. In 1944 he was based at HMS *Attack* in Portland (Weymouth) so having holidays there, including watching the Armed Forces Weekend, has helped me appreciate more fully his wartime role. On 6th June 2021, the seventy-seventh D-Day anniversary, the British Memorial at Gold Beach was officially opened, in remembrance of over 22,000 killed.

Back to the beginning

I began chapter 1: 'A Liverpool lad, born and bred in post-war Liverpool – a "baby boomer", summer-born baby and Scouser.' Why return to this? Well, it's a long time since I lived in Liverpool (1947-1967), although we returned there to visit Auntie Edie and Auntie Bel after we moved to Ashton. In chapter 9, I mentioned hearing Billy Graham preach, via live link, at Liverpool's Empire Theatre. That June 1967 night, I committed my life to Christ with a focus on God's plan. Another evening, I returned to hear Billy, and coincidentally met Chang, my Chinese school friend from Quarry Bank – he too chose to follow Christ.

My sisters Anne and Christina, and their husbands, live in Greater Manchester. So, some years ago I started visiting Liverpool, first with Tim, and then Sue. One Christmas, Tim and I visited Liverpool with John Elton (my brother-in-law) to take the tour of Liverpool's Anfield Stadium (having visited Manchester United's ground the previous year!). Around this time, we visited Boundary Lane (seeing Ogden's Tobacco factory) and New Grey Rock Close, to give Tim an idea of where I grew up. Also, Tim and I took the ferry across the Mersey on a chilly but lovely trip.

Sue and I visited in October 2014 and stayed at the Devonshire House Hotel (Edge Lane, Fairfield), not too far from the city centre. During this time, we met my sisters and saw Newsham Secondary Modern School's original premises and took photos. We also visited Newsham Park, St Margaret's Church, and St Michael's Roman Catholic Church. The Liverpool Irish Centre (previously St Michael's Irish Centre, until 2017) was located, from 1999, at 6 Boundary Lane. It was founded in 1964 on Mount Pleasant. Although I had Irish great-grandparents in Mum and Dad's families, I can't recall learning about Irish culture.

On subsequent visits, we stayed at the Travelodge on the Strand overlooking the Pier Head and Albert Dock, which are beautifully illuminated in the evenings. From 4th-8th April 2016, we visited again, travelling on the train. Unfortunately, I woke up feeling sick, and we missed our pre-booked departure from Bristol, so by the time I felt better we had to buy a further set of tickets at £104 for two singles or £105 for anytime returns. We chose the returns, but it was an expensive mishap! The next day, Tuesday, I felt fine, so we took the open bus tour on the top deck for fifty minutes, then saw the Museum of Liverpool for two hours, followed by the Mersey ferry ride for fifty minutes – which brought back memories. Wednesday was a cold day, so we chose the Maritime Museum for the *Lusitania* and *Titanic* exhibitions and the Atlantic War. On Thursday, Sue, tiring of history, went for a quiet cup of tea, whereas I visited the Western Approaches Museum deep under the street buildings at 1-3 Rumford Street off Chapel Street. It's billed as "explore Britain's top secret underground war bunker". Truly an amazing experience – I didn't know it existed when I lived in Liverpool. From here, the Admiralty controlled the Battle of the Atlantic; the museum notes that: 'The Operations Room has remained exactly how as it was left when the doors were closed on 15 August 1945.'[171] I wonder how much Dad knew about this while he was serving.

During our visit from 13th-17th September 2018, we enjoyed the open-top red bus for the Beatles' Tour. We had a great view from the top deck, where we could clearly see and hear the tour guide. It was advertised as ninety minutes, but as he liked explaining everything it lasted almost two hours. It was wonderful to see sites such as the roundabout at the end of Penny Lane, where I'd get the bus to Quarry Bank High School on Harthill Road. However, the tour guide reminded us about Liverpool's terrible Toxteth riots of 1981, related to racial disadvantages, which we'd seen, shocked, on TV.[172]

Later that day, we walked to the spectacular Roman Catholic Cathedral of Christ the King. Breathtaking in beauty. We felt the presence of God. At the Museum of Liverpool, we visited the space exhibition and handled an iron meteorite from Namibia, Africa.

Saturday also was a lovely step back in time as we caught the Merseyrail electric train to West Kirby in the Wirral, via Meols and Hoylake, to go along the North Wirral coast. We couldn't believe the return train fare for us two – it was so low we thought that was the return cost each, but it wasn't! The train was modern, clean and quiet, and the stations well cared for. At West Kirby, we walked on the path around the large man-made Marine Lake (fifty-two acres and five feet deep) looking over to Hilbre Islands and the River Dee to Wales. This was the Marine Lake my small sister Anne had fallen in on our day visit many years

---

[171] See 'Western Approaches HQ'. Accessed 23 January 2023 at Western Approaches (liverpoolwarmuseum.co.uk)

[172] See John Belchem, *Before the* Windrush: *Race relations in twentieth-century Liverpool* (Liverpool: Liverpool University Press, 2014). Focusing on Liverpool 8 it tells another story to my experiences.

before. After coffee, we took the train back to Hoylake Station. Here, I recalled the long row of shops with its toy shop where, as a boy, I had looked longingly into the window at model soldiers. Of course, the shop had long gone, but the lovely memory remains.

From Hoylake, we walked along the North Parade coast path, passing the Lifeboat Stations (old and new) towards Meols Parade and Promenade, enjoying the warm, dry weather, and the wonderful sea and beach views over Liverpool Bay. At Dove Point in Meols, we were on the North Wirral Coastal Park (which goes four miles to New Brighton). Meols Dunes (sandhills) are still there, but the considerable concrete sea and wartime defences at the promenade, the man-made embankment that I recall as a child, are gone, replaced by a quite different concrete front without its wartime features. But our old family photos clearly show them. I recognised the house that was on the seaward edge of Burbo Camp (see chapter 5) in the 1950s/60s. But the camp was considerably changed; now renamed the Wirral Beach Caravan Park with permanent caravans, it seemed smaller.[173] Rather than walk further to Moreton, we walked to pretty Meols Station with its flowerbeds, following a route our family used over many years – as a child it had seemed a long way! Then we returned to Liverpool.

On Sunday morning, we enjoyed visiting Liverpool's Anglican Cathedral, and participated in the Eucharist service; the first service I recall attending there. We also visited the nearby Faulkner Street featured in the BBC2 documentary *House Through Time* narrated by David Olusoga. The house was being filmed that day by another company. And we passed the beautiful entrance to China Town.

On Monday, on our way home, at Lime Street station, I

---

[173] See the *North Wirral Coast leaflet* in the 'North Wirral Coastal Park', Wirral Council 2022. Accessed 31 August 2022 at North Wirral Coastal Park | www.wirral.gov.uk

had a photo next to the statue of Liverpudlian comedian Ken Dodd, and saw the statue of Bessie Braddock, Liverpool MP for twenty-five years (1945-1970), known for her campaigning on housing; I recall Gran mentioning her.[174] Our journey was fraught, overcrowded and long, but eventually we reached Bristol after a lovely visit.

In 2019, regretfully we didn't revisit, but planned to return in 2020. Unfortunately, this was a non-starter because of the introduction of Covid-19 lockdowns and various restrictions starting in March 2020 and continuing into 2022. As elderly folk, we had more restrictions than others. Liverpool had some particularly high infection rates.

In comparison, we didn't need to go far to visit Sue's previous places in Wales: day trips to Barry, Cardiff Castle and meeting friends for coffee. We stayed at her Auntie Marion's caravan at Southerndown on the coast (near Porthcawl). Unfortunately, a storm subsequently demolished the caravan. One year, we'd had two lovely weeks in a caravan with Dad at Lydstep Haven near Tenby, on the South Wales coast.

What is my favourite street in Liverpool? It's Grey Rock Street, where I grew up. And I am not alone here. When Billy Butler was asked to name three streets that meant the most to him, he said: 'Grey Rock Street – where I lived as a young boy,' then Boundary Lane and Mathew Street.[175]

Like Billy, I'd love to walk down Grey Rock again, but it's long since been demolished, along with many of Everton's streets, thanks to the 1960s' slum clearances. The Mardi Gras club (see chapter 8) in Mount Pleasant where I was a member was demolished for a car park in 1974/75.

---

[174] Stephen Griffin, *Ken Dodd: The Biography* (London: Michael O'Mara Books, 2005/2018).
[175] Matthew Jacobson, 'On The Streets I Ran', 15 April 2021. Accessed 31 August 2022 at Matthew Jacobson, "On The Streets I Ran" - Explore Liverpool (explore-liverpool.com)

Liverpool's 1960s bands played there.[176] Thankfully we have our memories and photos.[177]

Reflections:

Polluting our neighbourhoods?

One thing that stands out for me when I grew up in Liverpool was air pollution, from burning fossil fuels for heating homes and producing electricity. Exhaust from cars and buses added to terrible smogs ("pea soupers"). So, what progress has been made over the decades? The number of vehicles on our roads has risen rapidly, and increased air travel adds to the pollution. The UK government introduced the first Clean Air Act in 1956, after the London smog that killed so many people and, of course, we experienced our lethal Liverpool smogs. Also established was a national survey for monitoring air pollution (black smoke and carbon dioxide), which has developed over the years to include automatic monitoring and more pollutants e.g. ozone, nitrogen dioxide, and fine particulates. Further legislation has followed.

However, there's still much to do as the Department for Environment, Food & Rural Affairs shows in *About Air Pollution*.[178] Vehicle emissions are too high. Moreover, in 2018 the government launched a new clean air strategy which states: 'Air pollution is the fourth biggest threat to public health after cancer, obesity and heart disease.' A new government

---

[176] Localwiki, 'Liverpool's destroyed landmarks, Mardi Gras Club'. Undated. Accessed 31 August 2022 at Liverpool's destroyed landmarks - Liverpool - LocalWiki

[177] For old photos of Everton see Ken Rogers, *The Lost Tribe of Everton & Scottie Road* (Trinity Mirror Media: 2010) and his website, with films. Accessed 30 January 2023 at: Home - The Lost Tribe of Everton

[178] Department for Environment, Food & Rural Affairs, 'About Air Pollution'. Undated. Accessed 31 August 2022 at About Air Pollution - Defra, UK

strategy set out to reduce particulate matter pollution.[179]

In December 2020, the BBC reported: 'A nine-year-old girl who died following an asthma attack has become the first person in the UK to have air pollution listed as a cause of death.'[180] Pollution from a busy London road materially contributed to her death, said the coroner's death certificate. For me, it is noticeable how very many more vehicles occupy our roads than when I was a child (a ten-fold increase since 1949). One author wrote: 'About six million people aged over sixty-five in England are at high risk of lung damage and asthma attacks because of toxic air.'[181] It reminds me of Uncle Alf, and how he suffered with only one lung.

Eventually, thankfully, the UK phased out toxic lead in petrol.[182] Yet, even today, wood burners grow in popularity, despite the air pollution particulates they produce; something which the UK government knows about.[183] Smoking used to be socially acceptable, and just about the only places where you didn't get smoking was inside schools (except staff rooms!) and churches. People smoked

---

[179] Department for Environment, Food & Rural Affairs, 'New Clean Air Strategy has been launched by Environment Secretary Michael Gove', press release 22 May 2018. Accessed 31 August 2022 at New Clean Air Strategy has been launched by Environment Secretary Michael Gove - GOV.UK (www.gov.uk)

[180] BBC News, 'Ella Adoo-Kissi-Debrah: Air pollution a factor in girl's death, inquest finds', 16 December 2020. Accessed 1 September 2022 at Ella Adoo-Kissi-Debrah: Air pollution a factor in girl's death, inquest finds - BBC News

[181] Justin Rowlatt, 'Toxic air puts six million at risk of lung damage', BBC News 11 February 2021. Accessed 1 September 2022 at Toxic air puts six million at risk of lung damage - BBC News He refers to a report by the British Lung Foundation and Asthma UK.

[182] Tim Harford, 'Why did we use leaded petrol for so long?' BBC News 28 August 2017. Accessed 1 September 2022 at Why did we use leaded petrol for so long? - BBC News

[183] See further Gary Fuller, *The Invisible Killer: The Rising Global Threat of Air Pollution – And How We Can Fight Back* (London: Melville House UK, 2018).

at home, work, in the streets, shops, clubs, cinemas and theatres. I saw enough suffering that I decided to never smoke, and I never did. Now I'm much older, I'm so glad of that decision. And despite enjoying the Swinging Sixties, I didn't do drugs.

Oldbury and Hinkley Point

Power Stations

I've not forgotten the nuclear power stations where I started my career as a young scientist (see chapter 10); rather, I reflect positively on them. Nuclear provides clean, low-carbon energy. It doesn't give the air pollution of fossil fuels, and doesn't emit carbon dioxide in operation. It provides electricity in a safe, secure and resilient way.

Over fifty years ago, I joined Oldbury Power Station as a health physics assistant. Oldbury contributed clean, low-carbon electricity during its long life. But in 2012 it was reported that its last reactor (Reactor 1) was shut down permanently after forty-four years of commercial operation because it was no longer economically viable. The site's twin reactors had safely generated enough electricity for one million homes over twenty years (137.5 TWh – terawatt hours).[184] It was a privilege to work there.

In 1974, I joined the health physics commissioning team at Hinkley Point B Power Station and was working on the plant when it started generating clean, low-carbon electricity

---

[184] Department of Energy & Climate Change and Charles Hendry, 'Oldbury Power Station shuts down after four decades of safe generation', 29 February 2012. Accessed 1 September 2022 at Oldbury Power Station shuts down after four decades of safe generation - GOV.UK (www.gov.uk) A kilowatt-hour (kWh) is the electrical energy used by a one kilowatt appliance in 1 hour. A megawatt-hour (MWh) is 1,000 times it and a terawatt-hour (TWh) is one million MWh.

in 1976. It finally shut down in August 2022. BBC West Business Correspondent Dave Harvey explains the history of the plant and its many benefits.[185]

Even though I left Hinkley to become a tutor, I remained involved in: (1) working with other tutors on the Hinkley Point B reactor simulator, (2) training Hinkley staff at the training centre, and (3) having a secondment with the Operations team. Also, at Oldbury Training Centre (which became Oldbury Technical Centre), I trained staff from Oldbury Power Station and completed secondments there. I also took course members on our Radiological Safety Courses to the nuclear plant for training in the radiation and contaminated controlled areas.

Science, technology, engineering and maths (STEM)

As a summer-born baby, I had educational disadvantages when I started school.[186] Later, finding I could understand, and like, maths and physics came out of the blue. But I now regard them as a God-given gift; although I still needed to concentrate and work hard to develop myself. Others have abilities in other areas, for example music, which isn't among my strengths; even if I liked the Sixties songs. One of the advantages of being a scientist has been my ability to help children struggling with maths. Also, I have worked as a volunteer tutor for a charity, teaching disadvantaged

---

[185] Dave Harvey, 'Hinkley B: UK's most productive nuclear power plant closes', BBC West 1 August 2022. Accessed 13 October 2022 at Hinkley B: UK's most productive nuclear power plant closes - BBC News

[186] Robert Long, *Summer-born children: starting school*, House of Commons Library Briefing Paper, 2 August 2022. Accessed 1 September 2022 at Summer-born children: starting school - House of Commons Library (parliament.uk) For England 'summer-born' means born between 1 April and 31 August.

primary school children maths. Besides this, I've tutored A-Level maths with a distant family member – he passed.

Many schools (some now called Academies) and colleges emphasize STEM subjects (science, technology, engineering and mathematics) for providing future careers in these subjects.[187] For example, Hinkley Point C Power Station has considerable STEM resources for helping teachers and pupils.[188] The Covid-19 pandemic and the development of vaccines has shown the need for research scientists, doctors and nurses. Further, because cyber security requires professional staff to defend the digital world, the UK's National Cyber Security Centre is helping young adults to explore this area with financial support for qualifications leading to careers.[189]

Earlier in the book, I mentioned items we didn't have when I was growing up. That's an eye-opening experience for children born in the computer and digital age, with their internet access via computers and various devices such as smart phones. But the Internet of Things brings new critical challenges such as cyber security, data security (who holds our personal data and who's using it?), facial recognition, virtual reality, personal privacy or "Big Brother" (as in George Orwell's *Nineteen Eighty-Four: A Novel*), and questions of what it is to be human and our future, an issue interwoven with the ideas of artificial intelligence and its implications. Christian author and academic John Lennox rightly remarks: 'You don't have to be a computer scientist

---

[187] See Mediaofficer, 'More young people are taking STEM subjects than ever before', Department for Education Blog: The Education Hub, 9 February 2021. Accessed 1 September 2022 at More young people are taking STEM subjects than ever before - The Education Hub (blog.gov.uk)

[188] See EDF, 'Inspire Education Programme'. Undated. Accessed 1 September 2022 at Inspire Education Programme | Hinkley Point C | EDF (edfenergy.com)

[189] National Cyber Security Centre, 'CyberFirst Overview'. Undated. Accessed 1 September 2022 at CyberFirst overview - NCSC.GOV.UK

to get involved in the discussion about where artificial intelligence and technology are going.'[190]

Besides technological challenges, there are justice issues. I recall the Reds, those ninety-seven Liverpool fans, who tragically lost their lives in the 1989 Hillsborough disaster in Sheffield, and Liverpool's long-continuing fight for justice. Also, there are racial and religious injustices. I remember the US civil rights protests against voting registration and segregation, with the shocking assassination of the civil rights leader Rev Martin Luther King Jr on 4th April 1968, at the Lorraine Motel in Memphis, Tennessee.

Terrorism remains a challenge. For example, on 7th July 2005, TV showed the horrendous London bombings, which killed and injured so many using public transport. Our daughter knew the sister of one young lady tragically killed that day.

In May 2020, George Floyd was killed by a white police officer in Minneapolis. His murder caused outrage, and produced the "Black Lives Matter" movement for other Black victims of racist brutality and injustice. In April 2021, Derek Chauvin was found guilty of Floyd's murder. Religious injustices continue worldwide. In its *World Watch List Report 2022* Open Doors UK identifies the high levels of persecution and discrimination of over 360 million Christians (one in seven of the world's Christians). Moreover, 5,898 Christians were killed and over 5,000 churches and church buildings were attacked.[191]

---

[190] John C. Lennox, *2084: Artificial Intelligence and the Future of Humanity* (Grand Rapids, Michigan: Zondervan Reflective, 2020). See his interview 'John Lennox *2084: Artificial Intelligence and the Future of Humanity*', 3 July 2021, YouTube. Accessed 1 September 2022 at John Lennox | 2084: Artificial Intelligence and the Future of Humanity | Talks at Google - YouTube

[191] Open Doors, 'World Watch List 2022: Trends', 2022. Accessed 1 September 2022 at Serving Persecuted Christians Worldwide - Persecution Trends - Open Doors UK & Ireland

Climate change and

nuclear energy's merits

One of the greatest challenges to our world now and into the future is climate change and its critical consequences. My book *Let There Be Light! Nuclear Energy: A Christian Case* addresses the merits of nuclear energy, answering questions and discounting myths. I am for renewables and also pro-nuclear, supporting the *Nuclear for Climate* position paper, a grassroots initiative of nuclear professionals and scientists, written for the COP26 summit in Glasgow in November 2021. It aims to open 'a dialogue with policymakers and the public about the necessity of including nuclear energy among the carbon-free solutions.'[192]

It champions nuclear energy's many merits. Nuclear energy is used for electricity generation (alongside variable renewables), but it can also be used to decarbonise sectors such as transport and heating, as well as generating clean hydrogen. Sure, there have been national commitments on carbon emission reductions. But Fatih Birol, the International Energy Agency (IEA) Executive Director, on Day two of the *Leaders' Summit on Climate* (called by US President Joe Biden) admits commitment levels are at their highest but these 'alone are not enough. We need real change in the real world. Right now, the data does not match the rhetoric and the gap is getting wider and wider.'[193]

The IEA estimates that global emissions for 2021 are a warning: they continue to increase, rather than decrease.

---

[192] Nuclear for Climate, *Net Zero Needs Nuclear*, 2021, COP26 Position Paper, p.1. Accessed 1 September 2022 at <u>COP26-Position-Paper.pdf (euronuclear.org)</u>

[193] *World Nuclear News*, 'Climate commitments are "not enough", says Birol', 23 April 2021. Accessed 1 September 2022 at <u>Climate commitments are 'not enough', says Birol : Energy & Environment - World Nuclear News (world-nuclear-news.org)</u>

We need to be technologically neutral (open-minded and humanitarian) when we suggest solutions to curtail carbon emissions. Ideology isn't good enough. Further, a report shows that Britain is already experiencing the effects of climate change.[194] Indeed, in July and August 2022, we had record temperatures in heatwaves and extensive droughts. Europe and other countries (e.g. Pakistan) suffered with heatwaves, wildfires and floods. Summer 2023 has also brought widespread heatwaves, wildfires, etc.

The Intergovernmental Panel on Climate Change (IPCC) in its Sixth Assessment Report (AR6) 2021 warns of the impacts and risks. Its April 2022 report by Working Group III *Climate Change 2022: Mitigation of Climate Change* sets out the energy options and the urgency for action.[195] See the Christian academic Katharine Hayhoe's helpful book: *Saving Us: A Climate Scientist's Case for Hope and Healing in a Divided World* (2021). I am glad that the government's *British Energy Security Strategy* (2022) includes accelerating building more nuclear power stations (large and small) and addresses national security.[196] The UK aims to achieve "net-zero" emissions by 2050.[197] In January 2023, a final report was published by Chris Skidmore MP

---

[194] Met Office, 'State of the UK Climate', 28 July 2022. Addresses the UK Climate 2021 report. Accessed 1 September 2022 at State of the UK Climate - Met Office

[195] *World Nuclear News*, 'IPCC sets out energy options for "liveable future"', 4 April 2022. Accessed 1 September 2022 at IPCC sets out energy options for 'liveable future' : Energy & Environment - World Nuclear News (world-nuclear-news.org)

[196] Department for Business, Energy & Industrial Strategy and Kwasi Kwarteng, *Statement on the British Energy Security Strategy*, Oral statement to Parliament 19 April 2022. Accessed 1 September 2022 at Statement on the British Energy Security Strategy - GOV.UK (www.gov.uk)

[197] See Mike Moorcroft, 'What is Net Zero and why does it matter?' JRI Blog 14 July 2022. Accessed 31 August 2022 at What is Net Zero and why does it matter? – The John Ray Initiative (jri.org.uk) The John Ray Initiative (JRI) is a Christian educational charity.

called *Mission Zero: Independent Review of Net Zero* considered the British Energy Security Strategy. It stated: 'Investment in new nuclear is a no-regrets option given expected increase in power demand and retirement of existing plants'.[198] But it said more detail was required from the government and earlier targets.

Remembering

Writing an autobiography inevitably brings back memories of family, friends, schools, teachers/lecturers, colleagues and entertainers, e.g. seeing Bruce Forsyth live in the Empire Theatre, and the bands I heard. There are, though, sad memories from Liverpool's Merseybeat era, for example: Brian Epstein's death; John Lennon's murder; Cilla Black's death, and that of Gerry Marsden of Gerry and the Pacemakers. Their *Ferry Cross the Mersey* is a favourite of mine.[199]

In October 2021, Billy Butler was fondly remembered for fifty years on local radio.[200] In the Sixties, I was a Helen Shapiro fan and kept a scrapbook. She was famous for her 1961 songs *You Don't Know* and *Walking Back to Happiness*, which hit the top of the UK charts. In 1987, Shapiro became a follower of Jesus.[201] Also, Sandie Shaw MBE (born 26 February 1947) was a successful singer in

---

[198] Chris Skidmore, *Mission Zero: Independent Review of Net Zero - final report*, last updated 13 January 2023, p.94. Accessed 14 July 2023 at Review of Net Zero - GOV.UK (www.gov.uk)

[199] See BBC News, 'Gerry Marsden: Funeral held for Pacemakers star', 16 January 2021. Accessed 1 September 2022 at Gerry Marsden: Funeral held for Pacemakers star - BBC News

[200] Lisa Rand, 'Billy Butler celebrates 50 years on the radio', *Liverpool Echo* 2 October 2021. Accessed 1 September 2022 at Billy Butler celebrates 50 years on the radio - Liverpool Echo

[201] Helen Shapiro, *Walking Back to Happiness* (London: Harper Collins *Publishers*: 1993).

the Sixties who, in 1967, was the first British entry to win the Eurovision Song Contest with *Puppet on a String*. She retired from music in 2013. I am "made up", or "chuffed", as we said in Liverpool, to have lived in post-war Liverpool in the Swinging Sixties.

Time passes so quickly that it's difficult to comprehend as the generations come and go. I recall 1962, when Cliff Richard and the Shadows sang *The Young Ones*, with the words 'we may not be the young ones very long'. True! Now in my mid-seventies, I look back and forward. My late parents are our children's grandparents and for our grandchildren (Harry, Stan, Esther and Lydia – and our latest, Zachariah, who arrived in summer 2023, following Tim's marriage to Amina in 2022), they are their great-grandparents. They lived, as I did as a boy, in a world very different from nowadays. The current challenges are many and immense, especially to safeguard our children's futures for generations to come. I hope, and pray, that this autobiography will inspire our children, grandchildren, great-grandchildren, and my wider readership, to enjoy living on God's good Earth and carefully look after it for the benefit of all its creatures, human and non-human. God bless. Peace!

Our Streets

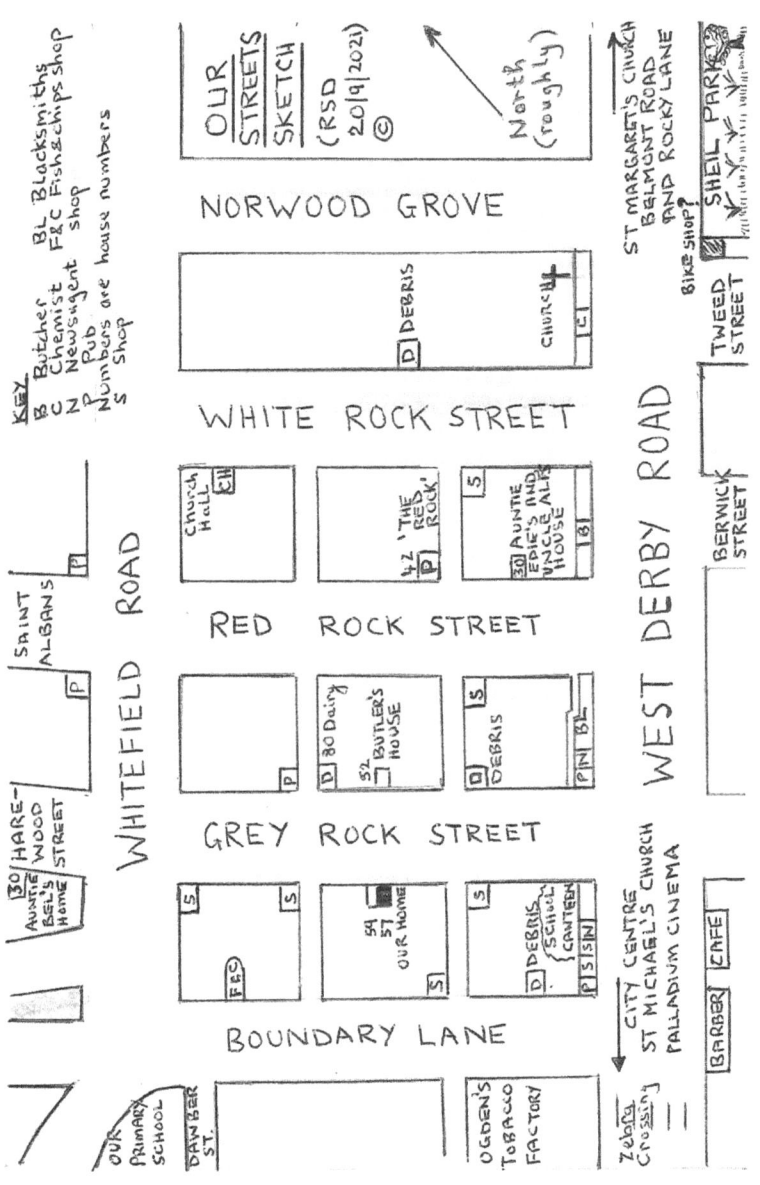

OUR
STREETS
SKETCH
(RSD
20|9|2021)
©

North
(roughly)

KEY
B Butcher   BL Blacksmiths
C Chemist   F&C Fish&chips shop
N Newsagent
P Pub
Numbers are house numbers
S Shop

ST MARGARET'S CHURCH
BELMONT ROAD
AND ROCKY LANE

SHEL PARK

Bike shop?

NORWOOD GROVE

D DEBRIS

CHURCH

TWEED
STREET

WHITE ROCK STREET

Church
Hall

42 'THE
RED
ROCK'

S

30 AUNTIE
EDIE'S AND
UNCLE ALF'S
HOUSE

18

BERWICK
STREET

SAINT
ALBANS

RED   ROCK   STREET

WHITEFIELD ROAD

30 Dairy

52 BUTLER'S
HOUSE

S

DEBRIS

BL

WEST DERBY ROAD

30 HARE-
WOOD
STREET

AUNTIE
BEL'S
HOME

GREY   ROCK   STREET

S

S

54
57
OUR HOME

S

DEBRIS
SCHOOL
CANTEEN

F&C

CITY CENTRE
ST MICHAEL'S CHURCH
PALLADIUM CINEMA

BOUNDARY LANE

OUR
PRIMARY
SCHOOL

DAWBER
ST.

Zebra
Crossing

OGDEN'S
TOBACCO
FACTORY

BARBER   CAFE

330

Lilian Dutch (née Thompson) family tree

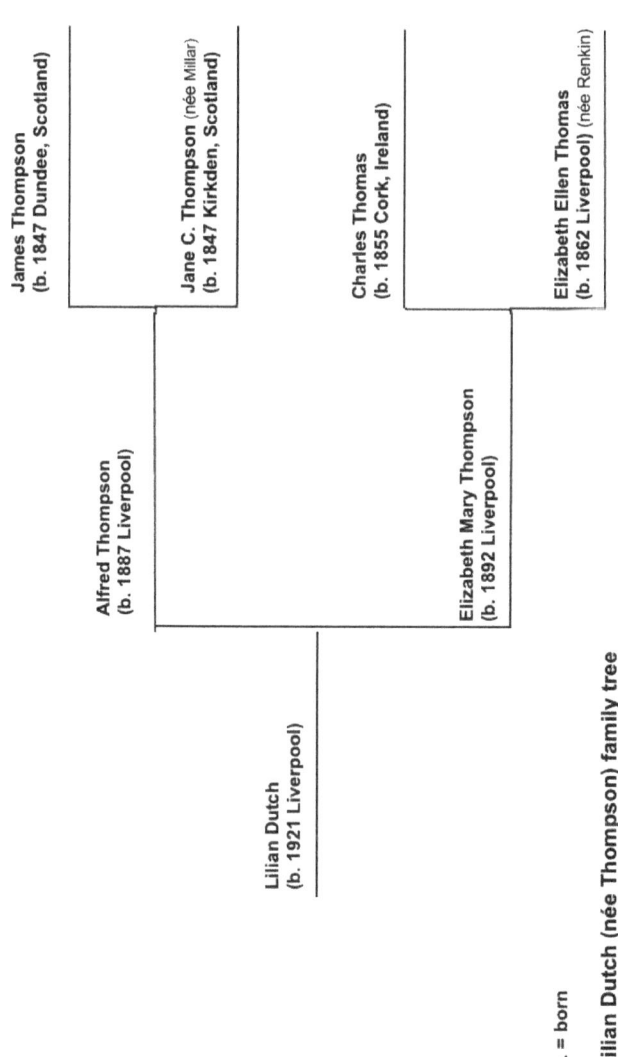

James Thompson
(b. 1847 Dundee, Scotland)

Jane C. Thompson (née Millar)
(b. 1847 Kirkden, Scotland)

Charles Thomas
(b. 1855 Cork, Ireland)

Elizabeth Ellen Thomas (née Renkin)
(b. 1862 Liverpool)

Alfred Thompson
(b. 1887 Liverpool)

Elizabeth Mary Thompson
(b. 1892 Liverpool)

Lilian Dutch
(b. 1921 Liverpool)

b. = born

Lilian Dutch (née Thompson) family tree

331

Summary of Education

Dates	Awarding Bodies	Qualifications
1966-69	University of Salford	BSc (Hons) Physics
1969-70	University of Salford	MSc Physics
1974-75 1976-78	Bristol Polytechnic: Council for National Academic Awards (CNAA). (Now University of the West of England)	Diploma in Management Studies (Postgraduate)
1979-83	University of London	Bachelor of Divinity (Hons)
1985-87	University of London	Diploma in Education (Postgraduate)
1993-94	University of Bristol	MA Biblical Studies
1995-98	University of Bristol	PhD in New Testament. Title: *The Educated Elite in First Corinthians: A Social-Scientific Study of Education and Community Conflict in a Graeco-Roman Context*
2003-04	The Open University	MEd Education
2009-11	University of Gloucestershire	MA Intercultural Studies

Acknowledgements

Thanks to my grandparents, parents, and sisters, who kept important documents and photos, giving me wonderful memories of Liverpool and Meols in the Wirral.

I am grateful for the memories of my sisters Anne and Christina, plus our cousin Alf Thompson, with helpful feedback on draft chapters. For Dad's life as a sailor, I have drawn upon the Royal Navy's records. The painting of his ship HMS *Grey Fox*, which hung in our Liverpool home constantly reminded us of his naval career.

In my school education, thanks to Mr Len Toft (Headmaster) at Newsham Secondary Modern School for Boys who created a brighter future for me, and other boys, when he introduced classes 4T and 5T for us to take publicly-recognised exams. Thanks also for my teachers, particularly Mr Ken Morton, our Duke of Edinburgh's Award leader.

Thankfully, Mr Toft arranged with Mr W.E. Pobjoy (Headmaster) Quarry Bank High School for Boys my school transfer at sixteen. I am grateful for three productive and happy years there before beginning a physics degree at the Royal College of Advanced Technology (RCAT) Salford, which became the University of Salford.

Thanks to the RCAT's staff who gave me a place in the Sixties when most universities required their students to have an O-Level in a foreign language. Thus began four valuable years studying physics with support from family, staff and students.

Liverpool's churches provided a foundation in faith. After we left Liverpool in early 1967, the summer return visit to the Empire Theatre (Lime Street) to hear the live link of US evangelist Billy Graham provided the deciding moment when I chose to follow Jesus and became a committed Christian. The university's Christian Union and churches provided friendship, hospitality and teaching. My friend

Dave Casey was on the same physics degree course; we shared student accommodation and attended the Christian Union and churches together. Thanks for his many recollections. Also, my friend Alan Ryden on our course recalled some names etc.

I am grateful for the opportunities to work as a scientist in the nuclear power industry; especially to the late John Edwards, our health physics commissioning team leader at Hinkley Point B Power Station. Thanks also to people who supporting my postgraduate theology studies, specifically the late Diane Treacy-Cole, my PhD adviser at Bristol.

Appreciation also goes to Peter and Jenny Kay, who confirmed my visits to Kenya and Burundi to teach in colleges, churches and conferences. Peter also commented on early draft chapters. Particular thanks go to Geoffrey Sutton (retired languages teacher), who devoted his time to reviewing draft chapters – twice – and reread the whole draft. Also, appreciation goes to David Wenham (retired scholar/author from Trinity College, Bristol), who once lived in Birkenhead (opposite Liverpool), and has provided feedback on all draft chapters. Moreover, thanks to my Bible study group for support and Katharine Smith (Heddon Publishing), who ensured my book became a reality.

Finally, special thanks to my wife Sue for her long-term support while writing over many years and during the Covid-19 pandemic. Our children Laura, Jess and Tim and grandchildren (Harry, Stan, Esther and Lydia) listened to my stories. Tim also gave feedback on all chapters.

Any errors contained within the book are unintentional and the responsibility of the author.